MW00454744

Rosicrucian
AMERICA

"Sora's informative new book is a must for those eager for the truth about the secret roles played by the medieval Knights Templar, the Rosicrucians, and Freemasonry in the founding of the 'New Atlantis.' Now more than ever the world needs the truth about the individuals and the tenets they held dear, which was the secret blueprint for the founding of America. What was long 'hidden in plain sight,' Sora skillfully 'brings into the light.'"

SCOTT F. WOLTER, FORENSIC GEOLOGIST,
HOST OF THE TRAVEL CHANNEL'S *AMERICA UNEARTHED*,
AND AUTHOR OF *CRYPTIC CODE OF THE TEMPLARS IN AMERICA:
ORIGINS OF THE HOOKED X™ SYMBOL*

"Steven Sora has done it again. Following up on his immensely popular *The Lost Treasure of the Knights Templar*, Steven has woven another tapestry of well-researched, entertaining narrative, which provides America with many of the answers that the nation's collective psyche currently seeks so desperately. Indeed, *Rosicrucian America* offers its readers a glimpse into the spiritual inspiration and alchemical transformation that provided much of the basis for the founding of the United States of America."

WILLIAM F. MANN, SUPREME GRAND MASTER OF THE
SOVEREIGN GREAT PRIORY—KNIGHTS TEMPLAR OF CANADA
AND AUTHOR OF *THE LAST REFUGE OF THE KNIGHTS TEMPLAR*
AND *TEMPLAR SANCTUARIES IN NORTH AMERICA*

"What fun I had reading this book! Steven Sora has connected so many of my favorite topics into one woven tale—a real page-turner. For 50 years I've been studying the German Pietists of provincial Pennsylvania, the authorship question of William Shakespeare, the far-reaching influence of Sir Francis Bacon and Dr. John Dee, and William Penn's hidden reasons for coming to America, among other topics in this book, but it took Stephen Sora to flesh it all out with the latest research and put it all together in one brilliant volume. Like the alchemical goal of a Rosicrucian, this book will transmute your appreciation for the destiny of America."

ROBERT R. HIERONIMUS, PH.D.,
AUTHOR OF *FOUNDING FATHERS, SECRET SOCIETIES*

". . . explores ideals that evolved through the Crusades, the Renaissance, and the Enlightenment. Both known and unknown adepts worked to weave together the threads of intellectual, philosophical, and spiritual principles that gave birth to a unique new nation: conceived in liberty and dedicated to the proposition that all men are created equal. That Rosicrucian vision survives to this day and is well presented in these pages."

JAMES WASSERMAN, AUTHOR OF
THE TEMPLARS AND THE ASSASSINS AND
THE SECRETS OF MASONIC WASHINGTON

"Textbook versions of early American history comprise little more than a propaganda veneer obscuring the occult forces that really drove the British colonization of our continent. Nowhere are these sub-rosa influences more credibly exposed and their leading conspirators better identified than by Steven Sora in his latest book, *Rosicrucian America*."

FRANK JOSEPH, AUTHOR OF *POWER PLACES AND
THE MASTER BUILDERS OF ANTIQUITY* AND
ADVANCED CIVILIZATIONS OF PREHISTORIC AMERICA

ROSICRUCIAN AMERICA

How a Secret Society Influenced the Destiny of a Nation

STEVEN SORA

Destiny Books
Rochester, Vermont

Destiny Books
One Park Street
Rochester, Vermont 05767
www.DestinyBooks.com

Text stock is SFI certified

Destiny Books is a division of Inner Traditions International

Copyright © 2019 by Steven Sora

All rights reserved. No part of this book may be reproduced or utilized in
any form or by any means, electronic or mechanical, including photocopying,
recording, or by any information storage and retrieval system, without permission
in writing from the publisher.

Cataloging-in-Publication Data for this title is available from the Library of Congress

ISBN 978-1-62055-906-2 (print)
ISBN 978-1-62055-907-9 (ebook)

Printed and bound in the United States by Lake Book Manufacturing, Inc.
The text stock is SFI certified. The Sustainable Forestry Initiative® program
promotes sustainable forest management.

10 9 8 7 6 5 4 3 2 1

Text design by Virginia Scott Bowman and layout by Priscilla Baker
This book was typeset in Garamond Premier Pro with Historycal, Gill Sans, and
Belwe used as display typefaces

To send correspondence to the author of this book, mail a first-class letter to the
author c/o Inner Traditions • Bear & Company, One Park Street, Rochester, VT
05767, and we will forward the communication.

*To my wife and best friend, Terry,
and to Aria, Isabel, Jackie, Jordan,
Millie, and Wyatt*

CONTENTS

INTRODUCTION
The Invisible History of the United States   1

CHAPTER 1
The Secrets of the Rosicrucians   7

CHAPTER 2
Sir Francis Bacon: The Man Who Couldn't Be King   26

CHAPTER 3
The Author(s) Known as Shakespeare   46

CHAPTER 4
All the Queen's Men   80

CHAPTER 5
Occult England   114

CHAPTER 6
King Arthur and Avalon in America   130

CHAPTER 7
Roslin, Henry Sinclair, and the Discovery of America   150

CHAPTER 8
Bacon's New Atlantis   182

CHAPTER 9
The Colony of the Virgin Queen   196

CHAPTER 10
The Rosy Cross over Pennsylvania   215

CHAPTER 11
The Rosicrucians and the American Revolution   228

CHAPTER 12
The Knights of the Golden Circle
and Their Plan for America   241

CHAPTER 13
Rosicrucian America Today   251

APPENDIX
John Dee's Influence on Ian Fleming
and His James Bond Character   255

Notes   260

Bibliography   268

Index   272

THE INVISIBLE HISTORY OF THE UNITED STATES

History, as we have been taught it, implies an America born from the grassroots movement of a large populace striving for freedom of worship as well as freedom from high-handed taxation. The truth is that a very small handful of individuals with lofty goals was the party responsible for seeking these freedoms. This group consisted of alchemists, geomancers, and philosophers, many of whom met in secret and risked everything on their new venture.

From its humble beginnings in a college in sixteenth-century England, this small circle of individuals has played an unusually great role in the history of the world. This true secret society has influenced politics, science, and the very foundation of the United States. The circle has been known by more than one name, but its most fitting name is "the Invisibles."

History is written by the victorious, so it should always be considered suspect. Europe before the seventeenth century was backward, illiterate, and unhygienic. People rarely bathed, drinking water was of very poor quality, and sanitation was at a minimum, allowing disease to be rampant and life expectancy to be short. It was not uncommon for whole families to sleep in one room, often with farm animals. Even royalty did not enjoy the standard of living we insist upon today. The

1

masses couldn't read, and if they could, they were often forbidden to read even the Bible. The priests were only slightly more literate yet somehow had been given the privilege of interpreting the word of God.

Then came the Enlightenment and the Renaissance, wherein men of science began to study astrology, astronomy, cartography, medicine, and metallurgy. No bell was rung to herald the advent of the Renaissance. There was no immediate signal that the bushel of ignorance that covered the light of learning had been lifted. The esoteric sciences, once known to the ancients yet subverted and forbidden during the Dark Ages, were not reintroduced without the vicious reaction of the church. Its monopoly on learning was broken, but not in an instant. The price for bending the rules was torture and even death.

For example, the sixteenth-century friar, philosopher, and mathematician Giordano Bruno believed that the sun was one of many stars in the universe. For refusing to recant this idea, the Roman Inquisition burned him at the stake. His colleague the polymath Galileo fortunately was spared execution because he recanted his theory that the planets circled around the sun. He was sentenced to house arrest. Earlier, Copernicus had been credited with the heliocentric theory of the universe but had refused to allow his work to be published until he was safely in the grave. Even Columbus had been brought before the Inquisition for proposing an adventure into the Atlantic.

The catalyst for the Renaissance was due in part to the maritime trade that connected the cities of the Italian Peninsula with those of the East. More dramatically it was due to the Crusades. Although these wars failed to take back the Holy Lands, the crusaders were able to bring back works of Greek astronomers and Islamic mathematicians. An unenlightened church and a less than intellectual royalty had brought about the Dark Ages. Ironically war, specifically the Crusades, broke that intellectual chokehold. Seeking to divert European princes from constant warfare, the church directed that a crusade be waged against the Muslim invaders who had taken Jerusalem. The Crusades, which took place over centuries, made East-West contact a necessity. They opened the floodgates of the arts and sciences as well as the writings of Greeks, Romans, and Egyptians—and variations on religion never before seen in the West.

French Templars and Italian merchants sailed home with new ideas and old texts that spread like wildfire, given that patrons of the arts and sciences, most notably the Medici family, hired scribes to copy the manuscripts. Scribes were considered artists, because they decorated the pages of their documents with colorful letters and designs. Later, thanks to the widening use of the printing press, copying such works became less expensive.

As a result of this influx of knowledge from the East, architecture, astronomy, cartography, shipbuilding, and medicine all changed for the better. The church, however, found itself under attack as gnosis challenged its dominance. Arianism, Catharism, and a host of variations on the church's narrow approach threatened the organization that had held near-absolute power for almost one thousand years.

The church reacted with violence. It tortured and burned the "heretics," initially wiping out one million people in France in the early thirteenth century.[1] Ideas and ideals were incorporated into practice among the Templars and put into use by them and their non-military order, the Cistercians. As a result, the church intended to destroy the Knights Templar, its strongest military arm. Despite its immense power, the church's actions were like putting proverbial fingers in the dike. The floodgates of learning were opening, and little could stop their momentum.

The light of learning could not be extinguished by the heap of ignorance that was Rome. The democratic ideals of Greek philosophers were once again available to a Europe that was dictated to by popes, kings, and landowning nobility. Translated from ancient languages, these ideals opened Europe's eyes.

Forced to remain sub rosa (under the rose), many of the new thinkers took protection by coming together as groups, or circles, and in their entirety became an Invisible College. This "college" would eventually spread from England to Italy, Germany, France, and the New World. Its curriculum consisted of an underground stream of knowledge. Secret societies survived even while the Cathars of France and Italy were being exterminated by the church. These societies survived the joint attack on the Templars and the arrest, torture, and death of many in what had been the church's most powerful orders.

Smaller circles of men banded together to help inspire each other on paths of discovery. Among such groups were a handful of men who stood out, both in terms of spreading knowledge and in forming and maintaining the secret societies. They ensured that these societies avoided detection and yet succeeded in their purpose.

Possibly the greatest of these individuals was the Englishman Sir Francis Bacon (1561–1626), an intellectual giant who would go on to be a founder of the Rosicrucians (the Order of the Holy Cross). Bacon was a philosopher and a writer. He was also the architect of what would become the American Revolution even though he lived and died much earlier in time, long before his work would come to fruition. And although he would not reach the "promised land" himself, his efforts launched the expeditions that would attempt to create a new society where a democratic ideal could be installed as a progressive model.

In this, Bacon and his circle became the driving force for the English colonization of the Americas. For Sir Francis Bacon, there was an Atlantis, and it was directly across the Atlantic Ocean. In the distant past the Americas had shared commerce with Europe. Bacon wrote, "You shall understand . . . that about 3,000 years ago, or somewhat more, the navigation of the world, especially for remote voyage, was greater than at this day." Bacon continued: "We lost our traffic with the Americas . . . navigation did everywhere greatly decay."[2]

Another one of England's guiding spirits of the day was Dr. John Dee. He was at once the most famous alchemist of the Elizabethan era—a magician and a wizard who had the ear of the queen. He was also possibly the most influential man in Francis Bacon's life. John Dee was a most important member of a secret group called the School of Night, which included such luminaries of the day as Sir Francis Drake; Sir Walter Raleigh; Christopher Marlowe; Thomas Hariot; George Chapman; and Henry Percy, the Earl of Northumberland.

They were also called the Dragon Men. They were the writers, the scientists, and the explorers who influenced England to join in on the race for the New World. And although they worked toward the same goals, they were not necessarily united. Infighting over leadership and land and favors from the queen and later king brought them to betrayal and murder—and even to *fake* murder.

For some, their efforts led to imprisonment, beheading, expulsion from court, and relegation to a life of poverty. Collectively, however, they succeeded in their primary aim: England's pursuit of the colonization of the New World. The Spanish sailed for gold and silver. The French sailed for furs. The English came to America to re-create Avalon and create the New Atlantis, and because it put idealistic notions in the forefront, it achieved a different type of success.

Tradition holds that a group of Rosicrucians landed at the Blue Anchor Tavern, which was conveniently located near the seaport in Philadelphia, with William Penn, who was sympathetic to alternative Christian religions. An anchor is a Christian symbol, and a blue anchor is a Rosicrucian motif, implying that Rosicrucian ideas were already being built into the architecture of the emerging nation. Rosicrucianism then spread south to Virginia and north through New England. Throughout it all, they had an influence on the Founding Fathers, as did Freemasonry. The difference was that Freemasonry survived the scrutiny of the public eye while the Rosicrucian tradition remained underground.

In the process of bringing new ideals to a New World, secrecy had to be maintained as a matter of security. Both Elizabeth I and her successor, King James, were suspicious of any ideal that threatened their divine right. Many of the original Bacon-authored texts, including his writings on Rosicrucian thought, his blueprint for the New Atlantis, and the disguised political statements garbed in comedy and history and attributed to Shakespeare, were brought to America and concealed in vaults. Secret vaults exist on Oak Island in Nova Scotia; under the Bruton Church in Williamsburg, Virginia; and in the Ephrata Cloister in Pennsylvania. Some have been exposed, while others remain hidden away, protected by a handful of guardians.

The Rosicrucians were even more secretive than the Freemasons, who describe themselves not as a secret society but rather as a society with secrets. The original Rosicrucians kept no membership lists. They have always called themselves the Invisibles, and they remain so today. Their *influence,* however, was and is not always invisible, as we shall see. In the pages of this book, we hope to bring their impacts and their influence from the shadows into the light.

CHAPTER 1

THE SECRETS OF THE ROSICRUCIANS

Rosicrucianism is not a religion, it's a tradition maintained by a secret society. Actually it is maintained by many secret societies—at least thirty-five separate groups, all of which claim to be the true Rosicrucian society. Some claim to have a direct line back to pharaonic Egypt; others claim a link to the Knights Templar; still others believe the fraternity was founded by a man named Christian Rosenkreuz, who was said to have lived in the fourteenth and fifteenth centuries. One writer, Tim Wallace Murphy, described Christian Rosenkreuz as an adept of Sir William Sinclair, the man who, in the fifteenth century, built the famous Rosslyn (also known as Roslin) Chapel, in Scotland.[1]

Other scholars would have outsiders believe that *Rosicrucian* is simply a generic term referring to studies and membership in a philosophical secret society. Others, like Canadian author and mystic Manly Palmer Hall, declare that the Rosicrucian society is composed of the intellectually enlightened who believe the secret destiny is a world order ruled by a king of supernatural powers descended from a divine race.

The modern Rosicrucian tradition can be dated to the late sixteenth century, and its reorganization might be credited to the English philosopher and statesman Sir Francis Bacon. Bacon had a passion for secrets and secret societies, and while a student at the exclusive London legal society, Gray's Inn, he created the Order of the Helmet. The helmet was actually the headgear of the goddess Pallas Athena, whose epithet was "shaker of the spear." *Pallas* is from the Greek word *pallo,* meaning "to brandish" or "to shake." Notably, the helmet of Athena, a gift from her uncle Hades, gave her the ability to be invisible.

Bacon would utilize this quality of invisibility throughout his life, given that he was the invisible man behind many written works as well as the founder of the Rosicrucian tradition, symbolized by "the Rose Cross." Its members were known as the Invisibles. They were considered as such because they published no lists of members and had no real hierarchy.

In addition to calling his followers the Invisibles, Bacon also called them his "literary sons." Much of his writings went from his friend and chaplain, William Rawley, into the hands of these nameless Invisibles.

POPULAR THEMES OF THE DAY AND THEIR REFLECTION IN THE LITERATURE OF THE TIME

The Rose Cross has existed as a symbol of higher meaning for at least one thousand years, and the rose itself has served as an important symbol for ages. Martin Luther used a rose and a cross as his emblem in the early sixteenth century, indicating the transcendence of faith.

English poets Edmund Spenser, Samuel Daniel, and Michael Drayton, in their own works, would go on to mourn the lost beauty of Rosalind and Rosamund. The English physician and author Thomas Lodge wrote *Rosalynde,* a pastoral novel published in 1590. *Rosalynde* examines the dilemma of all those who believed that the truth had been lost when the Reformation came to England. The red rose (found in *Rosalynde*) represented true holiness. It was also symbolic of the House of Lancaster, which fought against the House of York—whose symbol was a white rose.

The theme of Arcadia was another important motif of the day; it symbolized an idyllic world and the feminine role in it. Like others of his time writing on utopian themes and idyllic places, Bacon wrote the novel *New Atlantis,* which was not published until after his death. The world it depicted, a utopia of sorts, was not too different from the world that would later be articulated in Manly Hall's vision that described a learned society called Solomon's House that existed on an island called Bensalem (literally, the "son of Salem").

Salem is a Semitic word meaning "peace." The members of Solomon's House were gifted by God with the understanding of the works and secrets of Creation. Initiates wore white turbans bearing a red cross. The rules governing this utopia were identical to the rules in the manifestos of the Roscrucians. Unlike Hall's one-world government ruled by the supernaturally gifted and a divine order, Bacon's utopian world was a place where the learned shared their knowledge and received no payment for doing so. This was reflected in early Rosicrucian texts that advised members to act as doctors freely serving those in need.

Various other Rosicrucian documents began to emerge in 1605. One manuscript was *The Restoration of the Decayed Temple of Pallas,* which contained a constitution of the order. Within ten years the more widely known writings that would come to be known as the Rosicrucian manifestos started to appear on the continent. *The Fama Fraternitatis of the Meritorious Order of the Rosy Cross* is one of the most important. It was published in 1614 (although there is evidence that it had been circulating among esoteric circles for years prior to its publication).

This was succeeded by *The Confession of a Rosicrucian Fraternity* the next year. And in 1616, *The Chymical Wedding of Christian Rosenkreuz* was published. (It had allegedly been written in 1459.)

This Rosicrucian body of knowledge included information on alchemy, mysticism, and the Kabbalah. It also included a vision of social transformation. All this of course was heretical—at least to the Catholic Church—and was highly suspect to others.

TWO SEMINAL ROSICRUCIAN FIGURES:
DR. JOHN DEE AND SIR FRANCIS BACON

Although it is impossible to be certain, many of these Rosicrucian texts were most likely from the pen of a highly regarded figure of the time named Dr. John Dee. One of Dee's protégés was Sir Francis Bacon, who may have brought Dee's texts to Europe. Dee was a wizard, an alchemist, a prophet, a writer, a magician, a cartographer, and a spy. He was also the confidant of Queen Elizabeth I of England, serving as her astrologer as well as in other capacities.

It is worth noting that one of these Rosicrucian texts, *The Confession of a Rosicrucian Fraternity,* was originally published with illustrated commentary on John Dee's famous Monas Hieroglyphica symbol. This symbol combines the moon, the sun, the elements, and Aries into one odd figure and accompanies text that has defied explanation. This Monas Hieroglyphica symbol could be said to be a signature symbol of Dee's, and its inclusion in the manuscript links the book to him.

In any event, together Bacon and Dee grafted a tradition of thinking onto an underground stream of thought that had been around since the church came out against anyone who questioned its doctrine. Because it was dangerous, such knowledge was said to be sub rosa, as in "under the rose." (In Bacon's case, it was under the *Rosi Crosse,* or Red Cross.)

The concept of sub rosa dates back at least to Roman times, when paintings on the ceilings of banquet halls reminded patrons that what happened under the rose-decorated ceiling, especially under the influence of vino, stayed under that ceiling. Later, in the Middle Ages, a rose suspended over the table of a council meeting took on the same meaning: proceedings were subject to secrecy. In modern times the confessionals of Catholic churches sport carvings of roses, assuring the petitioner that confessions will remain between the the confessor and his or her priest. In similar fashion, Bacon's Rosi Crosse Literary Society assured its members that their discussions would stay within the group.

And as we shall see, even though Bacon was quite prolific, most of his writings were credited to others.

Many of Dee's writings were penned in secret and remained hidden for years; however, some of his works were designed for immediate publication. When Dee wanted to be, he was free to be himself in all his glory. He dressed and looked the part he played in Elizabeth's court: he had the ear of the queen and her courtiers, and, given that he served as Elizabeth's astrologer, Dee would influence the queen in many ways. His services included picking the most propitious date and time for her coronation. He also convinced her that England had rights to the New World as well as the need for a strong navy. From then on, Britannia ruled the high seas. As well, he was able to persuade her that King Arthur's Avalon was actually America. Intellectually she lived vicariously through her wizard. Dee would write on topics from Rosicrucianism to navigation. His estate at Mortlake held four thousand books, a crystal ball, and a magic mirror with which to tell the future. The secretive and anonymous works of Dee and Bacon became the basis for the modern Rosicrucian tradition.

LITERARY WORKS THROUGH TIME THAT REFLECT ROSICRUCIAN THEMES

Another indication of the power and influence of Rosicrucianism is reflected in the pervasiveness with which the message and theme of the Rosicrucian tradition has been transmitted in literary works through time.

A book published in 1914 called *Revolt of the Angels* by Anatole France posits that fallen angels have taken on human form and are preparing to topple God. One of them is named Arcade. Lucifer is the light-bringer who liberates knowledge for humanity. It should also be noted that most of the action in *Revolt of the Angels* takes place in the shadow of St. Sulpice in Paris.

In 1719, Daniel Defoe, a dissenter, wrote *Robinson Crusoe* (with the odd explanation that *Crusoe* was short for a German word). Page 1 of

Defoe's book declares: "I was called Robinson Kreutznaer—we call our-selves and write our names Crusoe." (The name Robinson Kreutznaer could be thought to be similar to the name Christian Rosenkreuz, and the name Crusoe resembles the word *cross*.)

Jules Verne said, "We have all written 'Robinsons' but it is a moot question if any of them would have seen the light had it not been for their famous prototype."[2] Verne's words show many writers have dis-guised characters or that the full identity of their characters may only be known to the initiated. Verne had been initiated into Freemasonry and was familiar with Rosicrucian doctrines although his name does not appear to be associated with that of any Freemason lodge. He was, however, known to belong to a group called the Fog. He said that this group was connected to the Rosicrucians, and he named one of his most well-known characters Phileas Fogg. Mr. Fogg was a member of the Reform Club. Is it sheer coincidence that the initials of the Reform Club (*RC*) are the same as those of the Rose Cross?

The journeys of Jules Verne's characters are similarly heroic to those of Perceval and Lancelot of Arthurian lore. His characters travel in the air, under the sea, and of course to the center of the earth. (*Journey to the Center of the Earth* has a central theme of death-rebirth.) And the names of Verne's characters often have secret meanings. In *Clovis Dardenator,* Verne's sea captain has the name Bugarach—the same as a mountain in the Rennes-le-Château area. D'Ardent was the title of Clovis, the most important Merovingian king. Another character was Robur the Conqueror (*RC*), who lived in a world of UFOs.[3]

Another book, titled *Inside Secret Societies* by Michael Benson, describes the story of *The Protocols of the Learned Elders of Zion.* In *The Protocols,* a Rosicrucian by the name of Maurice Joly gave a prescription for the New World Order. Instructing, one can guess, the fellow elite, he declared that statesmen do not have to tell the truth. They could take control of the currency, control public opinion, create war, spread hunger and disease, and influence the youth. Later these protocols were seen as a Zionist plot by the Czarist secret police. Some say that the

Nazis invented them, but their appearance in Russia dates to 1903. In *Rule by Secrecy,* Jim Marrs identifies the book as a Czarist plot for the pogroms against Jews in Russia.[4]

Bacon's message was quite the opposite. He believed in the ideals of freedom of thought, religious choice, and the tolerance of other religions.

THE INVISIBLE COLLEGE AND ITS MEMBERS

The Rosicrucian Enlightenment in England would come to include the most influential alchemists of the day. This group of like-minded individuals (known as the Invisible College, as we have previously established) included Sir Walter Raleigh, John Dee, Edmund Spenser, Elias Ashmole, Robert Boyle, and Isaac Newton, all of whom were scientists seeking to uncover facets of the spiritual in a changing world. They were joined by Welsh philosopher and alchemist Thomas Vaughan, English physician Robert Fludd, German physician Michael Maier, and Danish astronomer Tycho Brahe and others. And although these men were all illustrious for one reason or another, the real Invisible College consisted of the network of nameless adepts who joined them.

After half a century had passed, the Invisible College would officially mutate (in 1660) into the Royal Society, which still exists. A commemorative plate presented to the society depicts Francis Bacon as its "past" master (although we know that the Invisible College did not *formally* exist). A poem by Abraham Cowley written in 1667 states, "Bacon, like Moses, led us forth."[5]

Members of the Royal Society would include architects like Christopher Wren and inventors like astronomer Sir Paul Neile, whose expertise was in grinding glass for telescopes. Among the group, Laurence Rooke studied longitude, Abraham Hill studied the theory of money, and Elias Ashmole (a Mason) studied astrology, secret writing, and substitution codes.

Robert Fludd was another influential member. He was the son of Queen Elizabeth's treasurer and served in court alongside Francis Bacon.

Fludd had been educated at Oxford, where John Dee and the poet Sir Philip Sidney had left their mark. Influenced by esoteric tradition from his Oxford days, Fludd kept a low profile. He said that he was not a member of any Rosicrucian group, although he endorsed their goals.

The court was, at this time, sending money to France, where Louis de Nevers was finance minister. Fludd was the treasurer of the English military, yet his esoteric connections were more important than his patriotic alliances, and so he sent money to support the French. In addition, Fludd tutored Henry of Lorraine's children, including Charles, the Duke of Guise. As a tutor to the sons of Henry of Lorraine, Fludd could not afford to alienate the Catholics of France by claiming membership in the Rosicrucian society. Thus, when he appeared at the Frankfurt Book Fair in 1616 with a text called *A Compendius Apology for the Fraternity of the Rosy Cross,* which defended the Rosicrucians, he maintained that he was not of their order, however sympathetic he might be to them. Fludd's denial and defense of the Rosicrucians would become typical of the behavior of many writers and men of science accused or suspected of being part of the Invisibles.

Fludd participated in the translation of the King James Bible, which connected him to Bacon in that Bacon worked on the translation as well. While Bacon inspired a world in which scholars were free to pursue lines of study unfettered by the straitjacket of religion, not all "Rosicrucians" were of the same mind. The Guise faction was of course composed of arch-Catholics who persecuted Huguenots. It should also be noted that both Guise and de Nevers (mentioned above) were tied to the mysterious Priory of Sion. Robert Boyle would serve as its grand master. This connects the birth of the Rosicrucian tradition with the priory in Paris.

THE FAR-REACHING TENTACLES OF THE ROSICRUCIAN TRADITION

There is little doubt then that the early Royal Society; post–1717 Freemasonry; the Priory of Sion; the Knights Templar and its sister order, the Cistercians; and the real birth of the Rosicrucian tradition were *all* connected. Indeed, "Bacon's circle included many Britons who undoubtedly had access to elder secrets carried through the Knights Templar on into Freemasonry," writes prolific author Jim Marrs.[6]

One of the more prominent symbols of the Royal Society featured a depiction of the letter *G* in a star representing the glory of God, the great geometrician. This symbolism is also integral to Freemasonry. The famous astronomer Johannes Kepler wrote that geometry existed before the Creation and therefore "Geometry is God himself."[7] Saint Bernard, reformer of the Cistercians, famously referred to God as "height, width and depth"; in other words, geometry.

Indeed, the importance of the sacred geometry in Masonry at its higher levels is that pure thought emanates from the mind of God. Only those who can transform themselves to this higher level and greater understanding can accomplish this enlightenment.

Saint Bernard was a complex man who, in addition to promoting the Templars to the point that they were granted huge powers from the pope, also promoted the feminine aspect of the Divine. He was born in the town of Fontaine-les-Dijon, near Dijon, Burgundy, France. From Saint Paul's day on, in the eyes of the church, women had lost all standing. Bernard did all he could to bring that back. He authored prayers to the Mother of God, made pilgrimages to her sites, and elaborated on the subject of a god-mother.

A CLOSER LOOK AT THE AUTHORSHIP OF ROSICRUCIAN TEXTS

We discussed important texts in the Rosicrucian tradition earlier; we would now like to elaborate on one in particular. A tome titled *The Chymical Wedding* was said to have been written by a man named Johann Valentin Andreae in 1603. However, Johann Andreae spent his life claiming that he had not written *The Chymical Wedding*. In fact, he said the whole affair was a prank orchestrated by others, one that would cost him his academic career.

Another important factor is that the work contains other traditions derived from the Alexandrian Hermetists, Gnostics, Paulicians, Bogomils, and Cathars, and Johann was but seventeen years old at the time of its writing. This was deep stuff for someone so young. It was rumored that Dee and/or Bacon may have authored the work. Certainly they were more intellectually capable of producing it.

In any event, it's an open question as to who may have written the text and why another may have been credited for it instead. The "who" might be Bacon himself; the "why" perhaps because it might have hurt Bacon's own career.

The Chymical Wedding is an allegorical description of a magical wedding of a mythical king and queen. In February 1613 this wedding actually took place. Life imitated a work of art when British princess Elizabeth Stuart of Bohemia and Prince Frederick V were married. They had one ceremony in Germany (which was not a unified state yet but a collection of states known as the Palatinate, which was ruled by a prince of the Holy Roman Emperor). They then had a second ceremony in England.

When they married, Elizabeth wore a rose, and the ceremony was vastly different from a Christian ceremony. The archbishop of Canterbury objected to the ceremony, which he described as pagan. The guests, however, were important. They included Sir Francis Bacon, Fulke Greville, Johann Valentin Andreae, and other Rosicrucians.

The Rosy Cross had been nearly invisible until this wedding. However, with this public debut, Frederick and his bride exposed it to the citizens of their German homeland. The tradition of the Rosy Cross came to be the same tradition espoused by the reformers of religion.

It wasn't long before Rosicrucianism became part of the political landscape. After the death of Holy Roman Emperor Rudolf II, the Hermetist and friend of John Dee's, the Bohemian nobles chose a successor. Prince Christian of Heidelberg offered the crown to Frederick, though this would quickly be challenged by the Holy Roman Empire.

Frederick's court was frequented by the German alchemist Michael Maier; the aforementioned Robert Fludd, who was also a student of Dee's; and others known to travel in Rosicrucian circles. Frederick assumed the crown and moved his court to Prague. Prague at that time was a mecca for scientists—which included alchemists—astrologers, and those who studied the magical arts. In England the wedding of Frederick and Elizabeth Stuart was a great event. At a time when Catholics and Protestants were at odds, Queen Elizabeth, son of James I, was a defender of Protestantism. While some believed that Frederick simply wanted a Calvinist corner of the world, he actually wished for a new world culture of reformation. His influence was Prince Christian, who believed in the New Atlantis concept shared by Dee and Bacon.

In short, Frederick wanted a changed world. But it was not to be. Just days after he accepted the crown, Ferdinand II of the Catholic Hapsburg family took up arms to depose the young king. The dream would end one day at a place called the White Mountain (now part of Prague). Though many Catholics deserted, Ferdinand's Catholic army outnumbered the army of the Protestants and the Catholic Hapsburgs would eventually gain rule. Prince Christian was taken prisoner, and Frederick and Elizabeth fled the country.

This battle was the first of many in what became known as the Thirty Years' War. The Hapsburgs were victorious over what was called the Protestant Union, an alliance of the many Protestant states within Germany. During this protracted war, these states fell one by one. Other countries attempted to help both sides. The monarch of Protestant Sweden brought his own army to battle and would die on the battlefield. Armies from Hapsburg to Spain, France and Denmark, Scotland, Italy, and the Balkans marched and fought in Germany.

In the end, the Hapsburgs ended constitutional rule and established their own government, which lasted until World War I. This had been the most devastating conflict on European soil until World War I. German states lost half their population to the war and ensuing disease and starvation, and 250,000 Germans left their homeland for the Netherlands.

No longer welcome in their own state, they took up residence at The Hague, which had become a Rosicrucian court in exile for other refugees from Germany. More than 100,000 followed them from the Palatinate, particularly the Lower Palatinate in southwest Germany. The culture that had been formed in the Palatinate, a Rosicrucian variation of the Protestant Reformation, took on numerous forms. Later sects from the Palatinate would settle in New York and Pennsylvania, where they were known as Pietists, Moravians, Brethren of the Spirit, and later as the Amish and the Mennonites.

Created in England then brought to the German states, the Rosicrucians would next make their existence known in Paris in 1623. Mysterious placards started appearing around the city at that time. One read: "We, the deputies of our chief college of the Brethren of the Rosy Cross, now sojourning, visible and invisible, in this town, do teach, in the name of the Most High, toward whom the hearts of the sages turn, every science, without either books, symbols, or signs, and we speak the language of the country in which we tarry, that we may extricate our fellow-men from error and destruction."[8]

In other writings they actually claimed invisibility as a protection provided them by God. One Parisian lawyer said that he wanted to become one of the Brethren after an "Invisible" appeared out of nowhere, claiming that he had read the lawyer's mind. Catholics were incensed at the claims and manifestos of the fraternity.

WHAT EXACTLY IS ROSICRUCIANISM?

Unlike Freemasonry, which is most easily if not always clearly defined as an organization with a hierarchy, Rosicrucianism is much harder to pin down. Today the numerous groups that claim to be from the original foundation share much, but there is also much they don't agree on. The renowned nineteenth-century English essayist Thomas De Quincey claimed that modern Freemasonry was modified Rosicrucianism, most likely unaware that Bacon was the reason. The various arguments put forth the claim that the tradition dates back to the pharaoh Akhenaten in Egypt, others to the gnostics of the early church, others to the Knights Templar. All agree that Bacon and Dee had organized the esoteric tradition that exists today.

Any semblance to a true history of the Rosicrucian tradition is elusive. In one attempt, documents offered to the authors of the groundbreaking book *Holy Blood, Holy Grail* attempt to link the name "l'Ordre de la Rose-Croix Veritas" to the Priory of Sion.[9] Though since its publication, some of the material in *Holy Blood, Holy Grail* has been discredited, the documents, which date to 1188, posit that Jean de Gisors, first Grand Master of the Priory of Sion and also a vassal of King Henry II, said that Rosicrucianism was handed down from Egypt via the Greeks. This secret society was connected to the Templars until 1188. Later the alchemist Nicholas Flamel, artists Sandro Filipepi (Botticelli) and Leonardo da Vinci, occultist Robert Fludd, and scientist Robert Boyle were alleged to be leaders of this secretive group.

Jean Markale, in his book *Templar Treasure at Gisors,* says, "It is likely that Geoffrey de Bouillon would have had contact with the mysterious Brothers of the Red Cross."[10] The Red Cross was an emblem of the Sages of Light, an initiatory fraternity with gnostic tendencies. The Sages of Light are also known as the Sons of the Light, a tradition of earlier Zoroastrianism from the followers of the god Ahura Mazda.

Other early documents that possibly inspired Rosicrucian thought were translations of works rediscovered and translated in Italy in 1463. The Medici family sponsored these translations, which are known as the *Corpus Hermeticum.* They encourage the reader to practice the magical arts while remaining devoted to Christian scripture.

At the very beginning of this chapter we briefly mentioned Christian Rosenkreuz, the alleged founder of the Rosicrucian tradition. This figure was germane to the entire movement, whether or not he actually founded it. According to the lore that exists about him, in 1393 he went on a pilgrimage to the East and studied with Arab and Persian sages and Sufi and Zoroastrian masters. He returned to Europe in 1407 and introduced his colleagues and cohorts to a new discipline, which he founded as the Rosicrucian order. His 106-year life span became a secret number in Rosicrucian writings.

POSSIBLE SOURCES OF
THE ROSICRUCIAN NAME

There has been no definite agreement about the source of the word *Rosicrucian,* although it's believed by some to derive from *Roslin* and has been extant since the thirteenth century at least. Frederick Pohl, a biographer of the Scottish and Norwegian nobleman Prince Henry Sinclair, tells us that *ross* means "promontory or peninsula" and *linn* means "a waterfall or stream."[11] These Gaelic words might explain the name, although the famous Rosslyn (Roslin) Chapel is not near a headland.

A Scottish translation of *Roslin* may be defined as a "morass at a pool," another ill-fitting description. *Roslin* as a feminine name means "rose," while *Ross* as a male name could mean "rose-colored" and therefore more likely to describe a redhead. Christopher Knight and Robert Lomas, authors of *The Hiram Key,* claim that *ros* means "ancient knowledge" and *lin* means "generation."[12]

It might just be that *Roslin* (Rosslyn) is on an ancient ley line and that at some point this line was called the rose line.

The St. Clair/Sinclair family has been made famous by the authors of *Holy Blood, Holy Grail,* who made the connection between the French side of the family and the Scottish side. Various mysteries connect Rosslyn with another church in Paris called St. Sulpice. On an interior wall of St. Sulpice an obelisk acts as a gnomon, a sundial. When the sun shines into the church in late December its rays fall on the obelisk, marking the winter solstice. This light, part of the astrological clock, is the "rose line," the Paris meridian.

In 1669 the Academy Royale des Sciences hired astronomer

Giovanni Domenico Cassini to direct the Paris Observatory. It was he who established the Paris meridian. While the Greenwich meridian would overshadow it, the line is still on French maps as the "Paris Zero."

The Church of St. Sulpice is named for Saint Sulpice of Bourges, who had a high standing with the Merovingian kings. His feast day is January 17. One of the last Merovingian rulers was King Dagobert II, who was murdered in the Ardennes forest near Stenay on January 17 of 681. Another saint, Saint Roseline, shares the same feast day as Saint Sulpice—an odd coincidence.

Saint Roseline de Villeneuve lived from 1263 to 1329. Her feast day is of greatest importance in the calendar of those individuals of the Merovingian bloodline. Her father was Arnold of Villeneuve, who was known to history as a Catalan alchemist. He knew the secret of sweetening the soluble salt of the sea. Roseline had a brother named Helios (a name invoking the sun god). He was captured and put in prison on the island of Rhodes. According to author James Egan, *Rhodes* is a Greek name meaning "rose."[13] The island was called Island of the Sun. Roseline miraculously freed him. (Although this information is regarded as historical, it seems like a bit of a fairy tale.)

THE TRADITION OF ROSICRUCIANISM

The Rosicrucian tradition developed as man's image of the world was changing. Ancient man had a group consciousness. He identified with his tribe, his village, and later his town or country. There was little privacy, and the sense of being an individual was challenged at every turn. In the Middle Ages this would begin to change as people became educated. With learning came a sense of self-identity and self-awareness and independence from the dominance of church and state. The Cathar religion was one example of this. The word *religion* actually derives from a word meaning "to bind." To find the spiritual one has to be free from such boundaries; no institution or authority—no intermediary—can intercede in the spiritual journey. This is the true quest of the grail.

Rosicrucians believe the metaphorical way of describing their tradition is to say that Rosicrucianism is the ignition that lights the spark. It brings about a sense of self-awareness and puts an emphasis on the initiation of the individual. Without self-awareness and self-knowledge man is considered to be unconscious. The motto at the Oracle of Delphi was "Know thyself." The mystic George Gurdjieff said that we are asleep most of our lives and have to wake up through self-observation. Individuals cannot change what they don't know. They need to be free from actions that are done without prior contemplation.

Once an individual becomes self-aware, a transformation of consciousness has begun, igniting enlightenment and a proverbial lightbulb of ideas. This transformation might also be said to have begun with early Christianity. Indeed, Christian iconography the world over depicts the receiving of baptism by Saint John the Baptist with a dove over the head of the initiate. Saint John is sacred as the patron saint of the Knights Templar; the dove is the most important symbol of the Rosicrucians. This "baptism" represents true alchemy in that this transformative process allows individuals to have communion with the mind of God.

The goal of a Rosicrucian is alchemy, but not simply in the sense of transmuting lead into gold. Those who have achieved a successful initiation are said to be able to perceive reality on another level, to see one pattern within another, and have the ability to be aware rather than remain unconscious. In Rosicrucianism it is said that the rose light needs to reach from the heart to the brain. This is accomplished by the ability to use the third eye. The adepts can transform themselves by accessing spiritual forces. These forces are all around us, but, until man can develop his ability to reach the higher planes of reality, he is not aware of them.

A purer understanding of Rosicrucianism may not be so simple. A Rosicrucian is an individual above all, a freethinker, and one whose spiritual values are separate from his or her religious values. And while Rosicrucians might subscribe to some tenets of the Christian faith, their leanings would be more toward Deism.

Individual Rosicrucians might take on shared political goals that have nothing to do with the original philosophy of Sir Francis Bacon, therefore representing a straying of sorts from the organization's original mandate and intent. An example of another entity that lost its original raison d'être is the Knights Templar.

THE KNIGHTS TEMPLAR AND ITS CONNECTION TO THE ROSICRUCIAN TRADITION

The Knights Templar was a secret society that was made up of a religious arm and a military arm. It came into being to protect pilgrims traveling to the Holy Lands and was endorsed by the Catholic Church in 1129. It eventually fell out of favor when it became a powerful business with interests in banking, shipping, and property management.

Through time, as part and parcel of its contacts in the Holy Land, the Knights Templar had numerous dealings with secret societies and religious sects of the Middle East. The knights brought many treasures home from their foreign excursions—sacred artifacts, sacred texts, and philosophical writings—of which the West was not yet aware. These treasures included the works of Arabic and Greek mathematicians, astronomers, astrologers, and alchemists.

The Order contained individuals who were interested in the art of magic, the alchemy of metals, and the study of the Kabbalah. The hidden heirs to the Templars devised methods to pass on some of this sacred knowledge through Freemasonry, the Rosicrucian tradition, and the so-called Invisible College, which would, in time, become England's Royal Society.

Templars would apply the sophisticated knowledge that the East had to offer, particularly in the fields of architecture and engineering. Among other things, Templars became renowned masons. Indeed, bridges built by the Templars and Saint Bernard's Cistercians stand even today. The Templars also built cathedrals.

To build a cathedral not only means employing a master architect but also amassing men who know how to work with stone and mortar. These talented workers would come from near and far to work on architectural projects that would take months or years to complete. In an era when every stranger was suspect it was important for stonemasons and others to be housed, fed, and protected in similar company. So "brother-masons," or *frère maçons,* would form lodges wherein a traveling worker could find food, shelter, safety, and kinship. In England they became "freemasons," giving birth to the lodge system among Templars who were builders.

This system remains intact today but has extended its purview to include merchants, lawyers, policemen, and bankers. Code names and phrases, secret handshakes, and secret signs serve to further bind members of this fraternity to one another to the exclusion of outsiders.

In 1307, when the Knights Templar came under attack, many of them and their treasures went underground in Scotland. There, one of the country's most illustrious families became guardian of the outlawed and excommunicated Templars. As Templar circles grew into Masonic lodges this family was appointed hereditary guardians of Freemasonry.

The St. Clair family of France and the Sinclair family of Scotland were one and the same. In Scotland they would build their chapel at Rosslyn. The Rosslyn Chapel, as it came to be called, was named for the rosy red (blood) stream that flowed from Christ's wounds when he was crucified. Near the chapel was the headquarters of the Knights Templar in Scotland, at Templeballythorp.[14]

The nineteenth century featured a resurgence of Rosicrucian societies with many new Rosicrucian groups emerging. When Jules Verne was penning his famous works, the elite members of the Rosicrucian society were represented by a specialized order called the Order of the Golden Dawn. This society was born from the Societas Rosicruciana in Anglia (SRIA), which had been founded in London in 1865. It was divided into circles, and its membership numbered 144 individuals. They included writer and politician Edward Bulwer-Lytton, occultist

Samuel Mathers, Satanist Aleister Crowley, and Bram Stoker, the author of *Dracula,* which is said to contain secret rituals of the Rosicrucians.[15]

To join these societies one had to be a master Mason in good standing and interested in alchemy. But the Rosicrucian tradition was not limited to Europe. By the time of the American Revolution, the organization known as the Ancient and Accepted Scottish Rite became a newer version of Rosicrucianism. During the American Civil War, the Fraternitas Rosae Crucis was founded. We will delve more deeply into these other Rosicrucian societies in later chapters of this book.

CHAPTER 2

SIR FRANCIS BACON: THE MAN WHO COULDN'T BE KING

As we have established, Francis Bacon was one of the most powerful forces for change in the sixteenth and seventeenth centuries in which he lived. He was a Renaissance man versed in science, the arts, literature, government, and politics. He had an immense vocabulary and even coined new words. In a modern vernacular we would say that his day job was in government in one form or another. His real life's work, however, was in the fields of writing and philosophy as a founder and member of various clandestine circles and societies. He was a private person, and, as we know, he kept his secrets.

His secrets include the reorganization of Freemasonry and that he was one of the founders of the Rosicrucian movement. These were not the only secret societies with which he was involved. Shortly after his "father's" death he founded the literary Rosi Crosse Society at Gray's Inn in London.

BACON'S CLASSIC TEXTS AND HIS CONNECTION TO SHAKESPEARE

Francis Bacon authored and coauthored several texts that were credited to others. These texts became the basis of the modern Rosicrucian tradition. One such text was Bacon's posthumously appearing *New Atlantis,* which described a world where learned men were free to develop themselves and their thinking along progressive lines. Bacon would not be comfortable publishing *New Atlantis* while he was alive, though perhaps he thought it was his greatest work, given that he put his own name on it instead of crediting it to Shakespeare or Christian Rosenkreuz as he did with other material he had written. He does not mention the Rose Cross specifically by name in *New Atlantis* but does maintain, in the pages of the novel, that the New Atlantis was governed by the R. C. Brothers.[1] Nineteenth-century writer John Heydon called the New Atlantis the "land of the Rosicrucians" and attempted a rewrite of Bacon's greatest work.[2]

The New Atlantis was not a world to conquer or one in which riches might be procured. It was meant to be a place where man could be free of religious domination and war. And while Bacon and his colleagues may have sold others on the idea of riches, they really wanted a safe haven from church and state. Bacon was already creating such a world with the influence he and John Dee had on Queen Elizabeth. Indeed, Bacon and his circle of fellow esoteric thinkers would fund England's explorations in the New World.

New Atlantis was a seminal work of Bacon's. Another famous text attributed to him was *The Advancement of Learning.* Written in 1605, it argued that knowledge was discovered by observation. Up until that time the attainment of knowledge was accomplished via memorization and a reading of the classics. Bacon, however, maintained that experience was a better route to knowledge. At the time though, a deviation of this type was considered to be taboo, not unlike the study of science, which had been so strongly rejected by the church, with its conceptual stranglehold on the culture of the day. Consequently, *The Advancement of Learning* was bolder than it might be considered to be at present.

It's interesting to note that in this book there is a depiction of a ship sailing between two obelisks or pillars. Two triangles and two owls are depicted on the bottom of the page. This is significant in that another of Bacon's works, titled *Sylva Sylvarum,* contains Bacon's "emblem." It again is an illustration of two pillars (of wisdom?), which is fundamentally the same as the symbol that is employed by the Freemasons. The pillars are connected by the sun of wisdom (or, the *son* of wisdom?). The letters of this son of wisdom are *s–o–w*. We know that Bacon enjoyed wordplays and, indeed, here we have a good one: "Bacon" was the product of the "sow," and also of the "hog." He was as well the "little ham," or Hamlet.

Referencing the illustration of the pillars again, a ship is seen passing through the two columns, which may be likened to the ancient route to Atlantis that involved passing through the Pillars of Hercules into the ocean. As a founding member of the Virginia Company, whose lost ships also "discovered" Bermuda, and a founder of the company that reached Newfoundland as well, Bacon can be said to be the true discoverer of the world he envisioned.

The symbolism of the two columns was adopted into Freemasonry, and while Rosicrucian tradition thrived in the years before Bacon died, this same symbolism found its permanent way into the culture of Freemasonry. At least one contemporary writer said that Freemasonry is modified Rosicrucianism.[3]

The motto of this emblem was *Plus ultra,* meaning "There is more beyond."

Perhaps the juiciest of Bacon's secrets is that he is the odds-on favorite candidate for being the author of many of the works attributed to Shakespeare. This in part is due to the fact that many scholars believe that an illiterate butcher's apprentice could not have written the works attributed to the Bard. The Order of the Knights of the Helmet was, as we have learned, an illuminated secret group with Bacon as its head. A rationale for believing that Bacon may have penned the works attributed to Shakespeare lies in the fact that the ancient goddess Pallas Athena, to whom Bacon's Order of the Helmet was dedicated, was often depicted with helmet and spear, and her epithet was "shaker of the spear." Indeed, Bacon wrote a play titled *The Order of the Helmet,* which was performed in January 1594 and again in December of that same year.

The members of the Order of the Helmet were known to call Sir Francis Bacon "king" and the "prince of purple." However, given that it was dangerous for Bacon to be publically named in this way, and given that he wanted to continue to write plays, he needed a front man for his writings.

Bacon's motto was *Occulta veritas tempore patet,* meaning "Hidden truth comes to light in time." He would be more open in his writings in the last five years of his life, notably after the death of Queen Elizabeth, but until then he realized that he would not survive court life if it were known that he had authored politically contentious works such as *Richard II.*

Circa 1592, members of Bacon's circle crossed paths with the man known as William Shakespeare. Christopher Marlowe, whom some credit for contributing to the works attributed to the Bard, might have been the first to meet young Will. Marlowe in turn introduced Will into other circles. In 1592, Henry Wriothesley became a patron of the Bard. Henry was the third Earl of Southampton, whose surname was pronounced "rose lee."

In Southampton's role as a patron of the arts, he also acted as patron for writers Thomas Nashe and George Wither and lexicographer and translator John Florio.

The first narrative poems said to be Shakespeare's are *Venus and Adonis* and *The Rape of Lucrece.* Both were dedicated to Henry Wriothesley, who is considered to be the person to whom Shakespeare's later sonnets were also dedicated. He is thought to be the Fair Youth of these sonnets to whom the poet expresses his love.

Was a twenty-eight-year-old Shakespeare declaring his love for a nineteen-year-old? If so, it was a dangerous declaration to make. Homosexuality was not yet taboo, but a lowborn butcher's apprentice might be setting himself up for serious consequences if he publically instead of clandestinely declared his love for someone of the same gender.

Southampton obviously was the object of *someone's* affections, given the fact that these works were dedicated to him. The chance that the someone was a male would not be unusual in the Elizabethan court. Another candidate is Edward de Vere, the seventeenth Earl of Oxford. Oxford was twenty-three years' Southampton's senior and would have been well acquainted with him. Oxford traveled extensively, was fluent in French and Italian, studied at Cambridge, and, like Southamptom, who was highborn and lost his father at a young age, had also been a ward of Sir William Cecil, Lord Burghley. Oxford was also a participant in Rosicrucian circles. A portrait of him shows his hand placed atop a skull, which in turn is on a red cloth; this is reminiscent of Freemasonic ritual. Whether the relationship between Oxford and Southampton went beyond mutual affection is unknown, but if Oxford was indeed the author of these romantic verses, Southampton would not be put off by the attention.

In any event, in 1592, William Shakespeare suddenly received a large amount of money and bought the second largest house in his home-town of Stratford-upon-Avon. This was a deal that, if made between Shakespeare and members of Bacon's circle, could serve them all well. Plays written for the stage might be sold for five to ten pounds, so the "gift" of a large amount of money from Southampton to Shakespeare wasn't for the purchase of a body of work. It was to purchase his silence. The so-called Bard might better be called the "Beard," disguising the true author (or authors) of these very sophisticated works. (Actually, it should also be noted that Shakespeare was never called the Bard in his lifetime. A bard in the Celtic context was a learned man. Will was a butcher's apprentice who could not read and could hardly even write.)

Bacon, given all the obvious reasons why he might have written the works of Shakespeare, needed such a patsy. Marlowe, Henry Wriothesley, and Bacon, all highly educated, might have been amused at the audacity of the concept of crediting Shakespeare with such erudite literary endeavors.

Shakespeare, for his part, enjoyed the money.

The "Who was Shakespeare?" question came up in 1780 when a British clergyman by the name of James Wilmot decided to write a biography of one of two of his favorite writers. He would conclude that Shakespeare could not have written anything, and the works would have been composed by Wilmot's other favorite writer, Sir Francis Bacon. In America a schoolteacher and author, Delia Bacon, came to the same conclusion. While she was publicly scorned, the list of others who shared the same view included Ralph Waldo Emerson,[4] Nathaniel Hawthorne, Walt Whitman, and Benjamin Disraeli.[5]

From James Wilmot to Delia Bacon and beyond, Sir Francis Bacon is generally, not unanimously, the man assumed to have written the works attributed to Shakespeare. But do we have any real proof? There may be clues in the works themselves.

Francis Bacon was allegedly born in 1561 in St. Albans, a suburb of London, twenty miles north of the city. This home is referred to twenty-three times in texts attributed to Shakespeare, while the birthplace of Shakespeare—Stratford—is not *ever* mentioned in any of the thirty-seven plays and sonnets. From childhood, Bacon was considered a prodigy, and as an adult he would become versed in science, politics, languages, and law, having studied at Cambridge and Gray's Inn. He also enjoyed drama, although he may have regarded it as an amusement and a diversion, in comparison to his cohort Henry Wriothesley, who would not miss a performance.

Born into prominent circles, Bacon spent much of his time in the company of the highborn.

WAS FRANCIS BACON THE CHILD OF QUEEN ELIZABETH I?

Sir Francis Bacon's greatest secret is that he was actually the child of Queen Elizabeth and the Earl of Leicester. The earl Robert Dudley was born on June 24, 1532, a year before Elizabeth was born. They both were born into intrigue, which created life-and-death situations.

Elizabeth's father was King Henry VIII, and her mother was Anne Boleyn, who was murdered by Henry.

At eight years old, Elizabeth confided to Robert that she would never marry. She may have understood that because of her father's marriages, heads rolled, and the Tower might be only one small step away from marital bliss. Elizabeth and Robert Dudley had actually spent time in the Tower together, though neither were treated badly while there. Her imprisonment had been at the hands of her half sister, Mary Tudor, as a result of the Wyatt Rebellion that saw Lady Jane Grey and her husband, Guilford Dudley, executed.[6] Robert Dudley had also been imprisoned for being involved in a plot that pertained to his family. Elizabeth learned the hard way of the treacheries of being queen, and that lesson was never forgotten.

Elizabeth and Dudley grew up together and shared the same tutor, Roger Ascham. He found that Robert was better at math than Latin and Elizabeth was able in mathematics, passionate about history, and adept in languages from French and Italian to Latin and Greek and even Spanish and Flemish. Elizabeth and Robert were in love with each other but had to keep their love a secret. Elizabeth was taken by his wit and charm, but the relationship could not be allowed because Robert was not of royal blood, and it was custom that a royal could not marry a lesser noble. Robert Dudley would go on to marry Amy Robsart, and Elizabeth would attend the wedding. Be this as it may, a year after his wedding, Dudley was spending most of his time at court.

Elizabeth and Dudley also shared a friend, John Dee, with whom Dudley interceded when it came time to choose Elizabeth's coronation date. One of Elizabeth's first acts as queen was to appoint Dudley as Master of the Horse, which kept him at the court and close to her. Dudley and the queen continued to be close despite his marriage. In 1559 gossip began to spread about their affection for each other. The Spanish court of King Philip kept a close eye on Elizabeth, and more than one letter that was sent home declared that Dudley was in the quarters of the queen day and night.[7]

Dudley still wanted the queen's hand in marriage despite the fact that his wife Amy was still alive. Dudley and Elizabeth, with the hope that England would allow their marriage, did not want Amy to survive into the coming year. Amy was sent to live in the home of Anthony Forster, a friend of her husband's, because she was said to have a serious illness. At this time Dudley saw an opportunity to be king, and Amy was clearly an obstacle to that. A Mother Anne Dowe of Brentwood reported in writing that the queen was pregnant with Robert Dudley's child. For this Dowe would be put in prison.

Amy's sudden death on September 8, 1560, occurred when she fell down a staircase. Sir Robert was not present. The queen herself was implicated by the court gossipers, but on September 12, four days later, she and Dudley were secretly married at Lord Pembroke's house. Indeed, the Spanish ambassador to England would be tipped off that she was secretly married to Dudley.

One of the most powerful men in the court was Cecil, Lord Burghley. He kept his power by manipulation and the ability to judge the direction of the political winds. In April 1551, Cecil became chancellor of the Order of the Garter. He opposed the idea of Elizabeth marrying Dudley and would tell an agent for the king of Spain, Count de Feria, that Dudley wanted his wife Amy dead. While this might seem out of character for Cecil, who was deemed to be exceedingly trustworthy by the queen, it was obvious that Cecil wanted to maintain the status quo, particularly a tight grasp on his power. A husband for the queen might mean competition for the queen's trust.

In a letter dated September 11 the bishop de la Quadra, an Italian spy, told the Duchess of Parma that Cecil, Lord Burghley, was upset over the actions of the queen. He said that Cecil had been told by Dudley that he was thinking of killing his wife.

If Cecil was truthful, there is little question that Amy was murdered for convenience sake. Her body at the bottom of a stone staircase caused the queen to state, in Italian: *Si ha rotto il collo,* meaning "She must have fallen down a staircase."[8] The queen apparently told Cecil that Amy was "dead or nearly so."[9]

With no firm evidence of foul play, however, and with Cecil afraid to go against either the queen or Robert's influence with the queen, there was little evidence that a crime had indeed been committed. A jury convened and maintained that her death was accidental.

While Amy Robsart's death technically left the queen and Robert free to marry, he was not considered royalty. The Spanish agent de la Quadra, however, reported that Dudley had confided in him that the queen had said yes to his marriage proposal. If this were true, the two were not ready for the storm that followed. The English public, the English court, and the courts of England's allies and enemies all reacted in horror to the idea of a marriage between Robert Dudley and Queen Elizabeth. If the reaction of her subjects had not been bad enough, a dispatch by the Spanish envoy threatened that if she married Dudley, France and Spain would unite to remove her from the throne. One can only guess that the couple had never expected this reaction. The reaction put off their plans for a public wedding indefinitely.

One thing they could not put off, however, was Elizabeth's pregnancy. Many commented that her looks were consistent with those of a pregnant woman.

Amy Robsart died on September 8, 1560, and Francis Bacon was born on January 21 of the following year. This would imply that Elizabeth was possibly in her fifth month of pregnancy when Amy had had her fatal accident. When young Francis was born, the queen was in residence at York House, the home of Nicholas Bacon—the Lord Keeper of the Great Seal of England—but she had no engagements. According to Henrietta Bernstein, author of *Ark of the Covenant, Holy Grail,* "Research confirms Sir Francis Bacon was the rightful heir to the throne of England."[10] His mother and father decided they could never acknowledge him, though Elizabeth seems to have done so in secret. So instead of being born Francis Tudor, they decided that Sir Nicholas Bacon and Lady Ann Bacon, a powerful couple of the court, would oversee Francis's upbringing as his "parents." The child would be known to the world as Francis Bacon. It would be noted that Sir Francis Bacon resembled Dudley and not Sir Nicholas Bacon.

FRANCIS BACON'S EARLY YEARS

How had Nicholas and Anne Bacon been chosen to oversee the young Francis? Lord Burghley, Elizabeth's chief adviser, had married Mildred Cooke. Mildred's sister Anne Cooke became Anne Bacon when she'd married Nicholas Bacon. So Burghley simply picked his sister-in-law as guardian, and, as history will show, as "mother" of Sir Francis. In this, Cecil, Lord Burghley, again ensured his position as the center of Elizabeth's world. He knew where the bodies were buried, and he knew secrets that could threaten the queen.

Lady Anne Bacon was the daughter of Anthony Cooke. The Cookes were a prominent family with large landholdings in Stratford. Anne was at once a housewife and a tutor and a governess of the future King Edward VI. Unlike that other Stratford resident, she was versed in classical languages and started each day with Francis by recounting to him stories of adventures, myths, and morality tales. Her effect on young Francis cannot be overestimated; his intellect was sparked by her teaching.

Nicholas Bacon, for his role in helping to bring up young Francis, was given a new home where he raised the boy. The queen was a frequent visitor. Sir Edward Coke called Sir Francis "the queen's bastard." Bacon was also said to be called "little lord keeper" by the queen herself.

Other sources confirmed the queen's relationship with Leicester as well as the evidence of a love child. Indeed, the Scottish ambassador said that the queen called Leicester "my lord." But alleging that Elizabeth had given birth to Dudley's child was a dangerous thing to do, and in 1562 one Robert Brooks of Devizes was sent to prison for it, while another man had his ears cut off. As mentioned, a woman by the name of Anne Dowe was imprisoned for the same crime, and two men, Robert Gardner and Dionysia Deryck, were pilloried. In 1571, Parliament passed a law declaring that Elizabeth's natural issue to be the only ones who would be considered as successor. Was the law more concerned with putting an end to the incessant question of who would rule next? Or did the wording *natural issue* set the stage for a surprise? The wording was not *her legal heir*, which might have excluded Bacon.

Elizabeth visited the new home at Gorhambury that she had given to Nicholas Bacon the month before Francis started school. And in a letter to Anthony, Queen Elizabeth said, "It is not my meaning to treat him as a ward."[11] In other words, it was her intention to treat him as her son, rather than a ward.

Sir Francis was given the finest education, starting with Trinity College at Cambridge when he was twelve. Later he would write to Elizabeth from school, telling her how he suffered as a "lost" child. She in turn wrote back that he was her son and truly royal but would not ever rule her or England.[12] In *Hamlet,* a work attributed to Shakespeare but most likely authored by Bacon, Hamlet is the prince by birth who cannot inherit the throne.

In 1576, Francis and his brother, Anthony, were admitted to Gray's Inn to study law. It was at this time that Francis's "mother," Lady Bacon, would hear that Francis was engaged in homosexual activities. This matter worried Lady Bacon. She wrote a letter to his brother, Anthony, expressing her concern about the possibility of scandal caused by Francis's choice of bed partners. The letter may have fallen on deaf ears because Anthony was equally inclined.[13] But back then many of the most obvious male homosexuals took women as wives.

Being homosexual in the twenty-first century is quite different from how it was perceived in the sixteenth century. At the time, the labels heterosexual or homosexual were not applied, for there were no exclusive categories of behavior. A long-standing affair with a same-sex partner might be considered mutual affection without implying that sexual activity was taking place. Even if suspected, it was not openly discussed. A *coach companion,* a term used by Bacon's mother in her letter to Anthony, *did* have that connotation. And being considered a pederast or a sodomite did carry a price; there were criminal statutes against such practices.

In 1579, Bacon had a dream about his father's home being covered in black. Sir Nicholas died shortly afterward. The will left a great deal of money to all of Nicholas's children except Francis. This is the most telling sign that he had been the caretaker of Francis, not his real father. Most likely he felt that the queen herself would make provisions for her son.

It may have been at this point in his life that Bacon discovered who his true parents were and took issue with being raised as "a Bacon" and not as a Tudor. By now he had begun his career in law but railed in private that he would not be recognized by his true mother.[14]

It might have been his understanding of his unique situation or simply his intellect that made him a bit of a rebel against the absolute powers of the monarchy.

It was about this time that his secret society activity was born and the famous Rosicrucian texts began to be written.

KEEPING A LOW PROFILE IN THE ENGLISH COURT

It is certain that there were strong traditions of secrecy among the Rosicrucians. For instance, Rosicrucians in the time of Elizabeth believed that the rose represented silence.

Bacon himself was cautious in his writings but on occasion gave himself away. In one text he said, "I begin to be weary of the Sun."[15] This unusual phrase is seen again in *Macbeth,* act 5, scene 5, verse 55: "I 'gin to be weary of the Sun." A German translation in 1654 of Bacon's *De Sapienta Veterum* depicted Bacon as the head of the Rosicrucian society.

As a Freemason, Bacon's favorite code was the Kabbalistic cipher in which his name, Bacon, was the number 33. The 33rd degree became the highest rank in Freemasonry one could attain. Though Masons state very little about the importance of this number,[16] it is said to represent the interface of the familial world and the higher realm of spirit.[17]

Masonry opened many doors to Bacon: In 1584 he was admitted to Parliament, an impossible feat without money or connections. It is possible his letters, imploring that his royal status be recognized, worked. At this time in his life he was busy reading, learning ciphers, and assembling secret societies. Little of his writing could be in his name as he dared not annoy the queen, his mother. Meanwhile his real father, the Earl of Leicester, was made the Lord Governor of England and Ireland, the greatest power any sovereign had given to a subject. But Leicester would not live long enough to enjoy his new power.

Upon Leicester's death in 1588, the queen seized all of his lands, which was her prerogative. She also made Francis the Counsel Extraordinary to the queen. Sometime before 1591 he became involved with Robert Devereux, the second Earl of Essex, who became his advocate with the queen. Essex constantly recommended that Queen Elizabeth promote Bacon to other positions at court, and she always turned Essex down. This could be construed as evidence that he was not her son, although others may argue it's evidence that he was.

In 1595, when Essex failed to get Bacon the post he had hoped for, Essex gave him an estate worth eighteen hundred pounds. Essex may have regarded Bacon in the same way he regarded Southampton. He loved both men, but such love was not physical. Essex did all he could to help Bacon but in the end was not able to because his character put his own life in peril.

In any case, when Bacon did finally get close enough to his mother the queen to provide her with counsel, Essex began to appear to be out of control. Essex had been sent to Ireland to quell Tyrone's rebellion but felt outnumbered and unable to defeat the rebels. His return to England was considered a shameful defeat.

Essex then attempted to incite rebellion against the queen. Bacon interceded, but at this time Elizabeth was old and embittered at the perceived betrayal. On February 7, Essex staged a production of *Richard II*. This enraged the queen because *Richard II* centers on a plot to remove a sovereign from power. Bacon's position forced him to take the role of prosecutor in the falling out between the queen and Essex. As much as he did not want to take sides against his long-term friend and promoter, the verdict was guilty. Bacon might have hoped that the queen would not carry out the death sentence, but he did not count on the actions of others who had their own reasons to see Essex dead.

The queen wished for some sign of contrition from Essex. He sent her a ring, which somehow never arrived. She still did not have the heart to have him killed and at the last minute signed a "countermand" to the warrant for execution. Robert Cecil, the son of Lord Burghley, had other plans, however. Known to have felt threatened by Bacon and as someone who relished ridding his life of enemies, he rushed Essex to a quick and nonpublic execution, which was highly unusual for a political prisoner. (Generally executions were public and held at Tyburn in present-day London.)

Following the execution of Essex the queen became withdrawn. She lost weight as well as her appetite for the finer things in life. Eighteen months later she was dead. It is possible that her greatest fear had materialized: She herself might have been on the outs of power, possibly arrested and thrown in the Tower, and/or possibly executed—as her mother, Anne Boleyn, had been.

ROYAL REFERENCES TO BACON'S TRUE HERITAGE

Ironically, Bacon, as the son of the queen and the Earl of Leicester, would prosper after Elizabeth's death even if he never received the recognition he had hoped for. His friend Southampton never forgave him for his role in the prosecution of Essex. If Shakespeare as a front man was known to both Southampton and Bacon, it is significant that Shakespeare is strangely silent after Essex's death.

But if Bacon lost one friend, his stock increased with others. Within four months he was knighted by James, the new king. And although his mother had never given him recognition as a prince, he was, at least, raised to knighthood by the king.

With James as England's king, not only did Bacon's political career fare better but his writings could be more public, though not all of them. Notably he penned his *New Atlantis,* which depicts the search for a peaceful world where royalty ruled judiciously as a result of wisdom. This would have been a dangerous thing to be made public during the reign of Elizabeth. It might have been equally dangerous under James. Publication could wait.

When *New Atlantis* was eventually released the cover of the first edition depicted Father Time leading a female figure out of a dark cave. The words around this emblematic device were "In time the secret truth shall be revealed," another of Bacon's mottoes.

Bacon, despite his attraction to male partners, would, like others in the royal court, take a wife. He married the daughter of Lady Packington, Alice Barnham, in 1606. He was forty-six; Alice would turn fourteen on her wedding date. Love was less of an issue than money, and Bacon was the benefactor financially.

At the time of the wedding it was still a law in England that only royalty could wear purple. Sir Francis wore purple at his wedding. A man by the name of Dudley Carleton, not a fan of Bacon's, would write, "Sir Francis Bacon was married to his young wench yesterday in Maribone Chapel. He was clad from top to toe in purple, and hath made himself and his wife such store of fine raiment's of cloth of silver and gold that it draws deep in her portion."[18]

Bacon's first biographer, Pierre Amboise, wrote that Bacon was "born in the purple."[19]

Bacon's chaplain and secretary, William Rawley, also wrote

that Bacon was born in York House.[20] In other words, he was born a royal.

If the act of wearing purple was criminal, Bacon was not reprimanded. He became Solicitor-General, a position he had looked to attain for a decade.

THE CASE FOR BACON HAVING WRITTEN THE WORKS ATTRIBUTED TO SHAKESPEARE

Bacon's sponsorship of the voyages of the Virginia Company would lead to the establishment of the accidental colony of Bermuda. The Virginia Company shareholders included the Earl of Pembroke and Montgomery, to whom the First Folio of William Shakespeare's plays was dedicated.

As Bermuda became incorporated into the Virginia Colony it minted coinage called hog money, another Bacon reference. Bacon's crest was on one side and a picture of a sailing ship was on the other. (Bacon's role in creating a democracy was of course not approved by King James I, who would forbid the circulation of this "hog money.")

The Virginia Company sent Sir John Somers to Virginia in 1609 with a company of colonists. Somer's ship the *Sea Venture* was wrecked on Bermuda. The story of the sinking of the *Sea Venture* is said to be the basis for *The Tempest*. (We will discuss this in more detail later.) Bacon is on the list of those who had inside information on the records of this ill-fated journey, which might indicate that he could have written this "Shakespearean" work.

In 1611 the King James Version of the Bible was translated and edited. Bacon had a field day planting cryptic coded messages throughout. In Psalm 46, the forty-sixth word from the first verse is *shake* while the forty-sixth word from the end is *spear*. Bacon also illustrated the title page, and these intricate designs provided hidden meanings as well. Each of the ornaments conceals a Rosicrucian emblem, a Masonic emblem, or Bacon's name in code as can be seen on the original frontispiece of Edmund Spenser's *Faerie Queene*. The royal eagle of the Stuarts (a reference to King James) landing on the stump of the Tudor rose referred to the last Tudor queen, Elizabeth. One rose of the Tudor bush has its bloom turned away, which represents Sir Francis: the heir that was hidden from the public eye.

The first editions of the Bible were printed in the same manner as the Shakespeare plays had been, implying that there could be a connection between the two.

Bacon was everything that Will Shakespeare was not. He was a polymath who was born to royalty, studied law, understood court life, and, through firsthand experience and through his brother and those who were close to him, had extensive knowledge of the military, the navy, navigation, and faraway lands. Bacon was also versed in Greek and Latin and read the classics. He was fluent in European languages as well—a prerequisite for being the author of the plays attributed to Shakespeare. His characters were often public servants, as he himself was.

Bacon's position at court was almost always precarious. He wanted more than Elizabeth would give him and held out hope that the favors of the queen would be forthcoming. He could not take the chance of getting on her bad side. Those close to him who found themselves on the wrong side of the queen paid a steep price.

While Elizabeth was alive Bacon risked everything to avoid being seen as an author. Indeed, he claimed in a letter to explorer John Davis that he was a concealed poet. His own works that were not concealed display a vast vocabulary and the ability to coin new words and phrases. Opinions displayed in his public works are shared in his secret works. His notebooks held a collection of phrases that were employed in the Shakespearean plays. Works attributed to Bacon and Shakespeare share alternating light and dark letter *A*'s as emblems along with other symbols.

One of Bacon's closest friends was Tobie Matthew. A letter from Matthew to Bacon says that Tobie is returning the manuscript of *Measure for Measure*. Another letter refers to Bacon's authorship of *Julius Caesar*.[21]

Bacon wrote in ciphers and understood the concept of steganography in which a symbol known by the writer and the intended reader can change the meaning of what is written. In this science a picture is worth more than a thousand words, for it's the key to understanding whatever has been written. The literal Greek translation of *steganography* means "covered writing." "Steg-text" can conceal a written document within another written document. Bacon would hide significant letters among the capital letters of a text. He might have further concealed some of the writing by substitution.

In some of Bacon's writing he uses periods in inappropriate places. This too serves as a device to those who understand what they mean in terms of deciphering the cryptic text. He also had a vocabulary that went beyond the average Cambridge graduate. Bacon carried a notebook in which he recorded phrases and meanings. In other cases he coined new words.

In 1594 he began work on his *Promus* (literally "storehouse") *of Formularies and Elegancies*. He would write down words, phrases, proverbs, and colloquialisms in English, Latin, French, Italian, and Greek. These words, this expanding vocabulary, would be useful in writing the plays.

Promus of Formularies and Elegancies was not published until 1883. It is not hard to conclude that Shakespeare did not have access to the *Promus* and therefore did not write the words shared in *Promus* and the plays that were attributed to him.

While Sir Francis endured life with a lack of acceptance by Queen Elizabeth, his true mother, and the inability to claim his right as a Tudor, he had an even greater secret. He was responsible for at least some of the works attributed to Shakespeare.

THE "DEATHS" OF SIR FRANCIS BACON

On April 9, 1626, Bacon was at the home of Lord Arundel. Bacon had taken ill while studying the effects of snow (instead of salt), on dead poultry. The illness took the sixty-five-year-old man so quickly he could not return to Gray's Inn, where his belongings were, and instead went to Lord Arundel's home, where he died.

Or did he?

There are many rumors of famous figures who may have survived their own death. From King Arthur to JFK, from Elvis to Jim Morrison, many stories are told, and they may even contain some truth here and there.

In the case of Francis Bacon, there was little public mention of his death. There would be no funeral and no burial ceremony. There is, however, a vault under a tombstone in St. Michael's Church in St. Albans, England, but it was sealed. This last secret surrounds his death. But wait a moment. Is there a clue in the portrayal of him on the tombstone's monument, which shows Bacon wearing a hat? *A hat in church?* Was this perhaps his last pun?—that he kept a secret under his hat?

It is believed by some that he left that year for Holland, never to return. Holland, and particularly the city of Leiden, gave shelter to many who fled religious persecution in England. These people were known as Separatists and later would board ships such as the *Mayflower,* bound for the New Atlantis. Many of them, however, would bring their own brand of intolerance with them, which had not been envisioned by Sir Francis. Massachusetts especially was not a paradise of religious freedom, for it banned the playing of cards and dancing, and it punished those who had the audacity to miss Sunday services. Rosicrucian thought did survive as envisioned by both Bacon and his friend John Dee, however, in places like Pennsylvania, especially Philadelphia. There it would spread secretly and be carried under many names to other cities and states where Bacon's freethinking ideals would take root.

It's also possible that Bacon may have settled in Philadelphia or possibly Virginia's first capital of Jamestown, or even Williamsburg, where he might have lived to a very old age. It is also speculated that his final resting place may be on a piece of property in Williamsburg that's owned by the Rockefeller family; it may also contain his written works. This is a topic that we will explore further in a later chapter.

CHAPTER 3

THE AUTHOR(S) KNOWN AS SHAKESPEARE

Next we will turn our attention to the man known as William Shakespeare, and to the men who may have used his identity as an alias to convey ideas that they could not publicly claim. In uncovering the possible identities of this playwright, we will see how the men who wrote under Shakespeare's name are connected to one another. What do we really know about William Shakespeare? Let's begin with the research that's been conducted on the subject.

More than 150 years after the Bard's death, a British clergyman and Oxford-trained scholar, James Wilmot, decided (in the 1780s) that he would write a biography of William Shakespeare. To do this, he moved to Warwickshire, near Shakespeare's home. He went to Stratford-upon-Avon to collect stories about his subject, only to discover that there were none to be found. He attempted to look for books that his prized author might have owned. Surely a man displaying such a wealth of knowledge must have had a wealth of sources! While writers are generally voracious readers, book lovers, diary keepers, and keepers of correspondence, William Shakespeare wasn't any of those things. No library of works could be uncovered—not one single book. The author of *The Tempest* had included the line "Knowing I lov'd my books," but apparently Will Shakespeare hadn't much love for them after all.

Nearly frustrated, Wilmot decided that he should at least be able to turn up one of Shakespeare's plays, as the man was such a prolific writer. Again his attempt was thwarted. (Notably, it was years after Shakespeare's death that a folio of his work was first put together. This was not an original folio, as none are known to exist.)

What Wilmot did discover was that William Shakespeare had been born of illiterate parents, neither of whom could sign their name and instead signed with an *X*. They themselves owned no books, and so none would have been used in teaching their son to read. Stratford itself was no center of learning—the entire town had a total of three dozen books when the Bard was born. Barely half of its residents could sign their name. Out of those who could, only a handful could actually do much more than that. Of the nineteen government officials in Stratford, thirteen signed official documents with an *X*. John and Mary Shakespeare were not alone.

Wilmot passed along his findings to his friend James Corton Cowell, who then lectured on the subject. While Wilmot burned his own papers shortly before his death, the lectures of Cowell are preserved in the library of London's Senate House.

SCANT FINDINGS ABOUT OLD WILL

The date William Shakespeare was born was not recorded. His baptism on April 26 of 1564 *was* recorded, however, so historians simply backtracked three days to claim that his birthday was April 23, given that April 23 was the feast day of England's patron saint, Saint George. William was believed to have only been schooled in grade school, where he showed little ability. As we have established, as an adult he could barely sign his name. And each of his six known signatures are different, displaying evidence of a man uncomfortable with writing even his own name.

It is believed that at the age of thirteen Shakespeare left school; however, there is actually no real evidence that he ever attended *any* school. Young Will was apprenticed as a butcher's boy. It is doubtful that in the years he spent cutting meat that he acquired knowledge of English, French, Greek and Roman history, the ability to read Italian and Latin, the principles of law, an understanding of medical science, knowledge of military and naval terms, falconry and horsemanship—or even the ability to write a full sentence.

Sixteenth-century Britain was the only place in the world where English was spoken. However, from one county to another people could not understand each other's dialect. In Stratford, sanitary conditions were pitiful. Diseases due to poor diet included even scurvy, and they were spread by "the inconceivably filthy habits of the people."[1] There was no drainage of the streets, where pigs and geese roamed freely. At one point the municipal government passed an ordinance that offal be carted to dung heaps to reduce the smell. A dung mound, for which Will's father, John Shakespeare, was fined for noncompliance, stood in front of the Shakespeare family home on Henley Street.

Given these surroundings, there were worse things than working for a butcher, but the family was not accustomed to a reduced status. Once upon a time John and Mary Shakespeare had enjoyed a measure of prominence and prosperity in their small community. Mary, born Mary Arden, was from an old Warwickshire family. They had been considered Papists when the Reformation took root in England, and at one point two members of the Arden family had been arrested for suspicions of supporting a man named John Somerville, who had threatened the royal family. This did not, however, affect the family's status or wealth.

Mary married well beneath her, for John Shakespeare was the son of one of her father's tenant farmers. John's father, Richard, had also been a yeoman for the Arden family. A healthy dowry presented in both cash and land raised John's stature and helped him to get a good start in life. For a long time he was prosperous, owning two houses and holding numerous minor municipal posts. But in the 1570s, while son Will was still a child, his fortunes failed, and he was sued for inability to pay his debts.

Will took to poaching venison and rabbits, possibly to make up for his parents' inability to provide. He was said to have been whipped and on occasion imprisoned for his thievery.[2]

In November of 1582, Will took out a license to marry Anne Whateley of Temple Grafton. He was only eighteen. Anne was twenty-six and pregnant and was known to have socialized in the company of two or three males. There is more than a slight chance that the marriage was not entered into voluntarily by young Will. Today it might be called a shotgun wedding. The next day he took out another license to marry Anne Hathaway. Obviously someone had made a mistake—friends of the father of Ms. Hathaway had signed both bonds, indicating again a restricted knowledge of even rudimentary writing skill.

Anne would bear Will three children. Daughter Susanna was born in May of 1583, six months after her parents married. Twins Hamnet and Judith were born in February of 1585. They were named for neighbors Hamnet and Judith Sadler.[3] That same year, at twenty, the young husband had had enough of family life and disappeared. The seven years between 1585 and 1592 are regarded as the "lost years."[4] Scholars have hypothesized that Will might have gone to sea, traveled the continent, or been apprenticed to a doctor or lawyer, but—there is no evidence for any of this.

It might be surmised that he traveled with a roving band of actors where he learned a craft. There is no reason to believe this either, however, as actors had to be registered. So it would be likely that if Will *were* with a company there would be a record of it. Then again, he might have been behind bars as well. Again, a lack of evidence permits no valid conclusion.

There is, sadly enough, no evidence that the errant husband and father returned home, not even when young Hamnet died. But Shakespeare kept no diary, wrote no notes, shared no thoughts in letters, or in all likelihood, actually wrote *anything*.

Somewhere between 1590 and 1592, however, Will Shakespeare

does turn up in London. If we believe his biographers, who do not generally agree with each other, once in the great city he began writing plays, a considerable leap from his being unable to correctly spell his own name. He also joined an established acting company, which would perform these plays. Around this time he met Christopher Marlowe, who may have introduced him to the Burbage Theater and his own circle of colleagues.

Cue Christopher Marlowe.

CHRISTOPHER MARLOWE

Christopher Marlowe was born in 1564 and was the son of a Canterbury shoemaker. After receiving a scholarship, he was educated at the King's School in Canterbury and went on to study at Cambridge. As educated and talented as he was, he had a violent streak and would be brought up on criminal charges from street fighting to counterfeiting. His "friends" would testify to his heretical beliefs.

Marlowe's play *The Jew of Malta* was performed at the Burbage Theater in 1592. This play might have later served as a rough draft of *The Merchant of Venice*. *The Merchant of Venice* is a more refined work, but it is doubtful the butcher's apprentice had an edge over the Cambridge-trained Marlowe. Some even believe that Bacon had reworked Marlowe's play.

In any case, Marlowe lifted the plot and characters from a work called *Il Pecarone,* which was authored by Giovanni Fiorentino in 1558. It was published in only two languages: Latin and French. The pound of flesh, the defeat of the moneylender in court by a woman in disguise, and other important features were borrowed from Fiorentino.

Shakespeare of course was not proficient in Latin or French. If he were, and if he were literate, it might be assumed that he simply copied from Marlowe. But the "Shakespearean" play *The Merchant of Venice* also lifted the scene wherein the coffins are chosen from the *Gesta Romanorum.* Consequently, the true author of *The Merchant of Venice* would have to have been well read in more than one language.

The difference between Marlowe's work and that of the author of *The Merchant of Venice* is important. Marlowe wrote before the trial of the queen's doctor, Rodrigo Lopez, had occurred. Marlowe's Jewish villain, Barabas, named for the thief who was spared instead of Jesus at Golgotha, is a serial killer. He kills a convent full of nuns, a pimp, a prostitute, his daughter, two priests, and a slave. The villain in *The Merchant of Venice* is still a villain, but in this case it's because he's a Jewish moneylender. It was written after the execution of Lopez.

Lopez had committed a crime and in so doing had made a serious mistake. The crime was in his having suggested that he would poison Queen Elizabeth for his king, Philip II, if asked. His mistake was to badmouth Lord Essex, telling fellow drinkers of his diseases and what Lopez had had to do to cure him. The drinkers courted favor with Essex by directly conveying these indiscretions. Essex then wrote Anthony Bacon, the brother of Sir Francis, and told him that Lopez was a spy and a potential assassin. Sir Francis presented the case, and Lopez was taken to the Tower and executed.

Be this as it may, there is a case to be made that *The Merchant of Venice* was a version of the Marlowe play. Had some of the evidence of the Lopez trial been falsified? Had the true author of *The Merchant of Venice* wished to temper the anti-Jewish sentiment that had been caused by the trial? If the answer to the first question is yes, Francis Bacon might have borne the guilt of his own role in the prosecution. If the answer to the second question is yes, Francis Bacon was one who could also be suspected as author as he believed in tolerance and would write in *New Atlantis* that Jews should be free from any and all prejudice. Thus, Bacon may have written *The Merchant of Venice* to atone for his own involvement and ensuing guilt in the matter.

Another curious matter pertaining to *The Merchant of Venice* is that Shylock is not a Jewish name. However, a man by the name of Michael Lok was known to the Earl of Southampton and his colleagues. Apparently the earl, disappointed by Lok's role in funding an expedition to the New World, might have had something to do with this character. *Shy* in the year 1600 meant "shady." Following this line of reasoning, Shady (Michael) Lok could be rendered as the name Shy-Lok.

More Clues Connecting Marlowe and Shakespeare

It is not improbable that Marlowe could have penned some of the works attributed to Shakespeare. Many lines from Marlowe—what some might call flattery and others call plagiarism—are found in *The Merry Wives of Windsor, The Merchant of Venice, Twelfth Night,* and *Henry VI.*

A statistical study done by Thomas Mendenhall is based on the premise that the frequency of words and their use is "an author's fingerprint." The result of his study is that Marlowe and the author of the Shakespearean works shared the same fingerprint.

Marlowe was also believed to be the "dead shepherd" of *As You Like It.* This "Shakespearean" play, act 3, scene 3, line 14, contains a line that may allude to Marlowe: "It strikes a man more dead than a great reckoning in a little room." The author betrays showing an allusion to the murder of Marlowe. Another author, Sir William Vaughn, wrote *The Golden Grove* in 1600 and provides even more detail that places the blame for Marlowe's death on Ingram Frizer.

Theories about Marlowe's "Death"

On May 30, 1593, Marlowe was said to be writing *Hero and Leander.* George Chapman, of the School of Night, would finish the work, and *As You Like It* would reference it. On that same day of May 30, Marlowe's involvement in an argument over a bill in an English tavern, which doubled as a brothel, resulted in his death. An alternate theory is that Marlowe had indeed been murdered in the pub and the murder was initiated by Sir Walter Raleigh, a theory we will discuss further in a later chapter.

But was Marlowe actually killed? On the night of his alleged death, Marlowe was drinking at a table with three men who in one capacity or another had acted as agents of the queen's confidant and adviser Sir

Francis Walsingham. (Sir Francis Walsingham is not to be confused with his cousin Thomas Walsingham, who was a literary patron of Marlowe and others.)

One theory is that Marlowe was not killed and instead was hustled off to Italy. Indeed, researcher Calvin Hoffman, with the backing of the International Marlowe-Shakespeare Society, believes that Marlowe remained alive and well in Italy. Here, allegedly, he continued to write and actually sent his works home to England, where they were passed on to Shakespeare to claim as his own.

The greatest argument against Marlowe actually penning the works attributed to Shakespeare is that he was dead when some of them came to the theater. Rumors, however, of his demise might have been more than premature, as again he might have been alive and well and living in Italy. If his death in England in the pub had been staged, after his "death" he might have moved to Padua (Italy). At some point one researcher claimed a letter had been sent from Padua by Marlowe in 1627. An Italian doctor by the name of Pietro Basconi claims to have nursed an exiled recluse name Christopher Marlowe in that city.[5] Others point to the plays set in that country. They include *The Merchant of Venice, Two Gentlemen of Verona, Othello, Romeo and Juliet,* and *Much Ado about Nothing.*

Sonnet 29 provides yet another clue.

> *When, in disgrace with fortune and men's eyes*
> *I alone beweep my outcast state*
> *And trouble deaf hear with my bootless cries*
> *And look upon myself and curse my fate*

In Westminster Abbey a memorial window in the Poets' Corner is dedicated to Marlowe. It gives the dates of his birth and death. The year of his death is accompanied by a question mark, however. This might be considered as meaningful as Shakespeare's monument in Stratford, which depicts a man clutching a grain sack. (The real Will Shakespeare was known to have been, by his fellow townsmen, a hoarder of grain, as immortalized by a commemorative monument in Stratford.)

EDWARD DE VERE: ANOTHER CANDIDATE FOR SHAKESPEARE

In addition to Bacon and Marlowe, the Earl of Oxford, Edward de Vere, is believed to have authored some of the works attributed to Shakespeare. He too studied at Cambridge (as well as Oxford) and also studied law at Gray's Inn. He, like Bacon, had all the necessary background that Will Shakespeare lacked. He spoke Italian and French, was well traveled, had military experience, and was experienced in the sports of the aristocratic class, which were not generally available to a butcher's apprentice. He wrote poems and was said to have written plays too. He was also a better writer than Bacon when it came to tragedy.

De Vere was born into an ancient Norman family that traced its roots to France before the 1066 invasion of England and the Battle of Hastings. The first earl supported Mathilda against Stephen. The second earl served under King John while the third earl opposed him. The ninth earl, Robert de Vere, was a homosexual partner of Richard II. The affair brought disgrace to the family name and forced Robert into exile on the continent where, in the Netherlands, he would be killed by a boar. The de Vere family stock rose again when John de Vere helped the Tudor family take the throne. The twelfth earl was executed by Edward IV.

In any event, Edward de Vere was born in 1550 to John de Vere, who owned more than three hundred castles and mansions. His father loved the stage and supported a company of actors. His influence on young Edward was interrupted, however, for John died when Edward was only twelve. Before that young Edward might have received a great deal of his appreciation for the arts from the troupe of entertainers that resided at the de Vere house.

After the death of his father, young Edward lived at the home of merchant Sir Thomas Smith, who introduced him to the classical writers.

Then he was sent to London, like Henry Wriothesley, to be the ward of Sir William Cecil, later to be Lord Burghley. It may have been more of a technicality, for Edward had already begun his studies at Cambridge. Whatever time he actually spent in the Burghley household was enriched by Cecil's apparent insistence on continuing education. Edward was tutored in languages, in writing, and in art. He learned dance and sport—including riding, shooting, and falconry.

Both Cecil and Lord Robert Dudley took advantage of the young boy by trying to take over the landholdings that his father had left him. It would be decades before Essex could get back the properties that rightfully belonged to him.

Edward's education was his first priority. Even in the Burghley household he was under the influence of his uncle Arthur Golding. Golding was one of the great literary scholars of his day, having translated Ovid, and he had a great flair for writing. Golding also acted as the boy's tutor and would dedicate his *Histories of Trogus Pompeius* to the fourteen-year-old in 1564 and his edition of the Psalms to him in 1573. The works of Shakespeare liberally borrow from these two works, as well as Golding's translations of Ovid.

The Oxford-as-Shakespeare camp points out that Oxford had something of an obsession with the fall of Troy. He regularly mentioned features of the *Iliad* and Troy's aftermath when discussing other things. Troy is also regularly used in Shakespeare's works to describe suffering and loss. When Oxford wrote to Burghley in 1572 after the St. Bartholomew's Day massacre, he describes the scene in terms that Virgil used in *The Aeneid*. Shakespeare drew on Virgil and moreso on Ovid, employing both the original Latin and the Arthur Golding translations.[6]

Similarities have also been drawn between many of the words in Oxford's letters and words used in the Shakespearean sonnets. Author Joseph Sobran, in *Alias Shakespeare,* compiled a multipage list of phrases found in Oxford's writings and letters that he also found in *Richard II* and other Shakespearean works.

Venus and Adonis is considered to be an Ovidian poem, written in a style that might be hard to ascribe to the young Shakespeare. It's based on Ovid's narrative poem *Metamorphoses* and deals with a young man resisting the temptations of a more experienced (female) suitor. Edmund Spenser would use the same style of *sesta rima,* which is best described as a quatrain followed by a couplet. *Venus* was printed by a native of Stratford by the name of Richard Field, who certainly was already acquainted with young Will. Field's publication was trademarked with the Rosicrucian device of an anchor.

Venus and Adonis was followed by the *Rape of Lucrece,* which might be considered to be inspired by both Livy and Ovid. Ovid's *Fasti* is basically a sequel to Livy's work.

It's also worth noting that the sonnets would not bear an author's name until 1609, when they were published as Shakespeare's. None of William Shakespeare's plays included his name until 1598, although they would after that year.

It's also worth mentioning that, remarkably, Oxford was a relation, however distant, of Shakespeare's. Oxford's grandmother Elizabeth Trussell was related to Mary Arden, Shakespeare's mother. Oxford's father had married twice. The first marriage was to Dorothy Neville, a daughter of the Earl of Westmoreland. Catherine de Vere was born to this wife and is mentioned in *Twelfth Night,* which is attributed to Shakespeare. Oxford's father's second marriage to Marjorie Golding produced Mary de Vere and Edward.

Despite being able to afford dressing in the high fashion of a London dandy, and even dressing his horse in red velvet, Edward de Vere was a soldier like many of the de Veres had been. He also sat in the House of Lords as his right. He married Anne Cecil, who was, notably, the niece of Sir Nicholas Bacon. She was also the favorite daughter of Sir William Cecil. She would bear de Vere five daughters throughout their sometimes rocky relationship. Those who believe that the Earl of Oxford was the man who penned the works attributed to Shakespeare believe that she was the model for Ophelia.

When Oxford married Anne, Cecil reneged on the huge dowry that had been promised for the marriage. Cecil then told Oxford that if he went to Spain it would be paid to him.

Soldier, scholar, writer, and lord, Oxford and his family had their troubles nonetheless. Thomas Howard was a relative of theirs who happened to be in prison because of his role in the Ridolfi plot, a plot to assassinate Elizabeth I. Cecil played a role in this adventure, and Oxford was accused of attempting to free Howard from prison. Exposed, Howard was beheaded in June of 1572. It may have been that Oxford's charm, which had made him a favorite of the queen, had blinded her to his treasonous act.

De Vere's attempt to collect his dowry by traveling to Spain met with failure, and it was misconstrued that there were ulterior motives. He was suspected of sympathizing with Catholics, and, in particular, of meeting with Spanish Catholics. This second treasonous situation was also forgiven by Elizabeth. It was at this point that Oxford took time out from the political machinations at court to take a grand tour of Europe, which would include a visit to Italy.

He embarked on the tour without his wife. In Italy he saw the Jewish enclave, which was known as the ghetto, which had been built around a foundry. He saw the thirty-five-mile coastline of Bohemia and went to Trapani and Segesta in Sicily. He also visited Genoa. In Mantua he stayed with the Gonzaga family, whose huge estate featured a giant mural, *The Fall of Troy,* done by Julio Romano. Oxford's lengthy stay in Italy gave him intimate knowledge of Venice—its customs and culture and legal system. Perhaps, if he was indeed the author of *The Merchant of Venice,* he drew upon this experience of Italy in the writing of the play. Places in Italy that de Vere visited are in the plays attributed to Shakespeare. Places he did not visit are not present in them.

His trip cost him the equivalent of a million dollars in today's currency. When he returned he wasn't ready to tighten the purse strings. He invested the enormous sum of three thousand pounds in the exploratory voyage of Englishman Martin Frobisher, in part by buying a bond of the man named Michael Lok. Some have pointed out that this debt was echoed in *The Merchant of Venice* wherein Antonio (the merchant) borrows three thousand ducats for a shipping venture. Antonio's voyage was profitable and Frobisher's wasn't. There are also many more similarities in *Il Pecorone*, making it difficult to dismiss out of hand these connections between Oxford and Shakespeare.

There is little question that Oxford enjoyed and sponsored the arts. There are thirty-three works dedicated to him, and he maintained two theater companies. He was cited by author Frances Meres in 1598 as "the best among us for comedy."[7]

In 1920 an Englishman by the name of Thomas Looney proposed that the Earl of Oxford had written the plays attributed to Shakespeare. In 1975 the *Encyclopedia Britannica* posited that Oxford was the strongest candidate. He was presumed to have been buried in St. Augustine's Church in Hackney or in Westminster Abbey.

The Death of the Earl

It is believed that Oxford died on June 24, 1604. There is no known cause of his death although he complained of several maladies. He left no will. There is no record of a funeral. There are no memorials. Instead there are some unusually suspicious incidents that immediately followed his demise. On the day of his passing, many of his friends were arrested and their homes searched. Those rounded up on orders of the king for brief arrest included the Earl of Southampton, Baron Danvers, and five others, possibly to affirm their loyalty. As a eulogy to Oxford, James I had Shakespeare's company perform eight plays that were later attributed to Shakespeare.

The number of "Shakespeare" plays would drop off after the earl's death. Those who deny Oxford the credit maintain that *King Lear*, *Othello*, and *The Tempest* were believed all to be in an incomplete stage at the time of his death.

Othello was complete by 1604 and in any case was based on *Cinthio*, actually one of author Giovanni Battista Giraldi's works, which had been completed in Italian before 1573. An original *King Lear* had been written and performed long before the earl's death as well. *The Tempest* may have been based on a ship belonging to Essex that was wrecked, and updated after several accounts of the voyage and shipwreck had reached England. Indeed, the ship named the *Edward Bonaventure,* owned by Oxford, was wrecked in Bermuda in 1593.[8] Ben Jonson, who had not been a fan of Shakespeare's, wrote a satiric piece on *The Tempest,* named *Volpone,* in 1605, also suggesting that *The Tempest* was not written at a later date.

The Tempest includes passages from Arthur Golding's translation of Ovid. Remember, this is de Vere's uncle and tutor. *The Tempest* also includes passages from John Florio's translation of Michel de Montaigne's essays from 1533–1592. John Florio, who translated Montaigne's works into English and published them in 1603, was still alive at this time. Notably he had served as Henry Wriothesley's (the Earl of Southampton's) tutor. According to *The Oxford Companion to English Literature,* "No single source for it [*The Tempest*] is known."[9]

Bacon and Oxford remain at the top of the list of candidates who may have penned the works attributed to Shakespeare. Bacon had written on the value of keeping certain things hidden. So had Oxford. In 1589 the anonymous author of *The Arte of English Poesie* referred to noble gentlemen who had written commendably well and suffered to have these works published under the names of another. Of those, "of which number is first that noble Gentleman Edward Earle of Oxford," is regarded as the best.[10]

FURTHER CLUES AND CONNECTIONS

In any event, there is also no reason to deny that both Bacon *and* Oxford (as well as others) may have authored the various works attributed to Shakespeare.

Another case in point: Shakespeare is said to have written *Titus and Andronicus* in 1600. Sir Sydney Lee, a Shakespearean biographer, said there is reason to believe that this work had also been brought to Shakespeare by an author who wished to remain anonymous.

In short, it is very possible that William Shakespeare never authored anything more than a poor signature. It is also very likely that he played a role as front man for certain individuals, including (in addition to those discussed above) Francis Bacon, who needed to keep his light under the proverbial bushel.

Shakespeare's biographers can only *surmise* that he wrote plays given that there are no originals attributed to him. These plays displayed a worldly knowledge and included details of places far away in Italy, France, and Denmark, none of which Shakespeare had ever traveled to. These plays showed familiarity with horsemanship, falconry, and lawn bowling, though Shakespeare never participated in such sports. These plays displayed a vocabulary of twenty thousand words, five times more than that of a typically educated man. They even demonstrated an understanding of the slang that was used exclusively among Cambridge students. Shakespeare didn't attend Cambridge. In short, the plays exhibited many things that were outside of his limited realm of experience.

In 1593, Shakespeare would get credit for *Venus and Adonis,* which is very similar to Marlowe's *Hero and Leander.* Both works were written at about the same time; however, the evidence points to Marlowe's as being first by less than a year. Furthermore, both apparently are derived from Ovid. While Marlowe may have read Ovid in English and translated him as well, Shakespeare would not have had that advantage. The dedication of *Venus and Adonis* to Wriothesley, the Earl of Southampton, would also be very unlikely because a commoner like William Shakespeare would not typically dedicate a work to an aristocrat. More likely *Venus and Adonis* was penned by someone closer to Southampton.

Publisher Richard Field is listed as the printer of the work. Born in Stratford-upon-Avon in 1561, he came to London in 1579. He started his career as a printer with a seven-year apprenticeship to publisher

Thomas Vautrollier, who was printing what were primarily Huguenot titles. After Vautrollier's death, Field married his widow, taking ownership of numerous titles, including those by Ovid and Shakespeare. The Rosicrucian connection to the much wider circle of French Protestants would be important. Indeed, Field often incorporated symbols and even inside jokes on the frontispieces of his works. The cover of *Venus and Adonis,* for instance, included the distinctly Rosicrucian symbol we have discussed before: the anchor.

This might be a clue about the identity of the true author. Sir Francis Bacon was known to have participated in the revision of works great and small. And as we know, he was an expert cryptographer who left behind clues, even in the King James Bible. He might have improved on both of Marlowe's works as well as hidden clues within them. *Venus and Adonis,* for instance, contains three coded Bacon "signatures." And *The Merchant of Venice* contains a cipher referred to in Bacon's *Advancement of Learning.*[11]

MARY SIDNEY HERBERT

There certainly is no shortage of those who may have had a hand in the authorship of the works attributed to Shakespeare. They include Mary Sidney Herbert, the second Countess of Pembroke. Her marriage to Henry Herbert had been arranged by Robert Dudley and Sir Henry Sidney.

Mary Sidney Herbert is marginalized by history and in the shadow of her husband. Actually she was the most educated woman in England next to the queen. She had an extensive library with books in several languages. She spoke Latin, French, and Italian and read Hebrew, Welsh, and possibly Spanish. She had her own alchemy lab where Adrian Gilbert was her assistant (Gilbert was the half brother of Sir Walter Raleigh). She smoked tobacco, shot pistols, played cards, danced, and sang. She played musical instruments, was famous for her needlework, and bowled. She rode horses, hunted, and hawked. And she wrote. Similar to the works of Shakespeare, she coined new words for the English language, including *sea monster*. She was the perfect example of a Renaissance woman.

Her fourteen-thousand-acre estate was Wilton House, which she made a cultural center of England wherein she nurtured writers and poets in its academic environment. Philip Sidney, Michael Drayton, Edmund Spenser, Thomas Kyd, Christopher Marlowe, and Ben Jonson were frequent visitors there.

Like Dee she was very interested in musical codes and invisible ink. She sponsored other writers and indulged in her own literary endeavors as well. One of her works was uncovered in 2010. What role might she have played in Shakespeare's works? A letter that she sent to her son in 1606, found in the archives of her home, declared: "We have the man Shakespeare here."[12] Was it Will Shakespeare, or was she referring to another who might have penned work attributed to him? The First Folio (of Shakespeare's plays) was dedicated to her sons. Jonson refers to her as the Sweet Swan of Avon. Her symbol was the swan, and she had an estate on the Avon River.

Legend has it that Marlowe lived at her home after his "death."

SHAKESPEARE'S ASCENDENCY AMID RUMORS OF MISPLACED ATTRIBUTIONS

In 1594, Shakespeare's career took off. The company he belonged to played for the queen. The next three years he was active as a player in it. In 1597 he bought a house called New Place in Stratford. The next year the Globe Theater was built, and Shakespeare had a 10 percent interest in it. Robert Fludd, described as a Rosicrucian apologist, a student of the Kabbalah, and an astrologer, shared in the design of the building, drawing up architectural blueprints for it and inventing ways to create thunder and the illusion of burning cities. Richard Burbage and his brother Cuthbert each owned 25 percent of the Globe. Three other members of Lord Chamberlain's Men owned the balance.

The Globe was built close to the smaller Rose Theater, but in June of 1613 it would be destroyed by fire and rebuilt in 1614 before closing in 1642 at the hands of the Puritans, who had no taste for merriment. This second building would be pulled down in 1644. Today a modern re-creation stands near the site of the original theater.

The 1590s would treat Shakespeare well. In total he was given credit for nearly forty plays. He was also active on the stage and off, working as a player and a manager. However, there is no concrete evidence that he authored any plays at this time, or any other time for that matter. Will Shakespeare never referred to himself as an author. Neither did anyone in his extended family. These facts seem to support the commonly held belief that Shakespeare was not the real author of the plays attributed to him.

Others went so far as to publicly denounce him as a playwright. Robert Greene was a poet and a playwright and part of Edward de Vere's entourage of friends. In 1592 he lashed out at Shakespeare, calling him an "upstart crow" who bought the works of others and presented them as his own.[13] In August of 1592, Robert Greene, Edward de Vere, and Thomas Nashe were having lunch when they were joined by a man named Will. Will was the butt of jokes to Nashe and Greene; nevertheless, the four enjoyed lunch and a bout of drinking that went on late into the day. Will "Monox" was the name Nashe called him. It was a euphemism for Will, "my ox."

After the long lunch, Greene took ill. He hung on for days until finally passing away. Whether his illness was related to overindulgence or was a result of foul play—possibly poisoning—is unknown. In any event, the result was the same for young Will: he had one less critic claiming that the plays were not his own. Greene's death would serve to be a harbinger of Shakespeare's own demise.

Ben Jonson, Shakespeare's contemporary, said that Shakespeare had "small Latin and less Greek" and most likely no understanding of French or Italian.[14] This is important, because the plots that he used in his plays were taken from Italian works that had not at that time been translated into English. Jonson was possibly privy to the Bacon-Marlowe-Shakespeare connection. Jonson worked for Bacon at one point, but he may not have been aware that Bacon's works were getting to the stage via the Bard. He referred to Shakespeare as the "Poor Poet-Ape," a man "so bold a thief" who robbed the credit from the true authors.[15] Voltaire called him a "drunken savage."[16]

John Greenleaf Whittier said of the Bacon-Shakespeare issue: "Whether Bacon wrote the wonderful plays or not, I am quite sure the man Shakespeare neither did nor could."[17]

The works also display a sensitivity that Will the person seemed to lack. The real Will Shakespeare had abandoned his family and his hometown. When he returned to Stratford in 1610, or shortly thereafter, it was as a man who had acquired property, loaned money, collected taxes, regularly sued his neighbors over the smallest amounts, and hoarded grain in a time when food was scarce. He even refused to pay a small debt his abandoned wife had incurred in his long absence. This was not the graceful retirement of a successful writer or scholar. Instead, the life of the Stratford man was more like the real author's Shylock in *The Merchant of Venice*—he simply went home to count his money.

THE BACKSTORY: COMPETING FACTIONS IN ELIZABETHAN ENGLAND

In March of 1616, William Shakespeare was working in his hometown of Stratford, where he lived as a grain dealer, tax collector, landlord, and all-around businessman. He was in fine health and was coming up on his fifty-second birthday when something caused him to contemplate his mortality. He decided it was time to get his estate in order and to make a will.

What caused this sudden concern? Six days earlier, on March 19, Sir Walter Raleigh had been released from the Tower.

Sir Walter Raleigh was a man as large as his legend. Brought to the Elizabethan court as a young man, he won the eye of the queen with his handsome looks and his debonair attitude. He was a newcomer, and Elizabeth enjoyed his rough charm and lack of social skills. If the story of him placing his cloak on the ground in front of Elizabeth so she would not muddy her feet is myth, it was a myth created to describe the real man. Raleigh would earn his stripes but not without attracting enemies.

Sir Walter Raleigh was also the glittering star at the center of an orbiting circle of aristocrats and intellectuals. This circle of powerful friends included Dr. John Dee; Henry Percy, the ninth Earl of Northumberland, who was also known as the Wizard Earl; the scientist Thomas Hariot; writers Thomas Nashe and George Chapman; and many of the most brilliant men of science of the time. As we have established elsewhere, they were loosely organized as the School of Night and met at Raleigh's estate.

As its central figure, Raleigh had his finger on the pulse of the new ideas that were emerging in these times. While he would seem more the swashbuckler, he is credited with writing a book on the history of the world, complete with references to and discussions about Phoenician gods. Aware of Rosicrucian enlightenment, he fancied himself the Red Cross knight.

WHAT HAPPENED IN 1592?

In answering whether Shakespeare was the author of the plays attributed to him, we cannot ignore the fact that something very dramatic happened around 1592.

At this time, Sir Walter Raleigh's circle would split into two factions. On one side were Raleigh and Hariot and a handful of scientists, as well as the Earl of Northumberland. On the other side was what would become known as the Essex Circle. The Essex Circle included Sir Francis Bacon and his brother, Anthony; Henry Wriothesley (the third Earl of Southampton); Edward de Vere (the Earl of Oxford); Roger Manners (the Earl of Rutland); and Christopher Marlowe, as well as its central figure, Robert Devereux, the second Earl of Essex. Essex (Devereux) had inherited Leicester House and immediately changed its name to Essex House. His estate became home to a circle of intellectuals who could freely speak about science and religion and about government and philosophy.

The court of Elizabeth was a snake pit, and Raleigh's success had drawn the wrath of others who would be happy see him removed, primarily Essex, who was one of a handful of men who had captured the heart of the queen. Essex could be brash, impetuous, and dangerous.

Another enemy of Raleigh's was the Earl of Leicester, who had married Lord Essex's mother. Still another enemy was Christopher Hatton, a London businessman whom Elizabeth elevated to Lord Chancellor.

Bacon and the Essex circle did not appreciate the advances of Drake and Raleigh in the court of Elizabeth. Bacon wanted a New Atlantis based on philosophical ideals. Raleigh, despite his attempts from the 1580s onward to settle Virginia, did not always share in the higher ideals espoused by freethinkers such as Bacon. And Drake was a pirate who enjoyed raiding the Spanish Main for whatever could be stolen.

Shakespeare's pen—wielded by Bacon, Essex, Oxford, and others— could be used to get such pirates out of the way.

In trying to effect Raleigh's downfall, his enemies regularly told the queen that Raleigh's School of Night was actually a School of Atheism. This faction had great influence, and much of what they did was done behind the scenes. Raleigh knew that he had enemies, but his suspicions would, on one or more occasion, cause him to blame the wrong person.

The Bacon group plotted to work against Raleigh and ensure that he would fall out of favor with the queen. From 1592 to 1597 this did occur. Was it a coincidence that in those same five years Shakespeare became a very wealthy man?

DID THE CIRCLE OF ESSEX USE SHAKESPEARE AS THEIR COVER?

This relatively small group of men, on behalf of England, played some of the greatest roles in exploring and colonizing the New World. They also played a great role in the development of English literature. And although they could freely speak on such topics, few would dare to publish under their own name.

Then Shakespeare came along, and the Earl of Southampton immediately saw an opportunity. When Essex wished to see his sonnets to young Henry Wriothesley put in print, they were deemed the works of Shakespeare. When Oxford wished to fashion new iterations of tales he had read during his grand tour of continental Europe, he could publish as "William Shakespeare." When the Earl of Rutland was posted by the queen to Elsinore Castle in Denmark, he might have returned with enough ideas to assist in a new version of the age-old tale of Hamlet. And because Bacon understood that his political works threatened to ignite Elizabeth's wrath, he realized that a pen name could save his neck. Given that they had found a front man in William Shakespeare, the group was now free to write and say whatever they wanted. And thus did they become the patrons of Shakespeare.

Typically a patron funds the work of a writer, artist, sculptor, or musician. William Shakespeare benefited from the writings of others that were attributed to him and for being paid to act as the decoy.

That the Essex Circle went a giant step further in not only funding Shakespeare but also providing him with the plays he would claim to have authored is critical. The reasons for such subterfuge might have been more than one: some relatively unimportant, others as grave as a trip to the Tower.

A playwright earned very little in the Elizabethan age. While it was more than an illiterate butcher's apprentice might earn, these sums were nothing more than piddling trifles to barons, viscounts, and earls. The Earl of Southampton would later be financing expeditions to the Americas. Surely, in comparison, making Shakespeare the wealthiest man in Stratford was nothing to him. There was no economic motive in claiming ownership. Comedies and tragedies alike were plucked from one author and rewritten and edited by another, with impunity. But enjoying one's hobby without the risk of running afoul of the queen was worth paying Shakespeare to be a shill. Historical works with political overtones offered little to an author when weighed against the risk. Essex (Robert Devereux) lost his life for backing the production of *Richard II*. (While notably, the author, said to be Shakespeare, was not even reprimanded!)

This was life under Elizabeth, the Virgin Queen.

In support of this theory of attribution is the circumstance of Shakespeare's newfound wealth. Indeed, in 1597, Will was thirty-three years old and a man of means. As mentioned previously, he bought a pretentiously large home in Stratford as well as a portion of London's greatest theater. And one of the earliest biographies of Shakespeare tells us that his wealth derived from the Earl of Southampton, Henry Wriothesley.

The Earl of Southampton might have made the large payment out of his own pocket, for he was certainly wealthy enough. He also might have made his contribution on behalf of both himself and others, specifically those who had an aversion to publicity. The stage was not a reputable place, and actors were regarded as borderline people not to be trusted. Dukes and earls did not dare jeopardize their status for the very small amount of earnings that came from the theater business.

And again, Southampton was a young man with a great deal of money and a libertine lifestyle. Before his death he would have a wife, a mistress, and more than one male lover. He enjoyed the arts and was accused of being seen too frequently at the theater rather than at his government post. As previously discussed, he was part of an inner circle of intellectuals that would meet regularly to discuss common ideals.

In addition to Shakespeare, Southampton acted as a patron of others, including Thomas Nashe, a School of Night member. Nashe wrote under his own name, and his satire put him in Newgate Prison—a deadly place given that malnutrition and illness often commuted any prison sentence to a death sentence. Sir George Carey pulled strings to get Nashe released. Carey, through connections and ability, also successfully defended actors in "Shakespearean" plays who incurred the wrath of the Puritans.

Unlike the manner in which Puritans are displayed in American history, they were anything but seekers of religious freedom. In point of fact, they wanted their own religious intolerances to be accepted by others. Sir George Carey was the antithesis of the Puritan ethic; he had a penchant for smoking, drinking, and engaging in casual sex when the opportunity arose.

Nashe, to show his gratitude for Carey having gotten him out of prison, dedicated one of his few nonsatirical works, *Christ's Tears over Jerusalem,* to Lady Elizabeth Carey.

THE PEN AS A SWORD

Shakespeare's pen wielded its aspersions against Raleigh just as the Circle of Essex had intended. During this same time frame, two works attributed to Shakespeare were published. *The Rape of Lucrece* was loosely based on the expulsion of the Tarquin dynasty from Rome. The story of Lucretia was taken from Livy's recounting of it in *The History of Rome.* The point of publishing this at this time was to identify Tarquin the Proud as Raleigh the Proud. The underlying message of *The Rape of Lucrece* was that, like Tarquin, Raleigh would soon be expelled from London.

The other work was *Love's Labour's Lost.* This is one of the very few "Shakespearean" works for which a clear case of original authorship cannot be made. It appears to be exposing the School of Night, given that the Earl of Northumberland as Navarre is depicted as the leader, and his lords take vows not to look at women for three years so they can advance their studies without distraction.

Raleigh was also caricaturized in *Love's Labour's Lost,* a "Shakespearean" work that included a character named Don Adriano de Armado, who was identified as Raleigh. "Shakespeare" also created Holofernes, who is identified as Thomas Hariot—the astronomer who lived at Raleigh's estate. And he created the King of Navarre, who is identified as Northumberland. The Earl of Northumberland had already picked up the nickname the "Wizard Earl" for his work in alchemy. Attending lords in the play who were also identified include friends of Raleigh, who included the Earl of Derby and Sir George Carey.

Raleigh was sensitive to criticism, and when his enemies likened the School of Night to a School of Atheism (atheism being a very serious charge), he would have blamed William Shakespeare, not being aware that Shakespeare was only the front man of the literary work. The plays, however, were not the only reason Raleigh might wish revenge on Shakespeare.

When Raleigh was at the pinnacle of his career in the Elizabethan court, it would be his secret marriage that brought about his downfall. His romance with Elizabeth Throckmorton, a lady-in-waiting to the queen, led to a rushed wedding after she became pregnant. The queen had insisted that her ladies remain unmarried, and Raleigh understood that even a man of his status had no chance of changing the queen's mind.

The pregnant Elizabeth Throckmorton made her excuses and left London for her family home. The Throckmorton home was and still is known today as Coughton Court. It is just outside the town of Alcester. Halfway between Stratford and Alcester is the original home of Mary Arden, Shakespeare's mother. Not only was it a small world when the expectant Elizabeth Throckmorton returned home but the Ardens and Throckmortons were actually related as well. The extended family kept a few very important secrets, including that Shakespeare's father, grandfather, and mother were secretly Catholic. One secret that the Arden-Shakespeare family might have allowed to slip was the secret marriage of Elizabeth Throckmorton. As a result, Raleigh and his wife were put in the Tower.

Their stay in the Tower was not long, but the damage to Sir Walter's standing in court was long lasting. Shakespeare may have wondered if Sir Walter blamed him for the leak of his secret marriage and the ruinous results and whether he might seek real revenge. It would account for the short time between Raleigh's release and the writing of Will's will.

COLLEAGUE BEN JONSON

Shakespeare may have put such worrisome thoughts out of his mind when fellow playwright and player Ben Jonson came up from London. Shakespeare and his company had performed Jonson's plays years before. Jonson brought with him Michael Drayton, who was famous in his own day as one of Britain's most prolific poets. Jonson invited Shakespeare to a night out to celebrate the Bard's birthday.

He might not have been so happy if he knew what the night had in store.

Ben Jonson bears little resemblance to a poet. His first occupation was that of bricklayer, a job that toughens one up. He joined the military to fight in the Lowlands. It was customary at the time to have the soldiers on each side pick champions to fight each other. When Jonson was chosen, he killed a man in hand-to-hand battle and was proud of it. At home in England he killed another man in a duel. Given that dueling was against the law, he was arrested. His punishment for his conviction was to be branded on the thumb. He had a reputation for excessive drinking, street fighting, and four times was imprisoned. And yet, for some reason, Sir Walter Raleigh decided that he would be the best choice to tutor his son Wat.

It is possible that the reason was because Wat was quite the handful. Once at dinner with an important guest, Wat acted up so much that his father punched him. Not wanting to hit his father back, the young man punched their guest. Could the street-fighting Ben Jonson control him? It soon became obvious that this was a difficult job. In Paris, Wat and Jonson regularly drank to excess. One day Wat tied the inebriated Jonson to a cart, in a crucifixion pose, and paid men to wheel him around the city. It was at a time when Catholic-Protestant tensions were at their worst.

Jonson survived the prank, and the two remained friends.

After the long climb back into Elizabeth's good graces, Raleigh's situation improved. His enemies still included both Bacon and the Earl of Southampton, who backed voyages to the New World. They were threatened by Raleigh's fame and by his role in the settling of Virginia. When the queen died, James, the king of Scotland, took the throne as the English king. Numerous Catholic plots against him were uncovered, and although Raleigh had fought against the Spanish Catholics for decades, he was implicated in a plot against the new king. He was convicted on trumped-up charges and recanted testimony. As a result of this he was imprisoned.

Raleigh would spend thirteen long years in prison pondering the events that had led to his imprisonment.

The Bye plot was a conspiracy of English Catholics who planned to kidnap King James and force him to either convert or at the very least to place Catholics in powerful positions. The plot was poorly planned. English Jesuits actually reported it to the king for fear that things would get worse for them if the plot proceeded. The ringleader was William Watson, a priest who had rushed to Scotland when Elizabeth died.

Watson and two others were tortured into confessing and executed for their roles. Watson had given up George Brooke, with whom he had discussed the plot. Brooke was tortured as well and executed in December of 1603. He may have helped cast suspicion on his brother Henry Brooke, who was Lord Cobham, and a friend of Sir Robert Cecil's. Cecil was a paranoid hunchback who was threatened by both Bacon and Raleigh, and he delighted greatly in taking down his enemies. Cobham had been in touch with Spanish agents and had a much more serious plot in the works.

Part of the plot involved Brooke (Lord Cobham) taking delivery of a fantastic sum of money from Spain and carrying it through the Isle of Jersey to England. Here on the tiny channel island, Raleigh was governor.

This was the only real connection the plot had to Raleigh. It defies reason, as Raleigh had warred against Spain and regularly raided Spanish ships. Why would they allow him control over their money? However, Cobham named Raleigh as a coconspirator even though there is no other evidence for it. It did not matter that Cobham later recanted his inclusion of Raleigh in the plot. Cobham was executed, and Raleigh was sentenced to the Tower.

This is where the story takes a strange turn. Cobham's family had been, like Raleigh and his circle, the butt of jokes in *The Merry Wives of Windsor* and in a performance of *Henry IV.* So both Sir Walter Raleigh and Lord Cobham were victimized in works attributed to William Shakespeare. Raleigh might have blamed the secretly Catholic Arden-Shakespeare family for making him a scapegoat, for he had suspected them of the same thing in the past.

While Raleigh served his time, the real William Shakespeare had been sequestered in provincial Stratford, playing the role of small-town businessman. Those thirteen years that Raleigh was incarcerated allowed a great deal of water to pass under the bridge. It also allowed Shakespeare to lose touch with those he had known from his days as a "player"—an actor onstage.

What he didn't know was that Jonson had become the single best friend that Sir Walter Raleigh had. Their friendship survived the long imprisonment in the Tower endured by Sir Walter. Shakespeare may not have been aware that Jonson had become his most outspoken critic. Indeed, the full extent of the enmity that both Jonson and Raleigh felt for Shakespeare would never be known to the Bard.

Jonson lived up to the role of Raleigh's truest friend. He visited him often in the Tower, helped him write his *History of the World,* and attempted to be a surrogate father to Raleigh's son Wat (although he is most remembered for teaching him to drink and carouse). Jonson also might have performed one very important favor for his friend.

On April 23, 1616, Jonson and Shakespeare would meet. Will most likely put worrisome thoughts out of his head for at least one night, that of his birthday. As arranged, he met Jonson and the writer

Michael Drayton for dinner. What happened next has not been recorded in any detail. It is said that Shakespeare "drank too hard" and "died of a fever" the same night. Since a night of overeating and drinking rarely results in death, the tragic result may indicate that he was poisoned. Since no one else at their table was poisoned, it may be the case that he had been targeted by Jonson.

QUESTIONS LINGER AFTER SHAKESPEARE'S DEATH

Shakespeare had drawn up his will in March and, a month later, after the fateful dinner with Jonson and his pals, died. The signature he had put on his will, his sixth known signature, was not any better executed than his other signatures. Again, none of them resembled each other. If he had grown in experience and ability, this would probably have been more obvious at the end of his life. He hadn't, and it wasn't.

He did, however, have much more money. His will left household items, including a bed—actually a "second-best bed." However, as mentioned earlier, he left no books, letters, scribbles, and, notably, no folio of work. Generations of Shakespearean scholars would wonder why the "second-best bed" was all he bequeathed to his wife. Was it one last jab at the older woman who had forced a young Will into marriage? The second greatest question might address his lack of books. They would be much more valuable than household items and even a sword. Did he not possess *even one book*?

It was alleged, but not proved, that he had authored his own epitaph:

> *Good friend, for Jesus sake forbear,*
> *To dig the dust enclosed here.*
> *Blest be the man that spares the stones*
> *And cursed be he who moves my bones.*

Shakespeare's demise apparently had little effect on the world. It would be a half a century until a Nicholas Rowe attempted to create a biography for the man regarded by most as England's greatest playwright. Another half a century would go by before a man named David Garrick created a three-day jubilee that launched Stratford to tourist-mecca status.

Remarkably, Shakespeare's death received no notice either in Stratford or London until years later. If he had been recognized as a literary talent, one might surmise some public tribute at his death in Stratford, or some memorial in London. But he was not recognized as a playwright, or an author, or even an actor for that matter. The playwright Francis Beaumont, a contemporary of Shakespeare's, died just before him, and many works were composed in his honor. Jonson died after him, and his eulogies filled a book.

The Poets' Corner in Westminster Abbey is the burial place of Jonson, Spenser, Beaumont, Chaucer, and Drayton. There is absolutely no mention of Shakespeare there. He was buried in the village churchyard back home. Finally, in 1740, a bust of him was placed in the south transept, where the "lesser" poets were interred in Westminster Abbey.

Forty years after Shakespeare's death, Sir William Dugdale, who is one of England's most renowned antiquarians, came across a sketch of a bust of Shakespeare. Dugdale had been on a mission to make exact drafts of every important monument in Westminster Abbey as well as other principal churches. Sir Christopher Hatton, a very wealthy man who was a patron of Dugdale, felt that war was on the way and that there was a need to record the details of these monuments. Dugdale's work took him to Warwickshire. His *Antiquities of Warwickshire,* which was published in 1656, is considered his greatest work.

The bust of Shakespeare he encountered was said to have been made seven years after Shakespeare's death, the same year that the folio of the Bard's plays was published. The bust of Shakespeare depicted a sad-looking tradesman holding on to a sack of grain. The sack was a fitting monument to a wealthy man who had been accused of hoarding grain during a shortage. Somehow Stratford felt that this was an appropriate image of Shakespeare.

Surely a *writer,* however, would have been holding a book or a pen instead of a bag of grain! If Stratford-upon-Avon knew there was a celebrated playwright in their midst they apparently kept it a secret.

Sometime later a more elaborate bust of Shakespeare replaced the one of the man with the grain sack. The new bust featured a man holding a piece of paper in one hand and a quill in the other. The new bust might be more appropriate for a playwright. Seven years after the Bard's death, the folio of his plays was published. It did give Shakespeare credit for having been the author, along with commentary from none other than Ben Jonson, ironically enough.

Bertram Fields, in *Players: The Mysterious Identity of William Shakespeare,* asks if the printing of the folio in 1623 was the reason that the monument was replaced. The folio claims to be "Mr. William Shakespeare's Comedies, Histories and Tragedies." A letter that scholars attribute to Ben Jonson claims that errors in the originals are corrected in this edition, yet Jonson had made a comment that Shakespeare "never blotted a line."[18]

DELIA BACON AND OTHER SKEPTICS WEIGH IN

For sixty years after Shakespeare's death, there was no local celebration of Will Shakespeare. "Has it ever happened before—or since?" questioned Mark Twain, that such a celebrity gets no attention in the town of his birth and death.[19] Twain pointed out that biographies of the Bard, when discussing his identity, were replete with "perhapses," "maybes," "conjectures," "might have beens," as well as various other guesses and rumors.

James Wilmot decided that trying to put William Shakespeare in the role of the writer of "his" plays was and is impossible. He instead began to believe that Sir Francis Bacon had authored the famous plays, but for much of Wilmot's life he kept this theory to himself. He did tell his friend Cowell, and through his lectures word of his efforts and startling conclusions attracted others who believed that Shakespeare could not have been the author.

We have mentioned Delia Bacon (no relation to Sir Francis Bacon) earlier but will elaborate on her here. The daughter of a Congregationalist minister, Delia was born in Ohio in a log cabin in 1811. Although her formal education ended when she was fourteen, she read Shakespeare and went on to become a schoolteacher, writer, playwright, and finally a lecturer on the subject of Shakespeare. Delia was the first author to publish on the subject of Shakespeare's identity. Nathaniel Hawthorne would write the foreword to her book *The Philosophy of the Plays of Shakespeare Unfolded*.

By this time Stratford-upon-Avon had decided it had a basis for tourism, an opportunity that it could not afford to pass up. Suddenly objects that were said to belong to the Bard were fetching hefty prices by those who made a pilgrimage to Stratford. The legend took on a life of its own with new Shakespearean anecdotes and tales popping up all the time. Those who believed that Francis Bacon was the real author of the plays attributed to Shakespeare, and other heretics, however, persisted.

Indeed, in Connecticut, where Delia lived as an adult, her theories about Bacon and Shakespeare were tantamount to blasphemy, given that its largely Anglo-Saxon Protestant culture maintained that it was through their efforts and hard work that America was created. The Puritans, with their rigid religion, were actually as narrow-minded as any church can be. Bacon, on the other hand, as we know, promoted freethinking ideas pertaining to philosophy and science.

Delia Bacon had spent years doing firsthand research, which stopped short of unearthing the Bard's grave. Her extensive research also uncovered information about Sir Walter Raleigh, Edmund Spenser, Sir Philip Sidney, and Edward de Vere—the Earl of Oxford. All of them, Delia implied, had played a role in the writing of the plays but had concealed their involvement because, she maintained, they had much to fear if it was discovered that they were the playwrights behind the works.

Delia's close friend Samuel Morse studied codes and cryptography and claimed that Bacon had hidden secrets in Shakespeare's works even though he, as the inventor of the Morse code, could not decipher them.[20]

Delia Bacon's book *The Philosophy of the Plays of Shakespeare Unfolded* was met with waves of hostility and criticism, which may be seen as contributing factors to her deteriorating mental health. The stress she endured as a result of her claims and the breaking of relations with her family led her to have a breakdown in Warwickshire, England, where she was living by this time.[21]

Shortly after her early death, the twenty-two-page document that would be known as the Northumberland Folder was unearthed from the Northumberland House in London. It seemed to give evidence that it had been in Bacon's possession. It mentioned many of the plays, included copies of speeches that Bacon had written for others, and included the titles of politically sensitive plays that were not in the folder. This was not actual evidence that Bacon had authored the plays attributed to Shakespeare, but since the document is the only one to contain both Bacon's and Shakespeare's names, it did show that Bacon had at least possessed them.

THE DEBATE CONTINUES

The theory that Bacon wrote the Shakespearean plays is supported by the understanding that none of the known facts of Shakespeare's life qualifies him to write the texts attributed to him. At the same time *everything* about the life of Sir Francis Bacon qualifies him to have the necessary intellectual means as well as the necessary motive to do so.

To date, there have been four thousand books refuting Shakespeare as the author of the Shakespearean works. In 1857 a man by the name of William H. Smith published his own conclusions on the subject. And another man by the name of Ignatius Donnelly, a nineteenth-century lawyer, became one of the primary proponents of the theory that Bacon was the real author. He demonstrated that Bacon's love of cryptography was reflected in the Shakespearean plays, showing specific examples of where Bacon had hidden his own name in the texts.[22]

In the late nineteenth century, the physician Orville Ward Owen took up this code-breaking examination of the plays. In so doing, he invented a cipher wheel, and he was able to extract evidence that Bacon was actually the son of Queen Elizabeth and the Earl of Leicester. He also determined, by breaking Bacon's coded writing, that Bacon's manuscripts were in a secret vault. The vault unfortunately was under the river Wye, two and a half miles above its juncture with the Severn, in Gloucester, England—quite far from Owen's Detroit home. At great expense he managed to find the vault, but it was empty.

Another man from Michigan, Burrell Ruth, took up the torch. He believed that at some point Bacon's chaplain, William Rawley, had moved the manuscripts.

In any event, the key question in doubting the authorship of William Shakespeare is: How is it that the illiterate country bumpkin known as William Shakespeare could and did emerge as one of history's greatest authors? Now you know the answer. It was certainly not this country bumpkin who should be credited but rather some of the greatest minds of the era who, in addition to secretly authoring some of the best-known plays ever recorded, would also secretly shape the history of the world.

CHAPTER 4

ALL THE QUEEN'S MEN

Queen Elizabeth I had been on the throne since January 15, 1559, and ruled with a capricious but iron hand. On a whim she could arrest or execute anyone from the court to the countryside. Indeed, she traveled frequently to the country, staying at the estates of England's most powerful landowners, many of whom also had residences in town. She was so mobile not because she loved to travel but because she knew instead that her presence was usually rewarded with gifts for the honor it conveyed to the individuals she was visiting. At the same time, she was a single woman amid a large group of men who had many reasons to bend the queen to their will.

She had inherited from her father a fascination with the occult and specifically astrology. Before her coronation she sent Robert Dudley (the Earl of Leicester) and Blanche Perry, her personal attendant, to John Dee to oversee his casting of her horoscope. As mentioned elsewhere, Dee would go on to pick the date and time of her coronation.

THE WIZARD WHO WAS DR. JOHN DEE

"Dee. John Dee." This might be the introduction for this strange man who was the catalyst that initiated England's settling of the American continent. He was a magician complete with magic mirrors and a crystal ball, and allegedly he was adept at the art of levitation. He was living in the tradition of Rosicrucianism before he had even met Bacon and was an alchemist before alchemy became the science of chemistry. He was a historian and cartographer who was consulted by the famous cartographer Gerardus Mercator. He coined the term *Britannia,* induced the queen to establish the Royal Navy, and convinced her that, being a linear descendant from King Arthur, America was her inheritance. He dubbed the New World "Atlantis" while Bacon wrote his *New Atlantis.* Dee would also serve his country as a spy; his code name was 007.

England was a hotbed of political intrigue when Elizabeth took the throne in 1558. Plots and counterplots, assassinations and threats of war were constant. She needed those she could count on and trust to help her keep the throne. The queen trusted very few individuals and wanted any and all intel reported directly to her. Dee reported only to the queen and her master spy, Sir Francis Walsingham.

Despite John Dee's accomplishments and his impact on the world, historians on both sides of the Atlantic have tended to marginalize him. At the same time, Sir Isaac Newton was an alchemist who spent a great deal of his life attempting the "Great Work," the ultimate achievement in the dark art of alchemy. Yet Newton's reputation would remain unscathed.

The boy who would grow up to be Dr. John Dee was born on July 13, 1527. His father, Rowland, descended from an ancient Welsh family and held a minor post in the English royal household. His mother was Jane Wilde. At fifteen Dee left Chelmsford and its grammar school for Cambridge and a higher education. At Cambridge he studied logic and rhetoric, mathematics, geography, and music, as well as Latin and Greek. His true major, however, appears to have been magic.

He became infamous early on when he was part of the presentation of a Greek play. Through levitation or a stage trick "he caused a great scarab to rise and fly across the boards, carrying a man with a basket of victuals on his back."[1] Whether it was a stage trick or a magic trick, no one was certain, but he became known as a sorcerer.

He was a serious student and loved books and reading. To accomplish all he could he allowed himself only four hours of sleep each night. His reputation grew, both as a scholar and a sorcerer, a charge that might be hazardous to one's freedom or one's life. He crossed the English Channel to avoid such charges and attended the University of Louvain in Belgium.

Europe's cities held numerous secret societies in the sixteenth and seventeenth centuries. They included the Family of Love, the Palace Academy, the Confrerie d'Hieronymites, and the Order of the Holy Spirit, all of which represented possible threats to church and state. The Family of Love was particularly a threat to the crown, for it admitted commoners. Dee, before Rosicrucians even had a name, had his own sect built around him. He was not a Freemason, given that that secretive society had not yet been revised by Dee's student Francis Bacon, but he was knowledgeable about some topics commonly pursued by Freemasons. Dee did have a great interest in architecture as well as a great interest in navigation. He wrote that the building of King Solomon's Temple was not possible without the able assistance of Hiram's sailors. Hiram of Tyre had his own navy and educated Solomon's subjects in seamanship.

Edmund Spenser would refer to Dee as a god.

Dee's Associates and Influences and Their Connections to Rosicrucianism

One way we can trace Dee's Rosicrucian leanings is by referencing his servants, all of whom were involved with alchemy in one way or another. Roger Cook was one such servant. He remained in Dee's employ for fourteen years, from 1567 to 1581, then left, only to return in 1600. Then Roger Cook changed his name to Roger Cock, possibly because the rooster is a spiritual symbol, when he went into the employ of Cornelius Drebble, an alchemist, inventor, and man who was considered to be the most important Rosicrucian of his day. Drebble was an engraver and a glassworker from Holland who had come to England in

1604. He built the world's first navigable submarine in 1620. He also built telescopes and microscopes—and even hydraulics for the theater! Robert Burton noted in his book *Anatomy of Melancholy* that Drebble was a Rosicrucian and an alchemist. His scientific advancements led to his employment with the emperor Rudolf II of Prague.

Dee's other seminal assistant and pupil was Patrick Sanders. Sanders would go on to become a member of the Royal College of Physicians. Sanders edited a work by Roger Bacon, *Epistola . . . de secretis operibus Artis et Naturae,* which he dedicated to the Rosicrucians.

Dee's circle of contemporaries included Francesco Pucci, who, preceding Bacon's *New Atlantis,* had written *Forma di una republica catholica,* about a secret republic of good people from all lands, where colleges of men would meet in secret under the guise of merchant groups. They could thus reform their world and reunify Christianity. Bacon may have developed his ideas from Dee and Pucci.

Another influence on John Dee was Giacopo Brocardo. Described as a Christian Kabbalist, Brocardo wrote *The Revelation of St. John* and is considered a forerunner of Rosicrucian tradition. In his written works he maintained that the finding of Christian Rosenkreuz's tomb would precede the victory over the anti-Christ. He also claimed that a last age would end 120 years after Martin Luther was gone. Such claims did not grant him favor. He was arrested for reading forbidden works and forced by the church to flee the continent. In 1577, Brocardo was in the Dee-Sidney Circle.

It was Dee's wide-reaching circles that kept him safe throughout most of his life. Through the intercession of friends in high places he was allowed to return to Cambridge to get his master's degree. Following this he returned to London, where he was hired by the Duke of Northumberland to educate his sons. One of his sons was Robert Dudley, who would later introduce him to Elizabeth I.

Dee would then return to Louvain, where he studied and eventually taught. The school was a hotbed of occult philosophy, mathematics with a Pythagorean bent, and gnostic thought. He would also cross paths with Mercator. His ability with map projection would get him hired as a consultant for the Muscovy Company, which employed English merchants to trade with Russia.

He returned to England in 1589 with the title of doctor and lectured and wrote. In a short time his reputation had captured the attention of King Edward VI, who awarded him a yearly pension. At Edward's death, Elizabeth took Dee under her protection. He presented her with her horoscope while her sister Mary took the throne after Edward's death. He also drew Mary's horoscope, which at the time was a crime punishable by death. Imprisoned, he barely escaped conviction by the royal judicial council, the Star Chamber. Mary's time on the throne would prove to be very short in comparison to that of Dee's protector, Elizabeth.

Dee made the dark sciences an object of his study. He convinced himself that he could gain supernatural assistance, though not necessarily from saints. He believed that his powers could help unearth treasures. Since supernatural means of finding gold and silver were technically against the law, he had to get the queen's permission. Fairness dictates that Dee be judged by his time, for he was in good esoteric company. Thomas Hariot was a numerologist. Johannes Kepler, the famed astronomer, also believed that numbers ruled every aspect of Creation and, as a result, he cast horoscopes. His mother was accused of being a witch and was tortured and jailed for a year before being acquitted. Thomas Vaughan, Robert Fludd, and others had all studied alchemy.

Fludd, whom we have discussed before in a slightly different context, was a friend of Dee's and "inherited his mantle as England's leading exponent of esoteric thought."[2] While Dee would be ignored by England's scientific community after he died, Fludd was highly esteemed. They both shared the same thirst for knowledge in a new framework. Fludd endorsed the Rosicrucian tradition created or spread by Dee and Bacon, calling the "Brothers of the Rosy Cross" and their work with magic, alchemy, and the Kabbalah the highest good.

Fludd was a member of the Royal College of Physicians. Fellow member Robert Boyle had close ties to the Palatinate in Germany, where Rosicrucianism flourished and where many of Pennsylvania's immigrants would later originate from. Like his Rosicrucian colleagues, he never claimed membership in any esoteric order, but his letters are replete with references to the Invisible College.

Letters of others do attest, however, that their authors belonged to a Hermetic society. Boyle was one such case in point. He was born in 1627 and lived the life of a young aristocrat. He was also a founder of the Invisible College. According to author Michael White in his biography of Isaac Newton, "The real Invisible College was the network of nameless adepts who kept alight the alchemical flame."[3]

Boyle was also Sir Isaac Newton's teacher in the alchemical sciences. Boyle publicly claimed to be an Arian and not a believer in the Trinity. He claimed that the ancients were far more knowledgeable than the scientists of his day. His writings were mostly concerned with alchemy, and his numerous experiments with mercury discolored his hair. He is best remembered for what is known as "Boyle's Law," which states that at a constant temperature the pressure of a given quantity of gas varies inversely with its volume. At one point, Boyle had a nervous breakdown, which might have masked the deleterious effects of being poisoned. Yet he somehow managed to garner the respect that history never allowed Dee. In fact, he is regarded as the first modern chemist.

Why are Fludd and Boyle highly praised while Dee is not? Perhaps Dee went too far in attempts to promote himself at court, or perhaps he had reached too high in his role as Elizabeth's adviser. Perhaps we will never really know the answer to that question.

Dee's Life at Mortlake

The queen paid Dee enough to get by on, but not enough to live as he hoped. He needed a place to work and ample room for his assistants. When his mother became a widow she allowed him to take over her house at Mortlake, a suburb of London on the Thames. This would become Europe's finest private library, containing four thousand volumes. It was also home to Dee's magic mirror and crystal ball. (Dee also possessed another crystal ball that today is housed in room 46 of the British Museum.) Queen Elizabeth would send her ladies-in-waiting to see the mirror, and when they could not describe what they had seen, she would travel to Mortlake to see for herself.

With Dee's presence, Mortlake would become more of a private college than a country home. There were rooms set aside for visiting scientists and also some set aside as laboratories where scientific experiments could be done. Regular guests included Edward Dyer, who was the Chancellor of the Order of the Garter; Robert Dudley (the Earl of Leicester); Adrian Gilbert, who was a half brother to Sir Walter Raleigh and John Hawkins; Sir Philip Sidney, who was the author of *Arcadia,* and his sister Mary, the countess of Pembroke. One of Dee's closest friends was Walter Raleigh, whose social and intellectual circles overlapped with his own. Nearby Syon House, owned by Henry Percy, the Earl of Northampton, also served as a place where great minds shared similar interests.

In 1564, Dee put together what was considered his most important work, *Monas Hieroglyphica.* It is viewed as an alchemical text written in an alchemical language. He dedicated it to King Maximilian of the Holy Roman Empire. It is a puzzle to most, and, as mentioned earlier in chapter 1, he included on its front cover an odd symbol representing the moon, the sun, the elements, and the zodiac sign of Aries. Aries is the zodiacal month that begins at the spring equinox. Queen Elizabeth called upon Dee to explain the symbol. He was also asked to explain it to King Rudolf II, who is known to have had an interest in occult subjects. Dee concluded by claiming that a single four-letter word held the secrets of Creation (which the Jews believed also). The word was the secret name of God—a concept that might have had its roots in Egyptian religion. Historian Frances Yates concluded that the secret doctrine of the Rosicrucian documents was encapsulated in the Monas sign that Dee created.[4]

At Mortlake, Dee would finally have time to take a wife. In 1574 he married for the first time, but his wife lived only one year. He then married a woman by the name of Jane Fromond, who brought eight children into the world.

Dee had very little to invest on his own but was very interested in maritime exploration. In addition to assisting wealthy men like the Earl of Southampton with their investing in such ventures, he also sailed aboard Martin Frobisher's 1576 adventure to northern Europe.

The years at Mortlake gave Dee time to write on subjects as down-to-earth as creating a navy for England and as complicated as using trigonometry to measure the distance to the stars. He wrote on navigation and cartography, geography, and astrology, as well as on other topics that were more occult.

In 1577 he received a letter from Mercator that would influence his writings. Mercator said that the information he was conveying had been received by him from a man by the name of Jacob Cnoyen, a cartographer who in turn corresponded with Abraham Ortelius, a Flemish cartographer and creator of the first modern atlas. He referred to the "priest with the astrolabe," who most likely was a Franciscan friar by the name of Nicholas of Lynn who had taught the use of that key piece of navigational equipment two centuries earlier. The letter discussed other early visitors to the lands west of the Atlantic Ocean, including King Arthur and Prince Madoc of a Welsh royal family.[5]

That same year of 1577, Dee published his book *The Perfect Art of Navigation*. He had been working out its details in his circles, and his work influenced Sir Walter Raleigh. Raleigh, with funds from his own circle, would go on to send three expeditions to Virginia. While they were ill-fated, they would pave the way to the establishment of greater, permanent settlements. The colony and future state may have been called Virginia for Elizabeth, the so-called Virgin Queen. The flag that would fly over the colony depicted Bacon's goddess Athena with the spear and helmet that he had designed while attending school. Raleigh, although eventually executed by his country, would be remembered by the name of his estate of Richmond, which became the capital of Virginia long after his death. The name Raleigh is also preserved as the capital of North Carolina.

While Dee's influence made the case for settling the New World, he also had strong occult leanings. For years he had searched for enlightenment in the spirit world, and, as a result of his efforts, at last the archangel Anael would appear to him in a stone.

Dee had waited patiently for years for a happenstance such as this and claimed that it would provide his breakthrough to more hidden knowledge. Talmudic tradition maintains that this angel was a messenger who conveyed God's knowledge to man. The stone itself is said to be obsidian brought to England from Mayan Mexico. Today it is housed in room 46 of the British Museum, along with Dee's conjuring table and the other esoteric paraphernalia we have discussed earlier. His magic mirror is owned by the Walpole estate.

Dee also wrote in his diary that another angel by the name of Uriel visited him through his stone. Through angels and crystals Dee was regularly entertaining supernatural creatures who spoke to him and sometimes through him. He recorded his conversations with the spirits in his *Mysteriorum libri quinque* (Five books of mystery).

Despite Dee's odd side, he had more practical aptitudes as well. In 1580 he was involved in mapmaking and had a firm grasp on the accepted history and legends of the world. Explorers would come to him to discuss their planned ocean crossings.

On September 21, 1583, Dee headed to continental Europe for a visit. He was so regularly having visions that were he living in the 1960s instead of the 1580s, he no doubt would have been suspected of consuming LSD or magic mushrooms. It took months of travel, but at last John Dee arrived in Prague, where he was welcomed by the Hapsburg emperor Rudolf II. Rudolf was one of Europe's most eccentric monarchs. His court was home to dwarfs and giants, astrologers and alchemists. He patronized the occult sciences and enjoyed music, codes, and games. Dee may have believed that Rudolf might become his patron, but this did not materialize.

In 1589, Dee was welcomed home by the queen. Years of keeping his head in the stars had left his finances in disarray. He took a position as a university dean at Manchester College but bemoaned that its obligations gave him little free time to pursue his real work.

With Elizabeth's death in 1603, Dee lost his protector. James I, the new king, was against witchcraft and was not a fan of the occult. He had expressed this view in writing *Daemonologie.* At the same time, James was a product of Scottish Templarism, but the same Order that fought for the right of the Cathars to depart from traditional Christian dogma might not have always been so tolerant, which is reflected in James's bias.

John Dee Passes the Torch to Francis Bacon

Under James I, Dee was on his way out as Bacon's star was rising. The two friends understood the situation well, and Dee was said to pass along his secrets to Bacon. A man by the name of Jacob Cats published a book of woodcuts in 1655. One depicted an elderly wizard passing a lamp to a young man of the court.

The woodcut's title was *Lampado trado,* and the scene is alleged to represent Dee and Bacon. Between them is an open vault. Many have theorized that such a vault contained books, notes, or evidence of Dee's accumulated learning, which clearly needed to remain concealed. There was also speculation as to the whereabouts of this vault, with some believing that its location was beneath the river Wye in England or underneath the Bruton Church in Virginia. Or perhaps the vaults were actually a series of vaults buried deep below Oak Island, Nova Scotia. These are just three of the possibilities, and we will explore them more thoroughly in a later chapter of this book.

Dr. Dee could be considered the Merlin of his day, and Francis Bacon his Arthur. Bacon's round table, however, required secrecy. Here the woodcut of Mr. Cats offers up another clue. In the woodcut, the buckle of Bacon's shoe is decorated with a large rose. The rose symbolized the rose of the Rosicrucians. What is considered to be true is that

Sir Francis Bacon played an important role in the group when he was alive, and following his death he or those inspired by him would bring the secrets of Rosicrucianism to America.

Above Bacon's tomb in St. Michael's Church in St. Albans, England, is a statue of the young man with the same rose in his shoe buckle. (It's worth noting here that although Bacon is said to rest here, there are many who believe his resting place is elsewhere.)

While Dee did not get the respect afforded other scientists and philosophers, his influence carried forward into the twentieth century. One interesting influence is that which he had on Ian Fleming, the famous author of the James Bond stories. Fleming had links to the Rosicrucian tradition, and these are echoed in the Bond books. (For more on this interesting side story, please see the appendix.)

The wizard, magician, and spy that was John Dee left the material world in December of 1608. His legacy, however, survived him. Before he died he gave Queen Elizabeth a history lesson or two. The oldest story was that of King Arthur and its supposition that Arthur had never really died. Instead, he'd been seriously wounded and carried away by boat to Avalon. This is the basis of England's claim to a land in the western Atlantic.

The other lesson was about a fellow countryman of Dee's, Prince Madoc ab Owain Gwynedd. He too had been to America long before the Spanish, the Portuguese, and the French. Relaying these stories to Elizabeth was Dee's way of trying to convince her to continue to support ventures in the New World. But before Elizabeth could concentrate on such matters, she had to deal with more pressing affairs at home.

Her advisers, her parliament, and the English people all wanted her to marry and put a king on the throne. One by one she turned down the choices she had for a husband. She was England's Virgin Queen, not ready to allow a man to impose his will on her or her country. And marriage was not a sure bet of anything. Indeed, the religious climate of the day made either war or revolution a possible reaction to any marriage she might make.

She had her favorite insiders, however. They included Sir Francis Drake, whom she allowed to raid the Spanish Main; Sir Walter Raleigh, who would explore the American coastline south to the Orinoco; Sir Humphrey Gilbert, of a wealthy Devonshire family, whose goal was to reach Asia; and Martin Frobisher, who also sailed in search of the elusive Northwest Passage. A handful of older men who were happy to invest in such adventures also held influence in Elizabeth's court.

We will examine some of these favorites of Elizabeth in more detail next.

SIR FRANCIS DRAKE

Possibly England's greatest hero and certainly one of her most colorful figures was Sir Francis Drake. Born in Devon circa 1543, he may have learned to hate Catholics at an early age. His father had been a seaman who had retired from the sea to raise a family on his farm, but the Catholic revolt of 1549 forced Drake and others off their land. Francis would have been six when he was uprooted. Father and son worked the coastal trade ships, and Drake took to the ocean in his early twenties. He may have first sailed a slave ship, but merchant and naval commander John Hawkins accused him of abandoning his fleet. It is possible that he had no stomach for the slave trade. The ships could be recognized by their horrendous smell and offered little opportunity for glory.

Warring against Spain, on the other hand, could bring glory and accolades. From 1568 on, Drake raided Spanish ships and towns. In 1572 he captured the *Nombre de Dios* on the isthmus that later became Panama. Missing the opportunity to carry away bars of silver, he raided Cartagena and Santa Marta. In 1573 he crossed the isthmus with a mule train. He and explorer John Oxenham first saw the Pacific Ocean and vowed they'd soon sail that same ocean. Oxenham was captured by the Spaniards before getting the chance, however.

Drake returned to the Americas and several times joined with

Huguenot pirates, including William le Testu, to raid the Spanish. He was the Draco, or El Draque (the Dragon), which was a play on his name. The Dragon and his legendary attacks were the plague of the Spanish.

In 1575 he served with Essex in quelling the rebellion in Ireland. Soon after, the queen handed him the secret assignment that would be his claim to fame.

In 1577, Drake was assigned to raid the Spanish and leave Elizabeth blameless if he was caught. This trip was also meant to double as a mission of discovery. Backers included the Earl of Leicester (Elizabeth's lover); Sir Christopher Hatton (a wealthy London businessman); the Earl of Lincoln, John Hawkins; Sir William Winter and George Winter (who were navy officials); and Drake himself. George Winter's son John would serve as second-in-command and captain one of Drake's ships.

When Drake and his men were south of Safi, off the modern-day Moroccan coast, they began to raid the Portuguese and Spanish ships moored there. They then made passage through the Straits of Cape Horn. Next the small fleet raided the Spanish-controlled coast from Chile northward. Despite his fearsome name, the Dragon was praised by Spanish captives for sparing their lives. Drake's fleet desecrated churches and destroyed statues and paintings and even crucifixes, but they didn't rape or kill their captives. Drake was even known to free slaves who were part of the human cargo.

He traveled up the coast from Chile and Peru to California. Laden with the rewards of his piracy, he still managed to explore, which was the second part of his mission. He sailed through the Golden Gate by the future San Francisco and headed farther north. The fabled Strait of Anian, which was part of the Northwest Passage, awaited. He may have gone as far north as Alaska before crossing the Pacific and heading home.

By the time he returned to England he had been gone for three years and had circumnavigated the globe. With him he brought back Spanish gold, silver, and emeralds, which would support England's new navy for fifty years. He would be knighted by the queen for his bravery and his piracy.

What he was allowed to keep for himself is valued at 25 million English pounds in today's dollars. He bought a Cistercian abbey and the home of his rival Richard Grenville. Drake did have his setbacks, however, and a failed mission years later annoyed the queen, who sent him packing from court life. This was Elizabeth's nature. If one couldn't answer the question, "What have you done for me lately?" in a favorable way, the fickle queen was not amused.

The queen's dismissal mattered little to Drake. He had extensive landholdings from his second marriage and from his years ravaging the Spanish Main. Even in retirement the energetic Drake would build a water supply for the town of Plymouth, England.

The lure of the sea and the adventure of fighting Catholic Spain saw him return to action in 1595 only to meet his death in the first weeks of the following year. Dysentery, not a sword, was to be his mortal enemy. He was remembered as the Dragon Knight, again a wordplay on his name. A Spanish poem refers to him as La Drangontea.

The wordplay, however, was more than a mere play on words. Protestants of the time, especially the French Protestants who were known as Huguenots, had their own societies. The two largest of them were the Dragon Men and the Doves. Was it coincidence that both Columbus (Dove) and Drake (Dragon) had much to do with the navigational history of the world?

SIR WALTER RALEIGH

Sir Walter Raleigh, born in 1554, was younger than Drake by a decade. A Devon man as well, he was related to Drake and Drake's rival Richard Grenville. He was also related to Sir Humphrey Gilbert and Adrian Gilbert, who were his half brothers. Adrian Gilbert was an alchemist as well as an explorer, which was not unusual in that day and age. While Drake was mostly at sea, Raleigh belonged to a wide circle of intellectuals and other movers and shakers. He was well acquainted with John Dee, who was a great influence on all who took to the sea for England in the Elizabethan era. Raleigh was also close to Edmund Spenser and fashioned himself as the Red Cross knight of Spenser's *Faerie Queen*. In fact, when Raleigh reached the Orinoco, he noted: "which because it had no name we called the River of the Red Cross, ourselves being the first Christians that ever came therein."[6]

Spenser's *Faerie Queen* is an epic poem that was supposed to be complete in twelve volumes. It never was fully completed. When Spenser began it in 1590, he wrote a letter to Raleigh, which contained a description of the virtues of Arthurian knights. He describes the Tudors as being the heirs to Camelot, and Elizabeth as Gloriana, the Faerie Queen herself. This earned him a lifelong pension. His first book presents the Red Cross knight as the hero who bears the emblem of Saint George. This hero, garbed in white Templar-like attire with a red cross emblazoned on it, slays the dragon, as did Saint George. He then marries Una, but in the second and third books he is still on a quest. Una represents truth and personifies the true church, which is not the Church of Rome.

The Red Cross can be traced back to the Crusades but as a symbol may be even older. A pre-Christian goddess in Lorraine was Rosemerth. Her shrine in Sion-Vaudemont is where the Virgin Mary was announced to be the Queen of Heaven, a title given to Isis and the goddess by other names. Thus, a secret hidden with the sects beyond the control of Rome recognizes that a female deity exists as an object of worship.

The influence of John Dee and Edmund Spenser on Raleigh is important. Dee was a magician and cartographer; Spenser a philosopher and an author. Raleigh was well versed in their esoteric science and part of their inner circle. (It must be noted that through time the Rosicrucian tradition has been given credit for pioneering many aspects of science.) In 1595 the order had no documented identity. It was still an invisible creation of Bacon's and a secret branch of his secret Order of the Helmet.

While there are no recorded lists of those in Rosicrucian circles, one of the leading publishers of Rosicrucian literature was a man by the name of Johann de Bry. His father, Theodore de Bry, a refugee who fled the Catholics by fleeing to Germany, published Raleigh's *Discoverie*. Theodore was a goldsmith, editor, and publisher. He was also an engraver, and his self-portrait depicts him with his left hand on a skull, which was an ancient symbolic device in art known as a memento mori, a reminder of our transience on Earth.

Most likely family connections helped elevate Raleigh to powerful circles. On St. Bartholomew's Day, April 24–25, 1572, he was in Paris with Sir Francis Walsingham and Sir Philip Sidney. It was a day that would become the 9/11 of his generation. After the attempted assassination of Admiral Gaspard de Coligny, a military and political leader of the Huguenots, other leaders made demands of the French queen. Feeling threatened, Catherine de Medici ordered further reprisals. The king's Swiss guard began rounding up and killing Huguenot leaders. The wounded de Coligny was dragged from his sickbed, killed, and thrown out a window. The French Catholic populace took to the streets, killing all the French Protestants they could find. The violence spread to the countryside, and it is estimated that in total thirty thousand Huguenots as well as their important leaders were killed. The Vatican had a medal struck commemorating the jubilation at this genocide, while Tsar Ivan the Terrible expressed horror at the massacre.

The Red Cross knight who was Raleigh, having witnessed this religious fervor that allowed Christian to kill Christian over doctrine that few could read or understand, decided to create a new world that would not include the murderous Catholics and their treacherous church.

Returning to school in 1572 he met Thomas Hariot as well as John Dee. Before he was twenty, he attended Oxford and the Middle Temple, one of the four English Inns of Court where new barristers study.

In 1580 he was introduced to the court. There he met Edward de Vere, Lord Oxford, who was a favorite of the queen. Oxford loathed Raleigh's friend Philip Sidney and would soon find out that Raleigh was reporting to Walsingham, the queen's spymaster. Whether Raleigh knew it at the time or not, he had made a great enemy in Oxford. To Oxford and Bacon, Raleigh was part of the old guard.

Raleigh managed to stay out of the way and therefore out of trouble. Seeking honor through war, he went to Ireland to take part in the struggles between the Catholics and the Protestants that were transpiring there at the time. Here he would fight alongside Drake and Gilbert. The ferocity with which the Catholics were slaughtered earned Raleigh further favor at court, as well as the Durham estate and a monopoly on the wine trade. From his estate he collaborated with Dee, Sidney, Gilbert, and others in sending expeditions to America.

The queen, however, would keep him at court and would allow neither Raleigh nor Sidney to leave England. And although it was true that by and large the queen had the upper hand when it came to power and control, Raleigh understood that he possessed a weapon or two of his own. One was flattery, which brought him the greatest benefit. It is said that it was Raleigh who took to calling the American coastline Virginia to win the queen's favor. She in turn signed papers authorizing him to discover and settle that territory. He was knighted in the 1580s with the title Lord and Governor of Virginia.

He sent out three expeditions to Virginia, one of which became the ill-fated Lost Colony, whose entire population would disappear. He didn't travel on these expeditions to Virginia given that he was too busy with military service. He actually would not make passage to the Americas until ten years later when he went searching for El Dorado in South America.

Raleigh's Turbulent Second Act

If the pinnacle of Raleigh's career was in 1585, he soon received the other side of Elizabeth's favor three years later. As discussed earlier, he married a lady-in-waiting by the name of Elizabeth Throckmorton. This earned him a sentence in the Tower. She was ten years younger than he was. Her father, Sir Nicholas Throckmorton, had been the queen's ambassador to France. However, her family included Job Throckmorton, a Puritan rabble-rouser; a cousin Francis who had been executed for his plot to put Mary Stuart on the throne; and Thomas, who was a Catholic in exile in France. Raleigh should have asked the queen's permission to wed Elizabeth Throckmorton, but Elizabeth was pregnant with his child in 1591, so they decided to marry in secret. The baby was born in March of the next year. Somehow the secret marriage and child failed to remain secret. Instead the queen got wind of it and as usual reacted with anger at the perceived betrayal.

Both Elizabeth and her husband, Sir Walter, spent a brief time in the Tower, then were exiled to Sherborne Lodge. House arrest was more hospitable than a drafty cell, but Raleigh's career was still hostage to the queen's wrath.

But Raleigh was not one for sitting still or staying out of trouble. He was a central figure in the School of Night, and Sherborne quickly became the new meeting place for the group. This aspect of his intellectual career became a threat as well, for soon it was apparent that someone was out to get Raleigh. The events of 1592 to 1594 included his "outing" as a married man and his being accused of being an atheist because of his School of Night association. And then the heat was turned up. A member of his circle, Thomas Kyd, was arrested on April 22. The inquest, complete with torture, threatened to implicate others. Next Christopher Marlowe was arrested. Marlowe had one foot in Raleigh's circle and another in Essex's. Marlowe's murder the next month is explained as revenge on the part of Raleigh or a ruse to "disappear" the poet, both of which would have the same goal of protecting Raleigh and his circle.

The next year Lord Strange, who had just been made the Earl of Derby, sent a letter to the man the queen trusted the most, William Cecil, claiming that Raleigh and Francis Walsingham were going to assassinate Cecil. Strange was a patron of the theater and of Christopher Marlowe, Edmund Spenser, and purportedly William Shakespeare. Who was actually behind this plot is not obvious. Cecil, the queen's most important minister, worked against both Bacon and Essex and kept them in check in Elizabeth's court. They had the most to gain from Cecil's death, but it is also known that Cecil had a low regard for Raleigh. It might have been wishful thinking to wish Cecil dead, but most likely they or others hatched the plot simply to throw a monkey wrench in someone's powerful connections. If Cecil turned against Raleigh, it would benefit Bacon.

The mother of Lord Strange (Ferdinando Stanley) was Lady Margaret Clifford. According to the will of Henry VIII she would be heir to Queen Elizabeth, leaving Stanley heir to the queen after his mother died. Two days after Strange's letter reached Cecil, Strange took ill. A violent sickness such as his typically was an indicator of poisoning, but Strange would hang on for two painful weeks.

If Strange had been poisoned, who did it? The plot was complicated. English Protestants believed that Lord Strange would turn Catholic and thereby turn back the clock on renouncing the Church of Rome. Catholics accused Strange of the opposite: Strange obstructed a full restoration of the Church of Rome. Some accused the Jesuits of poisoning Strange.

Raleigh, as the preceding story illustrates, was always at the center of the action in Elizabethan England, and his many enemies, try as they might, could not get rid of him, although they did dent his career. It may have seemed to those who wished Raleigh out of the picture that he could handle all threats to him one way or the other. And then in 1596 the tables turned. Raleigh would return to favor at the expense of his greatest enemy, Essex. The Battle of Cadiz found Raleigh at his most heroic and Essex as a looter. Essex was then sent to Ireland, where he failed again. He was now on a slippery slope that would lead to his death.

Raleigh was seen as a culprit in Essex's demise by insiders of the court, but he managed to stay out of harm's way as long as Elizabeth was alive.

Raleigh's Life following the Queen's Death

After Elizabeth's death the attacks started again when Raleigh was implicated in plots to depose James I.

As we know, Raleigh spent thirteen long years in the Tower. During this time he wrote his greatest work, *The History of the World*. In it, he wrote that the stars were the determinants of man's fate. His unique view of the planets included the opinion that while Mars dries, Venus moistens. He believed that magic was a form of worship. His religious history would not be accepted by popular tradition, Catholic or Protestant. Instead he believed in the importance of a god named Dagon (also known as Triton). According to Raleigh's mythology, the goddess Derceta was impregnated by a young man and left her baby by a lake. The baby was changed by the goddess Venus into a fish. Dagon was the fish-man of the Philistines who brought knowledge. He is very much like the Merovee, the mythical ancestor of the Merovingians.

The sources for this work are unknown, but obviously Raleigh had been steeped in esoteric thought. His book was very successful, implying that the reading public was equally interested in the mystical world. It was the second of Raleigh's books. The first was about his trip to the Orinoco River in South America. Both would outsell publications of Shakespeare while the two men were alive.

Raleigh's release from his thirteen-year prison term in the Tower was conditional. He was once again to set sail to try to obtain riches in the Americas. While James wanted the English to steal gold from the native peoples, he did not want to risk war with Spain. There were two specific rules the king ordered Raleigh to follow: Don't raid the Spanish, and bring home the gold. He would disregard the first and fail at the second.

The price for his decision to raid the Spanish would be serious. In a battle against the Spanish, his beloved son Wat met his death on the Orinoco. Sir Walter was beheaded upon his return.

SHIFTING DYNAMICS IN
ELIZABETHAN ENGLAND

Drake and Raleigh—as well as other explorers such as Martin Frobisher, John Davis, and Sir Humphrey Gilbert—appealed to Elizabeth's adventurous nature. They were part of the old guard, which included the Cecils, Leicesters, Walsinghams, and Hattons. They would help the queen rule England, protect her from intrigues outside their own, and often be rewarded for being in the inner circle of court life.

But a younger group was emerging. Its members were interested in the arts and sciences. They were connected by Freemasonry, united in secretive circles, and ready to challenge the Old World. While Catholicism had lost control because of Henry VIII, Anglican Church elders were still ever watchful for heretical thought. It was still possible to face the executioner for heresy, and it was still easy to be thrown in the Tower for disparaging the queen. This small group would live dangerously, expressing heretical thought by challenging the notion that royalty enjoyed a divine right. When they expressed as much in writing, it was often kept within the group. When a public statement was made, it was often done through writings and plays attributed to another.

By 1588 there had been no successful colonies planted in the New World, no permanent settlements made. Some members of this younger inner circle would do much to change that. In 1588 the group included Sir Francis Bacon (1561–1626), age twenty-seven; Edward de Vere, the seventeenth Earl of Oxford (1550–1604), who was thirty-eight; Sir Philip Sidney (1554–1586), age thirty-four; Christopher Marlowe (1564–?), age twenty-four; Lord Essex (1567–1601), barely twenty; and Henry Wriothesley, the Earl of Southampton (1573–1624), who was only fifteen. All had wealth and/or connections, and many were interrelated. William Shakespeare was not part of the court, but at this time he had finished his apprenticeship as a butcher's boy and was twenty-four.

As established previously, these intellectuals banded together in various circles that expanded and contracted as alliances shifted and friendships waxed and waned. This was a continuation of a tradition that had begun with the old guard. At Richmond, built by Henry VII, the queen was close to the Walsingham estate where members of the circle of Sir Philip Sidney gathered. This was a favorite place of hers and, as we know, Walsingham was one of her most trusted agents. At Syon House, Sir Walter Raleigh, scientist Thomas Hariot, writer Christopher Marlowe, satirist Thomas Nashe, and others gathered. Mortlake on the Thames was, as we know, the home of Dr. John Dee and his grand library, where those exploring the New World came to access maps, charts, and nautical instrumentation. Visitors and regulars alike met to work, share ideas, and discuss science in these protected places, free from religious intrusion.

This circle would later be viewed as the inspiration for, if not the foundation of, the Royal Society. Somewhere between Syon House, the Invisible College, and the founding of the Royal Society in 1660, alchemists, heretics, Rosicrucians, and Masons came into favor, but then, with a downturn of fate's wheel, would just as quickly fall out again. Being a part of the court could be lucrative and dangerous in equal parts.

As we know, many of the most influential members of court at that time either were Rosicrucians or had links to the Rosicrucian tradition. It must also be said that not all of those who considered themselves Rosicrucians were active alchemists, astrologers, or explorers. But what they had in common was that they sponsored these pioneering individuals and supported them with money and friendship. They broke bread together as they engaged in spirited discourse about the most pressing matters of the day.

HENRY WRIOTHESLEY, THE EARL OF SOUTHAMPTON

The young Earl of Southampton is one man whose influence on the founding of America has been marginalized despite the funding he provided for its early exploration. Although he is not often discussed in the same company as other Rosicrucians, the tip-off that he was one is found in portraits of him wherein he is pictured with a gloved hand, his fingers pointing downward. His cuffs and gloves are emblazoned with Knights Templar symbols.

Henry as a young man appears to have been effeminate, though later in life he became more manly. He may always have been in search of a father figure, a man to play a guiding role in his life. Perhaps one such candidate was Sir William Cecil, who was much older than he was. Born in 1520, Cecil was Elizabeth's power in the English Parliament. He was her chief adviser for most of her reign, holding titles that included Secretary of State and then Lord Treasurer and Master of the Court of Wards.

It should be noted that Cecil, although a favorite of Queen Elizabeth, was generally not favored by the young at court. In 1563 he passed a bill forcing Englishmen to eat fish on Wednesdays. In *Hamlet,* Cecil is satirized in his identity as Polonius and called a "fishmonger." Where Sir Francis Bacon could not get away with such a depiction, "Shakespeare" did get away with such insults on a regular basis, but as explained in earlier chapters, "Shakespeare" did not visit court.

In any event, at a certain point Cecil wanted to see young Henry Wriothesley married, for he now had reached the age of seventeen and was marriage material. This point was not lost upon Edward de Vere (Oxford), who wished Wriothesley to marry his daughter Elizabeth. De Vere's fortune was very much diminished after a lifetime of free spending, and marriage with the wealthy earl would ensure Elizabeth a position among England's elite, which might help both father *and* daughter. But the young man refused. Henry may have been enjoying the good life of a wealthy young man in London and may have been the object of an older man's affections. And that older father figure may have changed with time. Initially perhaps it was Cecil, then the Earl of Oxford himself, and after that, Robert Devereux, Earl of Essex.

Henry would serve with Essex in the military action at Cadiz and be part of Essex's revolt against Elizabeth, for which Essex would be beheaded. Henry, on the other hand, would be spared by the queen.

CHRISTOPHER MARLOWE

We have discussed Marlowe earlier in connection with Shakespeare; here we will discuss his involvement in the court. An order by the privy council indicated that he performed a great service to the queen. The service was, no doubt, acting as a spy for the queen's spymaster. Francis Walsingham had recruited Marlowe, considering him both smart enough and reckless enough to be a spy. Marlowe's personal motto was "What nourishes me, destroys me."

Marlowe had been kicked out of the Netherlands for counterfeiting gold coins. In 1589 he was involved in a street fight that resulted in a man's death. Seemingly, Marlowe had few fears; that is, until his friend Thomas Kyd was arrested with papers considered both blasphemous and atheistic. Kyd, a long-term friend and a writer himself, had composed the violent *Spanish Tragedy*. Kyd would not survive his torture under interrogation. The real target of the investigation might have been Marlowe, for he had stepped on one toe too many.

In May of 1593 he was under warrant to appear in court for a most serious matter. Marlowe's life on the edge included an affair with the brother (Thomas) of Elizabeth's spymaster, Francis Walsingham, and membership in the secretive group of intellectuals called the School of Night. The members of the group had, as part of their aesthetic, vowed to forsake women; a point that was satirized in *Love's Labour's Lost*.

A Deeper Examination of the School of Night

A focal point for the members of the School of Night was Raleigh's home in Ireland, at the Abbey of Molanna. Raleigh had earned this estate for his role in quelling Irish unrest. Sir Walter Raleigh was a patron of Hariot's and gave him his estate at Molanna to continue his work on astronomy. Hariot would sail aboard Raleigh's first expedition and map the coastline of Virginia.

In England the circle met at Richmond and Sherborne. Later the group would move to Syon, the home of the "Wizard Earl" Northumberland, when Raleigh, locked in the Tower, could not preside over gatherings. The circle included John Florio, who translated the works of French essayist Michel Montaigne. These works were very influential in shaping the philosophy of Bacon and others. Montaigne's essay *Des Cannibales* is said to be a source, via his translator John Florio, of *The Tempest.*[7]

The group also included Florio's publisher, Edward Blount. Blount, it should be noted, also published the First Folio of Shakespearean works. John Florio was a friend of Giordano Bruno, who resided in the home of the French ambassador. There Sir Walter Raleigh, Christopher Marlowe, and Fulke Greville gathered. Other School of Night students included the poet Matthew Roydon and William Warner, a scientist.

Dr. John Dee of course was a member. George Chapman, who had translated Homer and wrote seven comedies of his own, was another member. In 1605 he and Ben Jonson wrote a satire called *The Isle of Dogs,* which was received as anti-Scottish. The king was not amused, and both Chapman and Jonson were put into the Fleet Prison. Raleigh, who had sponsored Edmund Spenser, also introduced him to the group. Francis Drake, Humphrey Gilbert, Richard Hakluyt, and Philip and Robert Sidney were members too. The Earl of Derby and Ben Jonson soon became regulars as well.

The School of Night attracted enemies and endured stretches of bad luck. Sir Walter Raleigh would be imprisoned and beheaded. Thomas Nashe and George Chapman were imprisoned and impoverished. Marlowe may have been stabbed. May have.

When Thomas Kyd was arrested with the blasphemous papers we mentioned earlier, he declared that the papers were Marlowe's. Since another friend of Marlowe's, Francis Kett, had endured torture only to suffer death by fire, Marlowe may have realized that a similar fate might be in store for him. The Elizabethan world apparently allowed ambiguous sexuality to exist at court but drew the line at treason and heresy. We can assume that Marlowe's connection to both Thomas Kyd and Francis Walsingham may have kept him out of harm's way prior to this time.

Heresy, however, unlike ambiguous sexuality, was a most heinous crime. Government agent Richard Barnes reported that to Marlowe religion was meant only to control man. He said if there be any "good" religion it would be that of the papists who knew how to bind man with numerous ceremonies and practices. If that was not enough to irritate a queen who had constantly battled a Catholic threat to her monarchy, Marlowe went even further. Barnes reported that Marlowe spoke of Jesus being a bastard and implied that Jesus and his disciples were homosexuals like themselves. According to Barnes, Marlowe said that the Jews had been right to kill Jesus.

It is possible that the irascible Marlowe *had* uttered such inflammatory comments, and it is possible that Barnes had added his own blasphemy to get rid of Marlowe. In any case, the matter was taken quite seriously indeed.

After facing an initial inquiry, Marlowe was allowed to remain a free man but had to report to the same committee that had investigated Kyd and Kett every day. Either he knew his days were numbered or he was tipped off by those who looked out for him.

On May 30, 1593, an argument over a bill in a tavern, which doubled as a brothel, resulted in Marlowe's death. Or did it? Marlowe was drinking at a table with three men who in one capacity or another had all acted as agents of Sir Francis Walsingham.

The Death of Marlowe

Walsingham was a very serious man who was in the long-term employ of the queen. Her spymaster, his motto was *Video et taceo,* which means

"See and be silent." He never betrayed a secret or said a loose word. His father was a lawyer who had died when the lad was two. There was money for Walsingham's education, and he had attended Cambridge and Gray's Inn. He was fluent in continental languages and had also studied in Padua. He had a dry sense of humor and was said to be unflappable in the most dire of situations. The queen had pet names for her men and threw merciless barbs at them; however, none dared return a quip. And yet when Elizabeth interrupted Walsingham, who was delivering a report to her, she called him a "Moor." Without missing a beat he replied, "the laws of Ethiopia, my native soil."[8]

Walsingham had uncovered the Duke of Norfolk's role in the Ridolfi plot to assassinate Queen Elizabeth. He placed insiders in another emerging plot, which he then brought down in the nick of time. His undercover agent was Robert Poley. Walsingham had code numbers for everyone, friend and foe alike. John Dee was Agent 007 and the Duke of Norfolk was 40.

Walsingham's job as spymaster was not always profitable. In fact it *cost* him money. This was rectified by his being involved in many projects whose financial return was great. The queen, Leicester, and Walsingham were the three largest investors in the remarkably successful Drake voyage of 1577–1580. Marlowe himself was an agent of Walsingham's, which may have begun when he was a student at Cambridge.

In any event, on the fateful night of May 30, 1593, Marlowe was stabbed in a tavern as a result of a petty quarrel with colleagues. The ensuing inquest was over in two days. Only three of those who had been present were asked to give testimony.

Despite the fact that Marlowe was a violent man who lived a violent life, some believe the whole thing had been a setup. Francis Walsingham and his brother Thomas had reason to either save Marlowe from the Star Chamber or at least make sure he did not, under torture, implicate others. Sir Walter Raleigh also had reason to fear exposure if Marlowe gave evidence about the School of Night.

Was Marlowe actually killed, or had his death been staged? The three men who drank with him included Ingram Frizer—the man who actually was alleged to have killed Marlowe—Robert Poley, and Nicholas Skeres. Frizer was a "servant" of Francis Walsingham. Poley and Skeres were among Francis Walsingham's spies. Poley had infiltrated the plotters of what would be known as the Babington plot, egging them on and then turning them in. Poley's cover was maintained by his imprisonment in the Tower for two years. Skeres had been part of the Babington plot and its foiling and undertook other assignments for Francis Walsingham as well.

Regarding the question of whether Marlowe's "death" was staged, the coroner William Danby accepted the improbable story that Marlowe had snatched a dagger from Frizer's belt and struck him with it. It caused only a superficial scrape. Frizer then grabbed Marlowe and plunged the weapon, all two inches of it, into Marlowe's forehead, killing him instantly. For the crime of murder, Ingram Frizer spent a month in custody, was released, and soon thereafter returned to the employ of the Walsingham family.

There is some speculation that if Marlowe did not die on May 30, he may have left England for Italy, where he remained in seclusion. Before the thirty-six-hour inquest was complete, someone's body was supposed to have been buried somewhere. If Marlowe was buried on June 1 as alleged, the location of the grave remains unknown.

To spare Marlowe the risk of torture, and others the risk of incrimination, Francis Walsingham may have intervened in the affair. Perhaps money changed hands, a dead man stood in for Marlowe, an inquest was rushed, and three agents received a slap on the wrist before returning to work for Francis Walsingham.

EDWARD DE VERE, THE EARL OF OXFORD

As previously mentioned, Edward de Vere was born into wealth and privilege in 1550. He was highly educated and a key member of the

School of Night. In chapter 3 we discussed his involvement in this group, as well as his possibly having been the author of some of the works attributed to William Shakespeare.

Edward de Vere received degrees from Cambridge and Oxford before going on to study law at Gray's Inn. In 1567, at the age of seventeen, he was involved in a notorious incident wherein he stabbed a man. Thomas Brinknell was an undercook in the employ of Cecil, and he died the next day. A jury ruled that Brinknell had started the altercation, and de Vere was acquitted. The episode was, however, to mark the beginning of a display of bad temper that would plague him all his life.

As an adult de Vere encountered financial difficulties. However, despite this, he still backed the voyage of Frobisher—an expedition to America—with an immense amount of money. His investment's return was zero.

Money or its lack thereof was not his only problem. He had privately endorsed the Catholic faith along with three friends. But for some reason they had a falling out, and Edward renounced his faith. In turn, he was accused of everything from disrespecting the queen and Jesus Christ to being a liar and a drunk, to "buggering" a boy on his kitchen staff.

He was also accused of having an affair with one of Elizabeth's ladies-in-waiting, Ann Vavasor. Here the evidence was greater. Ann had a child with him. Queen Elizabeth, who seemed to forgive almost everything Edward could do, threw him in the Tower for this indiscretion. He remained there for only a few weeks, unlike Sir Walter Raleigh's punishment for marrying Elizabeth Throckmorton. The damage was done, however; he had fallen from the queen's good graces.

ROGER MANNERS

Roger Manners, the fifth Earl of Rutland, was another man who was in the same circles as Bacon, Southampton, Oxford, and Essex. He was born at Belvoir, his family's estate, in October 1576. Manners enjoyed the sporting life as only those born into a great deal of wealth can enjoy. He hunted and engaged in falconry. (He also played tennis, which may account for the symbolic box of tennis balls given to the king in *Henry V*.)

His military experience was with Essex in Ireland as well as the Netherlands. He went too far in taking part in the Essex Rebellion, an attempt to overthrow Elizabeth. He paid a draconian fine for his very minor role. Later, when a production of *Richard II* staged at the Globe Theater in February of 1601 might have landed him in the Tower due to the treasonous nature of its content (commoners plot to kill a king), he was not punished. It may be that he already had been more than adequately fined. Under James I his fortune was restored.

Manners was close to Henry Wriothesley (Southampton) and William Herbert (Pembroke). He married Elizabeth Stanley, the only daughter of Sir Philip Stanley. The marriage has been referred to as platonic.[9] Manners did not have a long life, and on June 26, 1612, he died. His wife, Elizabeth, died two months after him, and it was rumored that she had poisoned him, an act that earned revenge from his family. Another rumor posits that Walter Raleigh was part of the plot to poison her.

ROBERT DEVEREUX, THE EARL OF ESSEX

Robert Devereux, the Earl of Essex, was descended from all of the great houses of England. Through Thomas of Woodstock, who was the Duke of Gloucester, the family traced its pedigree from Edward II. Robert was born in 1567, and despite the lineage and his glorified relations, he inherited little. When Robert Dudley (Earl of Leicester) married Lettice Knollys, Essex became the stepson of Robert Dudley, the illustrious favorite of the queen. The marriage would cost Leicester but help young Essex.

He was brought up under Burghley and sent to Trinity College at Cambridge when he was ten. At fourteen he received his master's of arts degree. At eighteen he was sent by his stepfather to the Netherlands, where England hoped to repress the influence of the burgeoning Catholicism that was developing there. In 1586 his title was head of the Cavalry, and after a famous charge at Zutphen in the Netherlands against the Spanish, he was knighted.

When Leicester returned to court life from war in the Netherlands, Elizabeth saw an aged man. The white-haired Leicester was somehow not as desirable as he once had been. His stepson Robert Devereux was more appealing, even given his young age. Soon Devereux had taken on Leicester's role completely. He spent nights in the queen's quarters, ostensibly playing cards.[10] The gossip was he would not return to his own quarters until the birds were singing their morning songs.

The downfall of Essex was due to those same characteristics that had initially brought him into the queen's graces. He was impetuous and a romantic. After the Spanish Armada was thwarted, Drake wanted to enact revenge for their attack with a quick attack back at the Spanish. Essex wanted to join in; however, the queen said no. Essex rode 220 miles on horseback in three days to board Drake's ship in Plymouth. The queen was furious that Essex had disobeyed her, that Drake continued on with his vengeful mission regardless, and that Sir Roger Williams took a detachment of soldiers to attack Lisbon.

The attack was a failure, although the queen did not punish anyone for this. Instead she did what she did best, which was to play her suitors. Young Charles Blount, whom Essex perceived as a rival for the queen's attention, was given a queen from Elizabeth's chessboard as a token of her esteem at his prowess.

Essex challenged Blount to a duel and was left bloodied. The queen was delighted that someone could teach Essex manners.

War between the Catholics and Protestants in France again gave Essex the opportunity to show his military skill. A drawn-out battle had cost England most of the men whom Elizabeth had sent, and again Essex came home in less than desirable circumstances.

Essex's court battles fared just as badly. He tried to secure for Bacon the position of attorney general, but the queen, at the time annoyed with Bacon, again favored the Cecil family instead. At this time, 1594, Essex brought the bad news to Bacon along with a reward: a piece of property valued at eighteen hundred pounds, a small fortune at the time.

Essex would go to war again, this time with the English attack at Cadiz. The day of his departure Robert Cecil was promoted to the queen's secretary. It was Elizabeth's style to make such a move. This was a position Essex had coveted.

The English were victorious at Cadiz, but the queen felt that she had been cheated out of her share of the spoils. Instead of securing treasure, Essex made looters out of his soldiers. Rumors of Spanish goods selling in London fueled the queen's suspicions, and Robert Cecil took her side by pointing fingers and making accusations. In truth, they had missed the treasure fleet that entered the Tagus two days after the English had left, even though Essex had wanted to remain.

When news came that a second Armada was being prepared, the attack on Cadiz would be repeated. This time the weather, not another army, would attack the English. The storms left the fleet unable to mount an attack, and thus the fleet headed to the Portuguese Azores to catch the treasure fleet that they had missed earlier. Essex and Raleigh separated, and Raleigh successfully attacked the Portuguese island of Fayal. Raleigh and Essex were left fighting each other over who was entitled to the booty. As they were preoccupied with this, the treasure fleet managed to elude them, and, worse still, a new Armada began making its way to England.

Again a fleet was hurt by the weather, and Elizabeth was horrified to see the country left without protection. Essex would be forced out of court for his role in the failings. Initially he was passed over for a title, while the original success of Cadiz was credited to Lord Howard of Effingham.

It was at this time that Francis Bacon became the confidant of the queen. Specifically she would heed his advice on Essex. Bacon owed Essex much, but clearly Essex was reckless. Was Bacon motivated by getting into the good graces of the queen and Robert Cecil, or did he have England's interests first and foremost? It is impossible to know for certain. In any case the stakes were raised when Bacon found himself being called a traitor in pamphlets that defended the earl.

When the Star Chamber met, Bacon was not in attendance. The chamber condemned the earl's actions (and inactions) in Ireland, his treaty with Tyrone, and his disobedience to the queen. The only punishment for Essex was to keep him isolated, first in Ireland and then in the Tower. Later Baron Mountjoy, the Earl of Southampton, and King James of Scotland discussed creating a fighting force in Ireland that would turn the tables on Elizabeth. James became too cautious to take further action, however, and Mountjoy (Charles Blount) was enjoying his role as commander too much to put any real energy behind the initiative.

Meanwhile, Essex was released to return to Essex House, and Bacon was asked by the queen for advice a second time. He again advised against the Star Chamber deciding the fate of Essex. But his voice wasn't heeded, and the queen insisted that he play the role of accuser. It was not a comfortable role for Bacon, and would get worse. When the eleventh-hour proceeding took place, Essex was forced to kneel at the end of a table. The chamber sentenced him to the Tower, but Elizabeth allowed him to return to Essex House instead.

Bacon again intervened on behalf of Essex. At this point he was risking his own position by defending the damaged man, but to his credit he was loyal to his friend. But Essex did not cooperate, instead sending Sir Gilly Merrick across the river to hire the players at Southwark to put on a presentation of *Richard II*. The message of this play was that a ruler could be deposed. The queen got wind of the performance and sent envoys to Essex. Once there, they found an armed mob of hundreds that could barely be controlled. The mob then began a march on London.

Once in London with the mob, Essex found that he had no other popular support. Worse still, the mob that appeared to be following him grew smaller. His own force was slowly deserting. He returned to Essex House with the queen's men on his tail. When artillery was brought out he surrendered and was brought to the Tower. At his trial, Bacon was the prosecutor. The days of defending his benefactor were over.

Essex and Southampton were found guilty. Southampton was spared while Essex was beheaded. Sir Christopher Blount, Sir Charles Danvers, Sir Gilly Merrick, and a Henry Cuffe were all killed.

The court of Queen Elizabeth was made up of some of the most wealthy and some of the most ambitious people of England. Wealth allowed them the pursuit of literary pleasures and wild adventures. Ambition could lead to imprisonment and death.

CHAPTER 5

OCCULT ENGLAND

The Tudors were an old Welsh family of little importance. The name is from the Welsh *Tewdwr,* meaning "Theodore." They would rise from obscurity in the fourteenth century when the Tudors' designated founder, Owen Tudor, married Catherine of Valois, the widow of Henry V. Queen Elizabeth's death would mark the last of the Tudor line. Elizabeth's father was Henry VIII, whose own father, Henry VII, had taken the throne as the founder of the Tudor dynasty. Henry VII's oldest son, Arthur, was next in line for the throne and married Catherine of Aragon.

Henry VII was the son of Edmund Tudor, who died three months before his son was born. Edmund's thirteen-year-old wife sought protection in Pembroke Castle, where the future King Henry VII was born. He would be raised there until the Yorkist William Herbert captured the castle. Henry was then raised as a member of the Herbert family until Sir William Herbert, the first Earl of Pembroke, was killed. His widow, Anne Devereux, then took Henry VII to the family home. He finally escaped and sought to take the English crown for himself.

He defeated the forces of Richard III at Bosworth Field. Henry VII had a smaller force, but Richard's army for the most part refused to fight. Famously remembered as begging, "My kingdom for a horse," Richard was killed and his reign thus ended in this decisive battle in

August of 1485. In the aftermath of the battle, Richard III's crown was taken from the bush where it had fallen and placed on Henry's head. Henry VII was now *King* Henry VII.

He was obsessed with the Arthurian myths and named his son Arthur. His hopes for his son becoming the new King Arthur were dashed, however, when influenza claimed the boy at the age of sixteen. It is possible that the interest in the historical or mythical Arthur was passed down in the family, culminating with Dee's attempts to convince Elizabeth that she had a destiny in the New World.

When Henry VII came to the throne England and Ireland were divided and isolated from Europe. They would remain isolated for the entire next century under the Tudor dynasty. Even in 1604, Ben Jonson commented on the situation: "The empire is a world divided from the world."[1]

In isolation, evil lurked everywhere. Part 2 of the play *King Henry VI* tells the story of the Duchess of Gloucester employing one Margery Jourdain, known as the Witch of Eye, as well as two priests and a sorcerer to reveal Henry's destiny and the destinies of the Dukes of Suffolk and Somerset. Together they fashioned a waxen idol of the king and melted it in a fire. It is unknown what the image revealed, but the fate of the duchess was to be imprisoned, the witch burned, and another dead by hanging.

Henry VII would live only seven more years, dying at the age of fifty-two. His daughter Margaret bore a son, also christened Arthur, but the child would not survive the year. Henry VIII then took the throne.

HENRY VIII TAKES ON THE CHURCH

When Arthur died, the younger brother, Henry VIII, married his widow. This may have kept England Catholic; however, Catherine only bore him a daughter, Mary, and not a son and heir. The survival of the Tudor dynasty was at stake. Henry needed to get the pope's blessing to annul the marriage and marry the attractive Anne Boleyn.

In 1529 an Englishman by the name of Richard Croke was sent by the king to gather evidence in favor of the annulment. Thomas Cranmer, who later became archbishop of Canterbury, instructed that both canonist lawyers and Jewish rabbis be allowed to provide an opinion. The book of Leviticus prohibits marriage between a man and his brother's widow. This fact might have supported an annulment for Henry. Deuteronomy, however, allows such a marriage, providing that there were no children from the prior marriage.[2]

When the pope denied Henry VIII a divorce, he embraced the Reformation and started the Church of England, with himself at the head as the equivalent of the pope. Anne Boleyn would give birth to the future Queen Elizabeth but was not able to produce a male heir to be king. Henry needed a new wife, and, as both king and religious leader, he had Anne beheaded as an adulteress. He then married Jane Seymour, Anne of Cleves, Catherine Howard, and later Catherine Parr.

According to the order of succession, Henry's son Edward VI, then Mary, then Elizabeth were in line for the throne. Edward took the throne at age nine and died at fifteen of consumption. He had been a Calvinist. His half sister Mary then took the throne and attempted to return the country to Catholicism. She married her cousin's son, the king of Spain. Mary died in 1558, possibly of stomach cancer, and at this point, Elizabeth ascended to the throne.

THE CHURCH REACHES
A TIPPING POINT

Queen Elizabeth followed in her father's footsteps and embraced the Church of England to make England predominantly Protestant again. Let's take a moment and look back at the dynamics at play when Henry VIII was in power. Things had changed dramatically when Henry pulled the proverbial rug out from under the church's feet. He did it mostly for selfish reasons: to marry someone (Anne Boleyn) who would produce a male heir to the throne (or so he thought). His revolt against the pope might have succeeded because of the haughtiness of the Vatican and its actions in the centuries preceding ascension of the Tudor dynasty in England.

Up until Henry VIII had tried to annul his first marriage to Catherine of Aragon, he considered the Church of Rome to be a necessary evil. He was not, however, a fan of the Reformation and despised Luther. He was possibly England's worst king and could have done with a bit of reforming himself! He typically sent friend and foe alike to the gallows, personally purging anyone who did something that didn't suit his fancy.

What might surprise many people about Henry VIII is that he was an intellectual, a sportsman, a musician, and an athlete in addition to being a king. He could quote scripture, compose a mass, and play several musical instruments. He also excelled at tennis, archery, dancing, jousting, and wrestling, and he could polish off an entire state dinner, which might last seven hours, with the best of them.

The king was indeed a catch, although his older brother, Arthur, was ahead of him to become the next king. In November of 1501, Arthur married Catherine of Aragon. Despite his tender age of fifteen, his marriage and life only had five months to go. Upon his death, Catherine denied the marriage had ever been consummated. Henry had his sights on her by this time, and that included her immense dowry. After church and civil officials deliberated on the legality of such a marriage, Henry married Catherine of Aragon, his brother's widow.

Seven months later their first child died in childbirth. A second child, a son, lived only for a few short weeks. Next a third and then a fourth child died in childbirth. Both were sons. In 1516, Catherine gave birth to a healthy daughter, Mary. Before she was two a marriage had been arranged for her with the dauphin of France.

Henry did not have to look far for female companionship as he was already enjoying an affair with a woman named Elizabeth Blount.

He had a son with Elizabeth; he would one day become the Duke of Richmond and Somerset and the Earl of Nottingham. He also had an affair with Mary Boleyn before his eye caught her sister, Anne, both nieces of the Duke of Norfolk.

It was for Anne that Henry would first request from the pope the blessing to marry and then deny his authority. It was Anne for whom the Anglican (English) Church was formed to rid the island of foreign interference that could dictate to a king.

The reason that his marriage to Catherine was not annulled was not because of the Christian imperative that what God brought together no man should tear asunder. It was because Catherine was the aunt of the emperor and the pope was his puppet. Popes granted other annulments to royals all the time.

OTHER FACTORS LEADING TO ATTACKS ON THE CHURCH

Henry VIII had been the first to challenge the church. But it was not just his protestations that had sparked a revolt against the Roman Catholic Church. Thomas More had written on the real Christianity in 1515 in his *Utopia*. According to it, the world should hold property and wealth in common, and personal property should be abolished. But the commoners, despite envisioning a utopia, lived in a country where two hundred knightly families and five thousand lower esquires lived idly, and justice for the common man did not exist.

Thus, for centuries the pressure was building, given that the church had power over all things from marriage to taxes and was not the benevolent father for whom the faithful had hoped. The church understood that knowledge was power and so created a monopoly on it. This was threatened by the Reformation, and the various new Protestant sects that emerged were branded heretical by the Catholic Church.

The church might have taken a stance that allowed for tolerance. Instead it reignited the Inquisition, placing popular writers and scholars alike, including Boccaccio, Petrarch, and Erasmus, on the "index"—a list of forbidden books. The Talmud, writings of Luther and Hus, texts supposedly written by King Arthur, prophecies of Merlin, and anything pertaining to magic and astrology were on the index. Jesuits and Dominicans competed in their scourge of science and art. Dominican Giovanni Carafa launched a campaign against Michelangelo's *Last Judgment*. Scandalized by its male nudity, he brought enough attention to himself to become Pope Paul IV. He started his own Roman Inquisition, mostly aimed at the Spanish in the south of Italy. In Calabria, in southern Italy, two thousand "heretics" were executed.

The pope was so hated by the people for his reign of terror that the holy office of Rome was attacked, buildings demolished, and records burned. Fortunately this pope was recalled by God himself within four years of having gained the title. The index survived into the twentieth century, and the list of authors it eventually banned included Dante, Robert Fludd, Descartes, John Locke, Daniel Defoe, Emanuel Swedenborg, Voltaire, Jean Jacques Rousseau, Jeremy Bentham, Victor Hugo, and Gustave Flaubert. The hatred and viciousness of the church survived the pope as well.

Philip II of Spain watched thirty-one heretics burned alive in Valladolid, an eight-hour display of religious barbarity. The preaching of Luther, Calvin, Knox, and others incited rebellion against the way things had been for a thousand years. Both Catholics and Protestants would from this point on not avoid any atrocity when warring against each other.

On January 17, 1562, the Edict of Saint-Germain, issued by Catherine de Medicis in France, was a countermeasure that bestowed religious tolerance on a troubled world. The powerful Catholic Guise faction opposed it. Later that year, the Duke of Guise was attending mass in Vassy, France. He complained that the Protestant mass being celebrated nearby was so loud he could hear them. He ordered the church to be burned with all inside. Hundreds died in the flames; two hundred more were killed outside.

ADDITIONAL CATALYSTS
OF CHANGE

Possibly the greatest challenge to the power of the church was actually a result of the church exercising its own power. The Crusades had been a series of disasters for Europe as hundreds of thousands of people and millions of dollars were lost in a series of misadventures leading to the fall of Jerusalem. The silver lining, as noted previously, was that the crusaders returned with knowledge and learning that had been kept from the people by the church. Italy was the first to benefit, given that cities like Venice and Florence were crossroads of the East-West traffic. And as mentioned earlier, classic works of Greek and Roman authors were carried home to Europe and translated.

The Medici court in Florence was possibly the greatest center of learning. Indeed, the Medici family made an industry of translating works that had previously been unknown. Philosophers like Marsilio Ficino and Giovanni Pico della Mirandola revived a movement known as Neoplatonism (given that Plato's works had been carried off from the fallen city of Constantinople). The *Corpus Hermeticum,* allegedly written by the Egyptian mystic Hermes Trismegistus, introduced a new breath of life to gnostic thought. It was believed to be the wisdom of the ages. Kabbalistic studies also developed even though many countries had expelled Jews.

Templars, having looted the Temple of Jerusalem and the texts, scrolls, and tablets protected there and elsewhere, contributed to the developing arts, sciences, and, occasionally, the black arts.

The new studies introduced and brought back previous practices that had been more prevalent during pagan times. Magic was the ability to capture or command another life force, such as angels or demons, to do one's bidding. Alchemy was the concept of either creating a transmutation of base metals or, on a much higher level, transcendence to a higher level of the human experience. Letters were magical, and words could conceal secret truths or even hold powers of their own.

Pico della Mirandola warned that such powers should only be used to capture the spirits of good beings like angels. Others began to fear pagan practices and dark magic even more.

THE QUEEN'S RELATIONSHIP WITH THE OCCULT ARTS

Queen Elizabeth was against these magical arts, but at the same time she consulted the astrologer John Dee to forecast her own life. To understand the paranoia of Elizabeth, it is best to understand what preceded her path to the throne.

The ability for the status of royalty to change so fast—as in the case of her mother, Anne Boleyn—would haunt Elizabeth, and the nearby Tower would always serve as a reminder that nobody was above such a fate. She was aware of the Shakespearean play *Richard II*, and while reading a historical document it dawned on her: "I am Richard II, know ye not that?" She complained that in recent months the play by that name had been staged as many as forty times.

Richard II was not simply historical but contained a message for the monarchy to act with restraint. Elizabeth herself was guilty of instructing Parliament that she was an instrument of God. This not only offended that segment of the population who was secretly Catholic, but it also offended Parliament that she was conferring the Divine on her rule. Not everyone saw the message in the play as a plea for restraint. When supporters of the Earl of Essex put on the play it was considered an act of rebellion. Many were arrested. Some were fined, and Essex, of course, was executed.

The night before Essex's execution Shakespeare's play was put on by the Lord Chamberlain's Men. Perhaps because Elizabeth had overcome threats to her rule, they were not punished. Did the queen know who was really behind the writing of *Richard II*? Did her successor?

Whether it was Oxford or Bacon or someone else advising the queen through their shill Shakespeare, she correctly considered Essex the threat, not the Bard. Her father's experience in butting up against the church and court politics was something she understood all too well, for it had posed danger to her personally.

This might have been hard for those who took their religion more seriously than the whimsical monarchy did. So many concealed their true leanings and waited for the winds of change to come around to their side again. Sir Francis Bacon was one of those who railed against the vagaries of both state and state religion that stunted science as well as murdered millions of people throughout history. Bacon lived during the same time period that the church arrested and cruelly tortured Tommaso Campanella for his book on faith and philosophy.

Campanella was born in Calabria, Italy, and joined the Dominican order before turning fourteen. He studied astrology in 1590, which was a reason he was brought before the Inquisition a few years later. He tried to create a community that shared goods and resources. This got him a much longer sentence in prison, where he wrote *City of the Sun*. Finally friends in higher places saved him. Campanella, later regarded as a spark that inspired the Rosicrucian movement, may have also inspired Bacon's *New Atlantis*.

Bacon was thirty-nine when Giordano Bruno was burned at the stake for refusing to recant the heretical statement that the Earth moved around the sun. Bruno had spent time in public debate in England before making the mistake of returning to Italy. It is possible that Bacon may have met him. At the time, however, Bacon's writings would remain hidden, due to fear of reprisal, while apparently William Shakespeare had no such fears.

THE IRON GRIP OF THE PAPACY

Henry VIII did not invent the Reformation, but he may have been the single greatest catalyst in keeping the rebellion against the church alive. For centuries prior to Henry the church had kept an iron grip on learning, science, and social mores, and it even made or broke kings. When the church needed heresy stamped out, the states did its bidding. The seeds of the reformation were evident following the Crusades, and not only in England. The Cathar movement may have been the first great threat to the Roman Church since Arianism. From Italy to the south of France this gnostic "heresy" preached that man's relationship with his god needed no middleman. To the church the theological aspect was serious, but the threat to the income-producing ability to tax was a grave one indeed. Cathars needed no legions of illiterate priests, haughty bishops, and faraway cardinals, nor a pope dictating just how to worship God or claiming their income. Their relationship with God was untainted with the horde of middlemen; it was pure. In Greek the term *kathari* meant "the pure ones."

In 1209 the church began an armed genocide with the mission of wiping out the heretics. It was a scorched-earth campaign that would bring death, poverty, and ruin to the south of France, the Languedoc. The genocidal purge of Béziers started the campaign as fifteen thousand men, women, and children were put to death for not accepting Rome's version of Christianity. A military officer asked the papal legate how they might tell who were Cathars, and the famous answer was, "Kill them all; let God sort them out."[3]

The crusade against the pure ones would climax in 1244 when a relatively small group of surviving Cathars were cornered at the stronghold of Montségur. After a long siege they agreed to a deal that allowed them to leave and be spared if they renounced their heresy. Two hundred marched out, refused to acknowledge their own faith as heresy, and went to their death by fire. They were burned in groups in a stockade.

Remarkably, a contingent of Knights Templar was among those defending the fortress of Montségur. In the end they were allowed to leave unharmed. Rome would take its time, but such conduct was never forgiven. The church and the French king would torture, kill, and burn hundreds of Templars at the beginning of the thirteenth century.

Sometime after the church burned fellow Christian Cathars, a backlash against the church began. The morality of this great power was not the issue. Instead, the English nation was questioning its ability to tax yet remain tax exempt. On occasion the clergy did contribute a tenth of their income to the state, but this was determined by the clergy. They were represented in the upper house of Parliament by their bishops and abbots. They wielded their power with few limits. If they had tenants on a church property, it was the church that had power over the tenants, not the government.

THE KNIGHTS TEMPLAR

The Knights Templar had been formed when the Crusaders took Jerusalem. It began as a handful of men with the mission of protecting pilgrims on the way to visit the Holy Land. After a decade, which many believe they simply spent excavating the Temple of Solomon, they returned home as heroes. Saint Bernard, the head of the Cistercian monks, endorsed them fully, and nobles from all over France rushed to pledge their riches and their lives to the Order, which grew rapidly.

The Knights Templar garnered the largest navy and became the largest property owner in Europe and North Africa in addition to founding the modern banking system, replete with many branches. A noble leaving London could deposit silver and gold in the London Temple and withdraw funds in Jerusalem. This made pilgrims less of a target, or at least less of a *valuable* target. Templar industry also had one powerful characteristic—it was not taxed.

This drew the ire of the French king and others who could not compete with the Order's many enterprises. The pope needed the Templars as an army that obeyed only him, despite the disobedience during the Crusade against French Christians. The king of France had a different agenda. He owed money and owed so much that even after confiscating the wealth of the Jews he needed more.

In 1291, however, the Templars' reason to be was gone. The last fortress of Acre fell, and the Templars returned home as an all-powerful monopoly, crowding out the business interests of others. Given that the Templar order was growing wealthy without tithing a third of their income to Rome, and they took business away from those who did pay the church's tax, they were less and less useful.

The pope was not ready to lose his army; that is, until the French king Philip was able to prove that the Knights Templar were guilty of all sorts of despicable acts, the most grievous of which was heresy. Most likely all the charges had been contrived, but that did not stop the king. He sent out secret, sealed orders to arrest the Templars and seize their wealth, which had been deposited in the Paris Temple.

What he did not count on was that with the world's largest army, the Templars had the world's greatest intelligence operation. The treasure was loaded on wagon trains and brought to La Rochelle. There it was loaded onto Templar ships, and the fleet escaped. A handful of men were left behind, including elderly knights.

The French king was even more vexed. He charged the Order with sodomy, heresy, denial of Christ, and worshipping Baphomet. Under interrogation, which could include being slow roasted over flames, stretched at the rack, and a multitude of horrors, many would confess to almost anything.

The Order's leaders having been thus killed, the Order itself dissolved. The power of the Templars was not broken, however. The organization remained aboveground in Spain and Portugal and underground in Scotland and England. It controlled banking in Switzerland, and its members were hired out as mercenaries in several countries. They also remained an invisible but powerful force in the affairs of various of the world's businesses and governments.

In 1333, Edward III decided to no longer pay tribute to the pope. This wasn't twenty years after the last Templar leader had been burned alive. Laws were passed to force the church to contribute a fair share of taxes on their own vast landholdings. Other laws granted the crown the right to intercede when Englishmen were sued by a foreign power—mainly the Church of Rome. England then stood as a buffer between the church and reformers like John Wycliffe. He famously claimed that no one but God had power over the souls of men and women. Worse still, there was no mention of a pope in the accepted scriptures of the church. On the last day of 1384, Wycliffe died, saving him from answering a summons to Rome. The seeds of the coming Reformation, however, were firmly in place by this time.

The century was also known for recurring outbreaks of the plague that would take one out of every three Englishmen. Labor shortages pushed wages higher, and laws were passed not only to restrict wages but also to take away a worker's right to move on to a new job. What Wycliffe had started against the clergy, Wat Tyler and others carried forward against the church and the powers that tried to enslave the working people.

The Peasants' Revolt of 1381, also known as Wat Tyler's Rebellion, spread to numerous towns and cities. No one holding power or wealth was safe. Tax collectors might be killed, clergy beheaded, and even the king himself was spared only by his ability to calm a crowd. The revolt was most likely not spontaneous but instead well planned. The crowd seemed to single out many of the properties that had been taken from the Knights Templar and given to the Knights Hospitallers.

The principal church of the Templars in London had also been given to the Hospitallers, and in the middle of the riotous carnage it appeared that their properties were protected. The mob took away the tax records and burned them in the streets, but the church itself was left unharmed.

In Clerkenwell this was repeated when the church that served as a priory of the Hospitallers was destroyed while a Templar church was again left unharmed. Apparently the rioters were not an unruly mob but were organized and executing a plan. Reports say that the spontaneous rebels had similar hooded "uniforms" from York to London.

At one point they took on the Tower of London. Only planning could have ensured that the drawbridge was down and the gates open. They simply marched in and took on whoever was targeted. The archbishop was beaten and the prior of the Hospitallers dragged out. Tax collectors and Franciscans were enemies of the common man equally. Such victims were beheaded before the crowd. The archbishop had his miter nailed to his head.

OLD WAYS MAKE WAY FOR THE NEW

This was the backdrop of the cultural world that Henry VIII entered, and he furthered the cause of putting a halt to the all-powerful church because of his own self-interest.

Henry's decision to break away from the Roman Catholic Church did not work for everyone in England. Many remained secretly Catholic; many others had already been inclined to join the various denominations that were emerging. As the church emerged from the Council of Trent (held between 1545 and 1563) with new energy and zeal to convert the world, the world wasn't willing to comply. A large number of Protestant movements sprang up regularly to challenge the old ways and new versions of the Reformation. From Anabaptists in Holland to Calvinists in Geneva, and from Knox in Scotland to Zwingli in Zurich, the world was in the midst of a religious revolution.

Many who left the Church of Rome had to decide which of a multitude of movements to join. Often these groups were persecuted, which served as an impetus to escape the new intolerance.

The vacuum left by the retreating influence of the church was soon filled with a variety of religious sects that were not truly Christian. John Dee influenced Catholics, Protestants, and Jews alike in preaching a blend of religion and the occult. Dee lived for several years in Bohemia with a noble family who had great interest in alchemy and the occult sciences. His philosophy would influence the printing of the Rosicrucian manifestos in Germany that called for a universal reform of the world through magic and the Kabbalah.

The reaction to such occult science created a backlash that might have surprised many. Reginald Scott's *Discoverie of Witchcraft* was published in London in 1584. The *Malleus Maleficarum* convinced Europe that witches did exist. James I seconded the motion in his work *Daemonologie* in 1587. When James I attained the throne in 1603, Dee could no longer count on being protected by people in high places. Dee's last years saw him defending himself against the charge of being a conjurer.

Ruwart Tapper, a theologian, condemned William Tyndale for being guilty of heresy. He had declared the Christian scriptures to be more important than the pope. He also printed the Christian scriptures in the modern languages. For his crimes he suffered in prison for over a year then was burned. Tapper said: "It doesn't matter whether those we execute are really guilty or not. What matters is that the people are terrified by our trials."[4]

Unlike Giordano Bruno, who was burned at the stake in 1600, Dee simply went about his business quietly, although impoverished. Less famous sorcerers were regularly killed. *The History of Witchcraft,* written by Montague Summers, contains a foreword declaring that while no one can be sure, the number of witches put to death between the sixteenth and eighteenth centuries was thirty thousand to several million.[5] Thirty thousand is the number more accepted by modern scholars. Most were of course old women and those whose neighbors did not like them around. The danger was greater for those with a following, including Dee and Bruno.

Shakespearean plays had more than a smattering of witches and sorcerers in them. Part 2 of *Henry VI* contains an incantation scene wherein the Duchess of Gloucester hires a witch, a conjurer, and two priests to reveal the destiny of the king and two dukes. The priests and the conjurer are sentenced to die in the gallows, the witch to be burned to death, and the duchess exiled to the Isle of Man. The story was based on a real incident and depicts it with some accuracy. In *The Tempest,* it's posited that the character of Prospero was very possibly inspired by John Dee. *Macbeth* has three characters who are not so much agents of evil as evil personified.

Emerging from the history described in this chapter, the court of Queen Elizabeth was responsible for the colonization of the Americas. The guiding lights of learning were John Dee, who taught all who would listen about navigation, and Sir Francis Bacon, whose philosophies inspired many. Surrounded by royalty and the wealthy, they brought many followers into their circles who would fund expeditions and provide both ships and colonists to the New World.

CHAPTER 6

KING ARTHUR AND AVALON IN AMERICA

While most of Dr. Dee's contributions to science have been ignored, he contributed greatly not only to cartography but also to getting Elizabeth to rally around the cause for claiming land in the Americas.

It is not exactly known how Dee convinced the queen that Arthur had made it to the Americas. Did his immense library at Mortlake once contain texts that did not survive into the present day? Suspicious residents would burn his house and his library, much like the burning of the home and laboratory of Dr. Frankenstein would be depicted as being destroyed. Dee's collection might have included many one-of-a-kind texts that could have influenced the queen and others. At the very least, Dee planted seeds that would be instrumental in settling the New World. While Queen Elizabeth dragged her feet by paying more attention to matters at home and raiding the Spanish for gold, under James I the seeds of exploration would grow.

Was Dee's claim legitimate? To understand the legends of King Arthur one has to realize that they evolved under a cloud of censorship. The Anglo-Saxons were invaders who had seized Britain from the Britons. They became the English, while the true Britons were forced north as well as into Wales. A royal bloodline passed from Arthur to Owain Lawgoch (or Glyndwr), who died in 1378. Wales then came under the rule of the Plantagenet kings, who deemed themselves princes of Wales. King Richard II was the eighth Plantagenet king, and he may have overstepped his bounds. He went so far as attempting to ban the Welsh language, and he prohibited writing in Welsh entirely. Then he began taxing the nobility. Finally the king was deposed in September of 1399 and sent to the Tower, where he died in early 1400.

KING ARTHUR AND HIS LEGACY

The man who would be regarded as a king had spent a lifetime defending Britain. Twelve battles culminated in a victory against foreign invaders, but there was still one more to be fought. It was the thirteenth battle, not a lucky number for Arthur or for the Knights Templar (many of whom would be arrested on Friday 13, 1307). Although Arthur's forces won the battle, he was badly wounded. This was at Camlann, and despite victory, the king had to be carried off the battlefield. He was taken west across the sea to recuperate, believing he would some- day return. While the life and battles of King Arthur are the subject of massive volumes, no one can agree as to exact dates or exact places in which these events transpired; some deny that he even existed at all.

There are several reasons for this. Histories were at best inaccurate in the fifth and sixth centuries given that few people could read and only a handful could write. Tales that were written down from tales told and retold were written and copied by hand. The invention of the printing press was still centuries away. This was the Dark Ages. There is, however, an additional overriding reason that the mystery of Arthur remained legend and not fact: politics. Arthur represented the Britons, the true people who inhabited the island we now know as England. The Angles, the Saxons, other Germanic tribes, and later Plantagenet kings who made Britain into England had no room for a British hero, so he was systematically edited, deleted, purged, and relegated to a medieval legend.

What couldn't be completely edited out provides a great deal of truth in the myth-history of Arthur. In the year 406 the Romans pulled out of the British Isles, leaving a power vacuum. A King Vortigern invited the Saxons in to defeat his enemies, but the Saxons came only to conquer.

Since the victors get to write history it becomes difficult to establish the truth. There is little agreed upon among the various tales of the "once and future king." There is, however, some agreement on the background, which provides clues as to where and when key events of the time took place. When the Romans came to Briton they brought with them a system of government from their home on the Italian Peninsula. While battles are remembered, the long years of history of peaceful development are not. Britain enjoyed a *Pax Romana* (Roman peace) in which many British families adopted the Italian economic model. Many Britons intermarried with Romans, and this created a noble class of landowners. It brought peace and progress, but at its core it needed the support of the Roman military, given that Picts in the north, Irish to the west, and Germanic tribes to the east all looked for the opportunity to take this prosperous country.

The chance came in the early fifth century. Rome came under attack, and military units were brought home to Italy. That power vacuum in England allowed the Picts to invade, and war raged for a decade around 450. King Vortigern, wishing to hold back the Picts and the Irish, made his deal with the devil by inviting in Germanic allies. The Saxons came, they saw, and they conquered. They also intended to stay.

Thus the Saxons had turned on Vortigern. Three hundred nobles were slain in an act of treachery that fatally weakened Britain. This was the first of the British versus Saxon wars. The original history written by the monk Gildas does not mention Arthur. Gildas does tell us that a series of battles was fought around Hadrian's Wall, which had been built to keep out the invaders from the north. It is safe to say that Arthur's enemies were initially the Picts and then the Saxons.

But Wales played a much greater role in all of these contests than most people assume. To understand the role of Wales is to understand the true history of Britain. As mentioned previously, the true British population was actually of Welsh descent and spread throughout the north of what is now England, separating Scotland from England.

Internal descent and external conquest had seriously hurt the Welsh culture, traditions, and knowledge of themselves. Richard II prohibited all writing in Welsh and suppressed the language, but worse was when Henry IV prohibited the importation of writing instruments into Wales. Printing presses would not be allowed there until the mid-seventeenth century. The onslaught against Welsh culture continued into the mid-nineteenth century; schoolchildren in Wales could not be taught in the Welsh language. Into the nineteenth century, speaking one word of the forbidden language was punished with caning.

THE ARTHURIAN LEGEND
IN LITERATURE

Possibly one hundred years after Gildas, a Welsh poem, *The Book of Aneirin*, describes Arthur as a great warrior. In the ninth century another Welshman by the name of Nennius provides us with details that the monk Gildas left out. Arthur was not actually a king, but he was Welsh and so were his people. Subsequent texts took the story and placed it elsewhere, given that Wales had become a backwater.

Geoffrey of Monmouth, who wrote *History of the Kings of Britain*, claimed that a secret book was given to him that contained an expanded tale of Arthur. The book was the property of Walter the Archdeacon of Oxford, and it was written in Welsh. This work and many others are now lost to us.

The *Life of St. David* and the *Annales Cambriae* are also considered basic sources. The *Annales* describes the Battle of Badon, where the victorious "Arthur carried the Cross of Our Lord for three days and nights on his shoulders."[1] John Dee may have been privy to such texts, some of which have never since known the light of day. He would have been familiar with *The Voyage of Mael Duin's Boat* in which a man named Merlin sailed the North Atlantic to a place called Avalon. Avalon was also known as Manannan after the Celtic sea god. While many like to posit that this is the Isle of Man, in getting there one did not pass by an island with fiery mountains (like Iceland) or columns or floating islands (icebergs), and the trip did not require weeks at sea. Another candidate is Manana Island, off the coast of Maine.

As mentioned earlier in the text, an aging Dr. John Dee would turn over the reins to his protégé, Sir Francis Bacon, who would then carry the torch. Bacon would be instrumental in obtaining for his friends baronetcies in Nova Scotia and lands in Newfoundland. Dee would die just before the first settlements would be planted in the latter locale. Bacon was remembered on a 1910 Newfoundland postage stamp as the "guiding spirit" in the colonization of this new-found-land. The stamp marked its three-hundred-year anniversary. It should be noted that at one time the new-found-land title was applied to a much greater area. Bacon was the guiding spirit in founding Jamestown, Virginia, and Plymouth, Massachusetts, as well. Arthur's mentor, Merlin, would be greatly responsible for the story of Arthur being reintroduced and entered as evidence in claims to the New World.

The legend of the Welsh Arthur became fair game to anyone who wanted to tell it in a different light. Arthur was placed in France, in Devon, in Somerset and Scotland—anywhere but Wales. Monks of Glastonbury went as far as unearthing the graves of a husband and wife whom they claimed to be Arthur and Guinevere. It was a crass attempt to bring in the tourist trade. Throughout Europe in this period churches and cathedrals were the destination of pilgrims who came to see and touch the sacred. Saints' bones, hair, and assorted body parts were bought, sold, and stolen to attract the faithful, who spent freely on lodging, food, "holy" water, and a chance to touch the remains of a saint. Monks who stole bones from the cathedrals of rival orders were not committing a sin, they were "translating," the practice of moving sacred objects and relics from one place to another, where honor could be bestowed on them. If one church lost the finger bone of a saint to a rival church, it was reasoned that they deserved to lose the relic.

This type of deception was prominent when the first tourism—pilgrimages—became important. So this throws much into question. Did Joseph of Arimathea come to Glastonbury in the months after the execution of Jesus? Supposedly a church dedicated to Mary existed at that site. This alone is historically significant as it would have been the first aboveground church; all that had come before it were underground.

Glastonbury was an important site for British Druids, and its significance was not lost on the early Christians who used it as a place of worship. Priests and attendants would carry banners that featured what appeared to be pre-Christian symbols, and oddly enough very similar to John Dee's Monas Hieroglyphica symbol.

When the monks of Glastonbury claimed Arthur as their own, they stole a legend. The story of an actual person was translocated from Gwynedd (in northern Wales) to Somerset. Geoffrey of Monmouth spiced up the details of Arthur's life with images from the legend of Hercules.

Tales of Arthur were also preserved in Wales, and recently documents hidden for centuries have emerged from family collections to help scholars unravel this history. Certain texts are still held by the Anglican Church in England, and the church refuses to return them to Wales. One document that has survived is the Llandaff Charters, which mentions Arthur by name, as well as his father, who is identified as being a king. (Llandaff was shown to be of much greater influence in the past than it would be in later times. Originally it was one of only three archbishoprics in the Isle of Britain.)

"To the victors belong the spoils," it has been said, and after the Norman Invasion of 1066 and throughout the centuries of the Crusades, a new Arthurian literature arose. The only people who might have actually called Arthur a king would not participate in reinventing him. Welsh texts served Geoffrey of Monmouth well, but when he wrote his *History of the Kings of Britain,* what he created is a product of history and legend, and Arthur's mother was now Igraine, the Duchess of Cornwall.

Utherpendragon visits her in disguise, pretending to be her husband. This ability to fool the king's wife was accomplished by Merlin's magic.

Most of the story takes place in lands held by the Khymry (the Welsh), but Geoffrey of Monmouth made it an English story. He manages to have Arthur conquer Iceland and Scandinavia as well, which most likely was his contribution to the original texts. He also writes that the mortally wounded Arthur was taken to an island in an attempt to save him. This island is the elusive Avalon.

His last days in a faraway place called Avalon provide us with a great mystery. No one knows where or if such a place ever existed. No final resting place for Briton's most beloved king has ever been found. That is, until Britain's most influential wizard came along. Dee had succeeded the ancient Merlin and provided proof as to the whereabouts of Arthur's resting place, which was in the newly rediscovered continent. Before Dee's time, the Isle of Man, Ireland, and the Scilly Islands had all vied to be the resting place of the king.

In his *Vita Merlini,* even Geoffrey of Monmouth himself had said that Arthur was transported on a ship (dismissing Glastonbury) and that his final resting place was across the deep sea. His pilot was called Barinthus, after the pilot that had served Saint Brendan and crossed the Atlantic. Taliesin (and later Geoffrey of Monmouth) says of Barinthus, "the waters and the stars of heaven were well known."

WEST TO AVALON

Could a sea captain have crossed the treacherous Atlantic? The answer is yes. Celts and the Norse had the ability to sail the Atlantic from very early times. What is referred to as the Nydam boat was found in Denmark and dated to the fourth century. It was capable of ocean travel, which coincided with the fact that in the historical record evidence exists of deep-sea fishing having been practiced for hundreds of years. A seventeenth-century Norse ship was seventy-five feet long and capable of carrying more men than accompanied the voyage of Christopher Columbus eight hundred years later.

One tantalizing clue of very early contact between the continents is found in the Celtic sea god Manannan, who may have been known as such on both sides of the Atlantic. Manannan, Manu, and the Vedic Noah share certain aspects, pointing to much wider contact than has been previously acknowledged.

The Irish Saint Brendan also made his trip to the Americas in 510 CE. And at least one Welshman, Prince Madoc, is on record as having made the crossing before Columbus as well.

In 1604, Pierre Dugua commanded an expedition that entered the Bay of Fundy with seventy-nine settlers and founded a settlement on St. Croix Island. This would later mark the border between Canada and the United States. The settlement didn't last more than a year as the waters of the bay froze, leading to great hardship. Exploring in the area, he landed on June 24 on what he named the St. Johns River of the future New Brunswick. Samuel de Champlain was his second in command. History remembers Champlain, but Dugua receives little attention.

Champlain is sometimes described as an ardent Catholic, but the real Champlain was much more complicated. He was born just outside La Rochelle, France, once a Templar stronghold and, after the demise of the Templar order, a stronghold of the Huguenots. The Catholic mass had not been said there for years. His mother was a Huguenot. His boss, the prominent Rosicrucian Pierre Dugua, had been born a Huguenot but married a Catholic by the name of Judith Chesnel. In modern times a mixed marriage such as this would receive no undue attention. During Dugua's and Champlain's lifetime it was another story. Catholics massacred Huguenots, and such genocide was celebrated by pope and king alike.

Remarkably the Pierre Dugua/Champlain voyage carried with it priests of Catholicism and Protestantism. Champlain's policy was one of peace and tolerance. This extended not only to Europeans but also to Native Americans, with whom he worked to maintain positive relations as well.

In 1601, Champlain married Hélène Boulée. He was forty, and she was twelve. She quickly learned the Algonquin language and impressed the Algonquin and helped facilitate friendly relations.

Among other early English and French explorers to the New World was Martin Pring. He was a protégé of Sir Walter Raleigh and loved the sea. On April 10, 1603, he left England for New England. Pring would land on the small island of Manana, off the coast of Maine.

Author Graham Phillips wrote *Merlin and the Discovery of Avalon* after physically tracing the Merlin voyage to the Americas. On the small island of Manana are a handful of standing stones similar to those found on the western coast of Britain. Phillips and his research partner, Glynn Davis, connected the ancient history of Merlin and Arthur to an expedition led by Pierre Dugua, who landed on Manana. According to Phillips, Dugua, who was connected to both Dr. John Dee and Sir Francis Bacon, had actually found the tomb of Merlin, an event kept secret by those in the know.

Sir Walter Raleigh was a friend of Dugua's, for, like Raleigh and Bacon both, Dugua had a vision of a tolerant New World. Dugua was also a member of the School of Night.

Did John Dee share other information with Francis Bacon as to the final resting place of Arthur? The evidence might elude us today as suspicious neighbors of the wizard Dee burned his remarkable library of four thousand books, and Mortlake, his home. Among his numerous volumes could other Welsh texts have been lost in the fire? We may never know.

The efforts of Sir Francis Bacon to create his New Atlantis in the Americas led him to found more than one expedition. In 1607, Bristol's Society of Merchant Venturers, which included Bacon, formed the Newfoundland Company. The new company had forty-eight members, of which the Earl of Northampton was one. They decided on a peninsula they would call the Province of Avalon on which to create a new colony. The name Avalon still graces the map of Newfoundland.

Does the rock-strewn coast of Avalon hide clues to the Avalon of Arthur? Maps of Newfoundland feature a large town by the name of St. John's in the region of Avalon. Avalon may have been ruled by a queen by the name of Argantia. Similarly, Argentia is another Avalon place-name in Newfoundland.

Someday the secret of the final resting place of Britain's most beloved king may be revealed. But King Arthur was not the only reason England had claims in the New World.

PRINCE MADOC

An odd monument stood at Fort Morgan in Mobile Bay, Alabama. It was erected by the Daughters of the American Revolution. It read: "In memory of Prince Madoc, a Welsh explorer, who landed on the shores of Mobile Bay in 1170, and left behind with the Indians, the Welsh language."

The story of the Welsh prince Madoc, who beat Columbus to the New World by 322 years, may have been forgotten except for the fact that it was written down by monks who labored in the abbeys of Wales. The monasteries of the isles of Britain and Ireland preserved much of the medieval culture of the period although time and catastrophe, along with periods of disinterest, has no doubt prevented much of the information from surviving to modern times. A Welsh bard, Gutton Owen, in the employ of King Henry VII, came across the story when researching the genealogy of the king. David Powel, writing in 1584, had described Madoc in his *History of Cambria*.

The prince's story is also recorded in Hakluyt's *Voyages,* compiled in the late sixteenth century. Hakluyt is the most famous of the early writers to discuss the discoveries of Europe's explorers. He is criticized because he often included fanciful details that sailors brought home, even though many of them later proved to be true. The details of his story are not the only reason that doubts were cast on their veracity. Some believe the entire story of Madoc was one more attempt for

England to claim a piece of the New World, given that Madoc was allegedly Welsh.

Madoc's adventure begins in Wales in 1170 with the death of his father, Owain Gwynedd. Upon his death his sons battled for the throne, which might have gone to the eldest if he was not regarded as unfit to rule. Another son had been born to an Irish woman, which was also deemed to disqualify him. This son, David, gathered together those who were loyal to him and killed one of the other brothers. Madoc, deciding that discretion was the better part of valor, left Wales at this point.

Madoc ab Owain Gwynedd sailed westward until he came to the "country" where the Spaniards would later claim to have been the first to explore since the time of Hanno. This land might have been the Americas, but more likely it was the Azores. Hakluyt insists that the prince had gone all the way across the Atlantic and then returned. The return trip went fine until it reached the island of Bardsey, where his ship was wrecked. Coincidentally, Bardsey is mentioned in the Arthurian legend.

Back in Wales the prince described the beautiful lands he had seen and gathered a large group of followers to make a return voyage of exploration and colonization. He crossed the ocean again with ten ships, which held both men and women. Possibly a thousand Welsh went on this voyage of settlement that was greater than any undertaken by the Vikings or those who would settle Plymouth Colony.

One criticism of Hakluyt is that he claims modern Mexico was where the prospective colonists landed. If the prince had been to America before the Spaniards it might add weight to British claims in that territory. Hakluyt also suggested that an earlier visit by a Welshman might account for some of the Christian practices and sacraments that the Aztecs employed. Montezuma gave a speech about white men who had come before to bring education to his people. These bearded white men left and promised to return.

In 1580, John Dee would include the tale of Madoc on his map.

Dee believed that Madoc had inhabited "Terra Florida or thereabouts." He led Elizabeth to believe that because of King Arthur's Avalon and Madoc's colonization that England had a role to play in the New World.

In 1583, Dee's map was followed by the publication of Sir George Peckham's *True Reporte*. The author had relied on an account of a man named David Ingram who had been left behind near the Gulf of Mexico when the fleet of Sir John Hawkins sailed away in 1568. Ingram walked two thousand miles and claimed to have encountered fantastic sites such as pillars of gold and a tribe whose language contained Welsh words.

A British historian, David Powel, updated a much older Welsh document in 1584 called the *Historie Cambria*. The author of this history of Wales was a Cadroc of Llancarfan, and his writings included accounts of three voyages of Madoc, which culminated in the settlement of the New World with men, women, and livestock.[2]

Given this proof of English precedent on American soil, England could then let the Spanish know that they were not swayed by the church's Papal Line of Demarcation, an arbitrary line that granted most of the New World to Spain and Portugal. A key part of the pope's language in making this papal decree implied that where discovery had been made it exempted countries from his papal line. Spain sent Hernando de Soto westward from Florida. In the four years it took him to reach the Mississippi River, he was said to have encountered abandoned fortifications.[3] Had they been made by an Englishman?

Clues of Madoc's Settlement

In 1608, Peter Wynne of the Jamestown Colony in Virginia reported that an eastern Sioux tribe called the Monacans spoke a language resembling the Welsh that he spoke. He was able to act as a translator. The Algonquin called these people Mandoag. In the 1660s, a Welsh sailor shipwrecked on American shores and said that he met a group of Indians who spoke Welsh and had a tradition of having sailed from the east.[4]

In 1669, Reverend Morgan Jones, a chaplain to the governor of Virginia, met up with a Tuscaroan tribe called the Doeg who understood his Welsh tongue. He preached the gospels in Welsh for a decade and wrote about his experience in 1686.[5]

In 1721, Father Charlevoiux, a Catholic priest, encountered the Iowa tribe. They claimed that their neighbors were a tribe called the Omans and that the Omans had white skin and fair hair.[6]

A French explorer, Gaultier de la Verendrye, in 1735 described the language of the Mandan as resembling the Cornish language of Brittany, a language with similar roots as the Welsh language. Another French explorer by the name of Pierre Gaultier de Varennes met up with Mandan people in present-day North Dakota. He claimed that they lived in domed houses on lined streets. They honored an ancestral spirit named Madoc Maho and understood Welsh. *Madahando* actually means a "person of renown, a chief," so it may be a case of deciding which came first.[7]

In 1791, John Williams published his own "Enquiry" into the story of Madoc and the Welsh in America. A John Evans took up the challenge of locating them and headed to the Southeast, only to end up in a Spanish jail. After being freed he joined the expedition of Scotsman James McKay and finally reached a tribe he believed were the Mandan people, seven hundred miles up the Missouri River from St. Louis. He claimed they were not Welsh speaking, however, much to the dismay of his benefactors.

Not everyone agreed with his conclusion.

A Revolutionary War captain, Isaac Stewart, traveling up the Red River from the Mississippi was captured. Like the chaplain, he was ransomed from the Mandan. His name for the tribe was the McCedus. He described their skin as nearly white and their hair red. He was told by them that they were from the east, and they showed him some writings in a language he did not understand.

Daniel Boone also described a blue-eyed American Indian tribe. He believed that they were Welsh in origin although admitted: "I have no means of assessing their language."[8] In 1804 then-president Thomas

Jefferson sent out an expedition to view just what the U.S. government had purchased in the Louisiana Purchase. Clark, of the Lewis and Clark expedition, commented on the blond-haired, blue-eyed native women they encountered.

A Benjamin Sutton described Welsh-speaking natives who owned a Bible.

The list goes on and on.

Madoc Slept Here

There are theories that Madoc reached as far north as North Dakota or Nova Scotia and as far south as Mexico, but the most favored theory is that Madoc made it to the Gulf of Mexico and landed in the vicinity of Mobile, Alabama. He may have explored Mobile Bay and sailed upriver and then headed back to the Gulf and the Mississippi River, which he may have found more navigable. But there is no reason to discount an upriver trip along the Alabama. The Alabama runs a roundabout course through the state to the northeast. At some point before Fort Payne had been built it was likely that a portage was necessary. Near that town in De Soto Falls, Alabama, another ruined fort was found; it dates to the twelfth century. The fort is in a state park named for the later Spanish explorer Hernando de Soto. In the park are the Welsh caves that Madoc allegedly visited.

Continuing in a northeast direction into Tennessee there is another fort that was built long before Columbus reached the American shores. When it was excavated the walls were found to be two thousand feet long, with a gate and a moat surrounding them. Archaeologists discovered no signs of it having been occupied and claim that it predated Madoc and the Vikings. Nevertheless it was built in a fashion reminiscent of similar forts in Wales. A third structure, with its cairnlike construction, is the Old Stone Fort near the river city of Chattanooga, again on the Tennessee side. These three forts are unlike anything built by the Cherokee. One of the three closely resembles the home of Madoc in Wales.[9]

Still another fort is found across the border in Georgia, a short distance from Chattanooga. This fort is also protected in a state park called Fort Mountain, and it is also unlike anything constructed by Native Americans. The Cherokee claimed that the "moon-eyed" people lived here. They had blond hair and fair skin, and it was claimed that they could see better at night.

The sites in Alabama, Tennessee, and Georgia are described as being more representative of similar sites found in twelfth-century Great Britain than those built by Native Americans.

A course correction from northeast to northwest might have brought Madoc to Paducah, Kentucky. It's claimed that he founded the city of Paducah and is possibly even buried there. Legend has it that somewhere in the vicinity he was buried with an epitaph that begins "Madoc Ap Owen was I called." Although this is mentioned in *The Gentleman's Magazine* of December 1789, no grave remains today.

In the Paducah area, the Native American tribes believed that a white Indian tribe had once been defeated by a red tribe. One writer in the early twentieth century described a battle between the two tribes along the Ohio River. On the site of the battle he claimed that armor depicting the Welsh coat of arms was borne by skeletons of the dead. *Kentucky* is a Native American word. It means "dark and bloody ground."[10]

Perhaps a final battle between Europeans and Native Americans involved a slaughter of one side or the other. Another possibility is that Madoc's people brought pox, one of the many diseases that Europeans were resistant to and Native Americans were not. Smallpox and chicken pox could both be fatal to those with no resistance. Circa 1200 CE the once great pre-Columbian mound city of Cahokia simply became a ghost town. Unlike cultures in the southwestern United States that might have died out because of drought, no such explanation would cause Cahokia to simply cease to be. The only explanation was that plague was the culprit. Ohio too had been depopulated for a time.

Had Madoc, like Cortéz, unintentionally carried a weapon worse than the sword?

A Cherokee chief by the name of Oconostota told of white people who had crossed the ocean and landed in Mobile Bay. Despite building stone fortifications, they were forced to move on and settled in Kentucky. They may have continued north from the juncture where the Mississippi River meets the Ohio River.

The tribe that did survive in that area is the Mandan. They are unusual in that some members had red hair and blue eyes. When the nineteenth-century painter George Catlin returned from living with the Mandan about 1838, his portraits were considered fakes because the Indians were considered more European than Native American. His published works about the tribe contain his belief that they were descended from Europeans. Their canoes were described as resembling Welsh hide boats rather than hollowed-out logs. Indeed, their way of stretching hide around a wooden frame to build a boat was exactly the manner by which a Welsh coracle was built. He even claimed that the name Mandan derived from Madawgys, which was given to the prince's followers.

The Mandan people even have their own flood story. This in itself is not unique, but most people who speak an Algonquian language usually employ the symbolism of a large turtle to represent the new earth. The Mandan story features a leader by the name of Numank who commands his people to build an ark and save themselves from impending disaster. In the annual celebration of this event, Numank is depicted as a white man.

There is more evidence that the Mandan stories and author and painter Catlin were right. Sir Walter Raleigh wrote that he met a tribe whose language was clearly derived from Welsh.

The Mandan were the eventual victims of a European import: smallpox. They did not survive to confirm or deny their origins, so we are left with the testimony of a handful of accounts and the paintings and writings of George Catlin.

In 1832, Catlin may have had the last word. He compiled a list of Welsh-Mandan word similarities including *pan*—the Mandan word for "head"—which was *pen* in Welsh. *Gwyn* meant "white." When Welsh and Cornish sailors aboard Drake's ship navigated the dangerous straits at the tip of South America they encountered birds they called white-heads. We know them today as penguins.

The Welsh word for boat was *corwyg;* the Mandan word was *koorig.* The word for *paddle* in Welsh was pronounced *ree* and spelled *rhywf.* The Mandan word was *ree.* The color blue in both Welsh and Mandan was *glas. Bread* in Welsh was *barra* and in Mandan *bara.* The adjective *great* was *mawr* in Welsh and *mah* in Mandan.

In 1844, six years after Catlin returned east, smallpox nearly wiped out the tribe. Survivors banded together with the Hidatsa and Arikara, who also had been hurt by the epidemic.

Since Columbus sailed the ocean with the blessing of the king and queen of Spain and the financial backing of Italian bankers, it is not remarkable that the results of the voyage were thoroughly recorded and quickly known throughout Europe. Equally thorough, the sagas of the Vikings were records of their early ocean crossings, the formation of colonies, and even the details of who married whom. The discovery of L'Anse aux Meadows and other evidence in Canada gave credence to the fact that there had indeed been an early European presence in the New World.

The veracity of unofficial voyages, however, have a greater degree of skepticism to overcome. Written records of Madoc are discredited as serving nationalistic goals. Eyewitness accounts are not believed. Legends of American Indian tribes are simply regarded as tales. Had Madoc's people not assimilated into the culture but instead conquered or wiped them out with plague, we might be celebrating Madoc's Day.

In the harbor of Mobile Bay, Alabama, a commemorative plaque dedicated to Madoc once stood. It has since been removed, and there are no plans to replace it.

NICHOLAS OF LYNN

If the tales of Madoc and Arthur are regarded as legend, another early Atlantic crossing has a great deal of evidence to support its veracity. In the mid-1300s, an English friar by the name of Nicholas of Lynn was a member of the Franciscan brotherhood. At a time when the Viking trading stations on Greenland and Newfoundland were fading in influence and importance, the church in Rome was still sending bishops to its most western outposts.

The church had been appointing bishops to oversee Catholics in Greenland from 1053 on. Adam of Bremen mentioned Iceland, Greenland, and "Vinland" in his *Descriptio Insularum Aquilonis* of 1072.

The North Atlantic went through a very warm phase between 1100 and 1300, which would have aided those who wanted to cross the Atlantic Ocean. In 1121 a bishop by the name of Erik left Greenland for Vinland and was never seen again. In the late thirteenth century bishops were still being sent to Greenland, although Pope Nicholas reported that the Sea of Gardar was visited less frequently than it had been because of the cruel ocean. Plague and much colder temperatures prevailed. Around 1368 the last bishop was sent to Greenland; he would die ten years later. He may have traveled aboard a Sinclair family ship, as the Sinclair family was conducting trade with Norway at that time.

The plague and possibly colder climate reduced the numbers of brave colonists. So did attacks by Inuit people. One man who made several voyages to Greenland and points west mapped the unknown or hardly known lands he traveled to and from between 1330 and 1360. This is forty years before the Sinclair expedition to Nova Scotia and New England. This man was Nicholas of Lynn.

His travelogue, *Inventio Fortunata,* was presented to King Edward III of England. It also found its way to Venice, where it was used by the Franciscans as part of their world map. This map included what they called the Norwegian kingdom, which extended from

Norway to Greenland and beyond. The map identifies Newfoundland, Nova Scotia, and Cape Cod. This should not be much of a surprise as it is believed that these lands were reached by the Norse explorers. The map also depicts the peninsula of Florida.

Historians tell us that it was Ponce de Leon who discovered Florida in 1513. Yet it was on the De Virga map of 1414 CE, one hundred years before. That map was informed by data from Nicholas of Lynn. Still another map, the Cantino map of 1502, depicts Florida. The tip of Florida is opposite Cuba and is named Ilha Ysabella. This name most likely is derived from a visit with Columbus post-1492, possibly by Amerigo Vespucci or John Cabot.[11]

East from Venice it depicts Cathay (the ancient word for China), which again is no surprise as Marco Polo and Venetian merchants and priests traveled the Silk Road to China. One of the most widely traveled explorers is hardly known outside of Italy. Giovanni de' Marignolli was born in Florence and took his vows for the Franciscan order, just as Nicholas had done, at a young age. Around the same time that Nicholas was heading west to the Americas in 1338, Giovanni de' Marignolli was heading east. First he went to Constantinople, then crossed the Black Sea to Crimea. He traveled through Uzbek and stayed in the ancient city of Armalec for a while before crossing the Gobi Desert to Peking. His adventure was not over, for he went on to visit Ceylon, Java, Sumatra, and sailed through the Persian Gulf on the way home.

Such voyages did not invite the doubting-Thomas historians as they were made over land for the most part. The same historians, however, claim that voyages in the other direction could not have ever happened (despite showing up on pre-Columbian maps). The presence of these voyages on maps is strong evidence that they did exist.

John Dee collected every map and chart he could and corresponded regularly with Mercator. It was Mercator who sent a letter and the friar's map to John Dee. The letter included a short biography of Nicholas.

The Franciscan order that Nicholas had entered was called the Greyfriars as this was the color of their robes. The order was known for its world travels in the service of their order and of their kings. Nicholas attended Oxford University, where he studied the sciences, including geography, astronomy, and mathematics. The biography referred to as the *Norfolk Biography* mentions a voyage that he took to the North Pole, although such a claim receives little regard from modern historians.

The letter and Nicholas's map circulated to other mapmakers, including Christopher Columbus, Abraham Ortelius, and Bartholomew Las Cases. While few have ever heard of Nicholas, he also wrote a text on practical navigation and the use of astronomy. It is very likely that Dee might have used this text as reference material for his own writings, including *The Art of Navigation.* By including Prince Madoc of Wales as a very important colonizer long before Columbus and by claiming that Arthur sailed to Avalon in Newfoundland after his last battle, Dee convinced Queen Elizabeth that she had a right to the New World.

CHAPTER 7

ROSLIN, HENRY SINCLAIR, AND THE DISCOVERY OF AMERICA

Just south of the city of Edinburgh in Scotland is one of the greatest pilgrimage sites of the modern esoteric world. It is the Roslin Chapel, where one might say that the connection between the Knights Templar and Freemasonry is revealed. Freemasons, Rosicrucians, and Hermetists consider it one of the most important places in the world. Now, having been made famous by *Holy Blood, Holy Grail* and *The Da Vinci Code,* Roslin is also on the tourist trail as one of Scotland's must-see sites. Alternately spelled Rosslyn or Roslin, the chapel is the destination of thousands of visitors who come from around the world.

Roslin once served as the ancestral home of Scotland's most powerful St. Clair (or Sinclair) family. The chapel is officially Christian, dedicated to the apostle Matthew, and it could be said that the connection between Celtic paganism and Christianity is revealed in Roslin's stones. Its motif is a strange blend, combining Christian symbols and pagan influences from the ancient Celtic and Nordic religions. It was dedicated on September 21, 1450, which is Saint Matthew's feast day, but, more telling, it's also the autumnal equinox.

This, combined with the Celtic Green Man, serpents, and fallen angels that adorn the chapel, would be reason enough to believe it had been a pagan place of worship. It might be said that this is a double-blind, however. One worshipper might see the Christian aspects of the chapel, while another, possibly an initiate to the secret arts, might see something completely different.

The Roslin Chapel is also replete with symbols of Freemasonry including the Apprentice's Pillar, the Journeyman's Pillar, the Master Mason's Pillar, and other Masonic devices. It was built in the fifteenth century, long before Freemasonry was actually established in any official sense. For this reason it might be said that the chapel hinted at or revealed secrets that might otherwise have remained secret until much later.

The Scottish form of Freemasonry grew out of the Templar organizations. After 1307, Templars were outlawed, and travel for them could be dangerous. As we have previously established, the lodge system of the earliest masons offered protection, lodging, food, and often employment to brother masons.

THE SECRETS OF ROSLIN

The secrets of Roslin are hidden in plain sight. The St. Clairs were prominent in the order known as the Knights Templar. The family that originated with the Norse invasion of northern France is connected in Paris to the Church of St. Sulpice and to the Scottish branch of the same family, from Edinburgh to the Orkneys. They fought the Islamic tide in Jerusalem and in Spain and brought home their fallen family members to be buried in the crypt below the chapel. The images of the grail cup in a chapel designed to recall the Church of the Holy Sepulchre in the Holy Land may hint at a truly great secret: the ultimate destination of that most sacred object. The eight-pointed rose in a depiction of the grail cup is a Templar design.

Another secret is that the chapel contains carvings depicting aloe and maize, which are found in North America. The evidence of corn in a fifteenth-century European chapel indicates that its builders were aware of what lay on the other side of the Atlantic. This imagery in the chapel was first observed on a voyage made between 1397 and 1398, a century prior to Columbus.

The Norse origins of the family might have served to preserve a record of numerous pre-Columbian voyages to America, as recorded in the sagas. If they had not been aware, another voyage in the fourteenth century gave Henry Sinclair the inspiration to make the voyage. This was the voyage of Italian adventurer Nicolo Zeno, who had sailed out of the Mediterranean to explore the world simply for his own sake. The St. Clair clan would know that Columbus was not the first to cross the western seas; in fact, they played a role in influencing his voyage.

William St. Clair founded the chapel. At the time he was the hereditary grand master of all of the Masons in Scotland. He was also a member of the Order of the Golden Fleece, which was a French order. And in addition to that, he was a member of the Order of the Knights of Santiago (Saint James), a surviving Templar order. This was one of several former Templar organizations that had sprouted in Iberia. The Knights of Christ would use the Templar red cross on a white field as their flag. Columbus married the daughter of one of these Genoese-born knights who sailed on behalf of the Portuguese king and the Knights of Christ. Columbus retained the Templar flag on his sails.

The voyage that William St. Clair recorded in stone had happened five decades before.

THE SINCLAIR-ZENO EXPEDITION TO THE AMERICAS

Henry Sinclair (St. Clair) had, in the late fourteenth century, decided to consolidate his power. His fleet sailed along Scotland's northern coasts and among the islands farther north. At the same time, Nicolo Zeno of Venice had been on an adventure of his own, exploring the same lands. In addition to the cold and treacherous seas there were more than a few dangers. The Norse had been in the area for centuries and were not above tricking a ship into becoming grounded on their shores.

On tiny Fer Island, this was the predicament in which Nicolo found himself. Denizens of that small island had a tradition of claiming anything that strayed near their island as fair game. Whales were enticed into a trap, and humans of the island would gather when the signal was made. A whale caught in such a trap was killed and butchered as the whole island took part in the killing and the bounty. No moral distinctions were made for humans. Indeed, a ship might be given a signal to land, or it might just strand itself too close to shore. In any case a grim fate awaited the unlucky. In Nicolo's case, before the island's inhabitants could kill his men and steal their cargo, Sinclair appeared. Besides the event turning into a last-minute rescue, the meeting between Sinclair and Nicolo and his crew would become important for another reason.

The St. Clair family and the Zeno families both had great power in their own countries. Both could count family members who were leaders and heroes. Members of the Sinclair family were considered kingmakers in Anglo-Norman lands long before the 1066 invasion of Britain had transpired. They were the Norsemen who, under Rollo, had landed in France and demanded land from the French king, and they hadn't been refused.

The Zeno family ruled the mercantile state of Venice, and one Carlo Zeno was revered as the "Lion of Venice" when, in the late 1300s, his fleet rescued their city-state in the eleventh hour of what had been a disastrous war against the Genoese that had raged for centuries. Both families had played roles in the Crusades. Upon meeting Sinclair, Nicolo would send for his brother Antonio, telling him that he was in the employ of a "prince" who wanted them to map the northern islands of the Atlantic, including the coast of Greenland. Nicolo died just before the journey was made.

In actual fact, however, Henry was not a prince, which would confuse his identity in later writings. In his own Norse-influenced world he was a jarl serving the Norse king Haakon. Later the Norse word *jarl* would morph to become the English *earl*. The Italians had no such title, so *prince* would have to do.

Those who plied the seas for reasons of exploration, trade, and fishing had no academies in which to learn their craft. Experience was foremost, and learning from those with experience was secondary. And so it was from an Orkney fisherman that Zeno and Sinclair learned of the world beyond Greenland.

This Orkney fisherman would tell, to the Zeno brothers and Henry Sinclair, of his adventures fishing in the banks far to the west. He had possibly traveled beyond even where the Norse explorers had sailed.

History doesn't record when cod fishing began off the Grand Banks, but we do know that the rich fishing found there had attracted European fishermen from long before Columbus. They left no records, as fishermen are inclined to keep the best places secret. They were not discovering new worlds for glory or gold. They simply brought home fish.

Basque cod fishers and whale hunters would sail west to these rich fishing grounds. They often wintered in the bays of the New World and traveled home with their catch in the spring. They left shacks and place-names on the map but were never regarded as discoverers.

The nameless Orkney fisherman who shared his knowledge with the Zenoes and Henry Sinclair claimed he had spent twenty-five years in the Americas. He had been part of a fleet of fishing ships farming the seas off the coasts of Newfoundland and Labrador. They were blown off course and taken prisoner by natives of this land. Many were killed, but the Orkney fisherman taught his captors the use of fishing nets. Fishing with nets was an art developed in the Orkneys, where the nets were rumored to be as long as sixty yards and as wide as fifteen yards. Apparently the Indians were impressed and grateful for the bountiful rewards derived from using this technique.

The Orkney fisherman claimed that the people in what is now Newfoundland spoke a language he didn't know. They also had books written in Latin. The fisherman was a celebrity in the New World and, over time, was invited to visit more than twenty chiefs in the country. He may have been as far south as Florida or even the Yucatan. He was finally allowed to trade and was able to build a ship to carry him home. Like Marco Polo, he had been gone for more than two decades and had great stories to tell.[1]

The tales impressed Henry Sinclair, as did the fisherman's claims of having met other Europeans in his travels.

In 1398, six hundred years ago, a Scottish seafarer (Sinclair) and his Italian navigators (including Antonio Zeno) sailed a small fleet across the North Atlantic to Nova Scotia and then explored the northeast coast of New England as far south as Rhode Island. Physical evidence of the voyage exists along their route, and written evidence exists in Europe, as it does in the lore of northeastern tribes that greeted the earlier explorers we have mentioned herein.

Sinclair and party left a trail of physical evidence that begins in Nova Scotia—where they made landfall—and continues to Westford, Massachusetts, where they inscribed the heraldry of one of their knights in stone. They continued on to Fall River, where a suit of armor was left behind, and ultimately to Newport, where a controversial tower was built.

They used the same technique as the Norse had in exploring and settling Iceland, Greenland, and probably Labrador as well. They populated their fleet with Orkney sailors who were armed with years of experience sailing in Greenland, replete with knowledge of the lands beyond. While island hopping was dangerous in the fourteenth century, it was easier than crossing vast expanses of ocean as Columbus would do nearly one hundred years later. The journey from place to place, like that of Cabot and Verrazano, would take place in a matter of days. Landfall was made in 1398 at a town that is today called Guysborough, on the Chedabucto Bay in present-day Nova Scotia. Zeno recorded the place as "Trin."

DOCUMENTS OF THE JOURNEY CORROBORATE ITS LOCATIONS

Historian Johann Forster wrote about the Sinclair-Zeno voyage in 1786 and identified the man Zeno called the "prince" as Henry Sinclair.[2] One hundred years later, geographer Richard Henry Major would concur with this assessment.[3] In 1951 an article by William Herbert Hobbs and a book by Frederick J. Pohl covered the expedition in much greater detail and located the most likely landfall of the party.[4]

Geologist and professor William Herbert Hobbs claims that the landing took place at Tor Bay. He bases his conclusion on descriptions recorded in the letters that Zeno sent home to Venice. When Sinclair and party entered the harbor they had seen a hill in the distance (Nova Scotia is very flat and has one high hill in what is now Antigonish County, which is visible from afar). After making landfall they gathered food by fishing and stealing birds' eggs. (Extensive fisheries and rookeries exist there even today.) Sinclair sent one hundred men to cross the "island." When they returned they reported another sea (the Northumberland Strait) and a spring where pitch ran into the ocean. (A spring of asphalt, a phenomenon that is very rare, is found in Stellarton, Nova Scotia). This site was a few days' march inland from the Atlantic Ocean. Hobbs had been the first to show that "a spring from which issued a certain substance like pitch" was most unique. There is, in fact, only one place that such a rare phenomenon existed besides Stellarton, and that was in Trinidad in the Caribbean.

The name Stellarton derives from a form of oil-charged coal (called stellarite) that runs throughout the region in a very thick seam. It was exploited by a coal company by the name of Stella Coal. Zeno also described a "smoking hole," which could have been caused by lightning or a man-made fire that smoldered for a long period of time.

The soldiers also reported encountering people who were very short, who had run away from them and hidden in caves. In actual fact, the Indians known as Mi'kmaq, who were native to that area, were a shorter race than most North American natives. They had been described as timid by other European traders, but they had the ability to travel great distances and had experience in trade. The large number of strange-looking men would have undoubtedly surprised the Mi'kmaq and caused them to flee. The fact that they hid in caves further confirms the geographic location, for there are very few caves in Nova Scotia and the area immediately surrounding Stellarton is where these caves are situated.

Frederick Pohl, who wrote extensively on early European discoveries in the New World, would later add much weight to the observations of Hobbs and pin down even more specific locales and dates for the Sinclair-Zeno voyage. Recognizing that sailors often created place-names for the religious day celebrated on their day of discovery, Pohl was able to calculate Sinclair's landing date. The safe harbor of the Sinclair-Zeno expedition was, as we have previously noted, called Trin, and the month, according to the Zeno letters, was June.

Pohl found that in earlier times the eighth Sunday after Easter is always the date of the celebration of the Holy Trinity. It's known throughout the world as Trinity Sunday. He verified with the Vatican that this date was celebrated in the fourteenth century and from there narrowed down possible dates of Sinclair's landfall. Since the Trinity feast could be celebrated as early as March, and the records from Zeno maintain that the expedition reached the harbor in June, there were very few dates that matched the dates cited in the Zeno letters. Trinity Sunday, and Sinclair's landing in Nova Scotia, was on June 2, 1398. This was ninety-seven years before the next European is recorded as having reached Nova Scotia and ninety-four years before Columbus "discovered" the New World.

Henry Sinclair liked the new lands he was discovering. The fish and game were abundant, the climate was moderate, and the harbors appeared to be good for shipping. He declared that he would someday build a city here and leave Scotland behind.

Perhaps his crew wasn't quite so enamored, because they wanted to return home before the seasons changed and the Atlantic crossing became even more dangerous. It was agreed that Antonio would captain the expedition back to Scotland with all who wished to return, while Henry and a smaller group would stay on and continue their explorations.

Zeno returned to Scotland, first stopping in the Faroe Islands. He recorded the voyage and immediately sent his story back to his brother Carlo in Venice. It is the narrative of Zeno, in the form of letters and maps sent back to Venice, that the voyage was recorded. The Zeno maps and narratives were not published until 160 years later, leaving a blank slate of a historical record until that time. When they were published, they were accepted as being true, and the maps were incorporated into maps by Ruscelli (1564), Mercator (1569), and Ortelius (1574). England and France dominated the New World by this time, and their sea captains used the Zeno-Mercator maps but were constantly on guard for the possible announcement of a Venetian claim to territory in the New World, which never came.

Apart from the letters Zeno sent home, we have no other written records of this expedition. Nor do we know what happened to the crew once they had returned home to Scotland. Sinclair did explore the New World further, and one of the Zeno letters says that he built a "town in the port of the island newly discovered by him." Since Zeno had most likely not seen the town, this is still supposition.

OTHER EVIDENCE OF SINCLAIR'S PRESENCE

Other evidence of the Sinclair overland travels has been preserved.

If Sinclair had sailed or marched along a coastal route to explore what would come to be called New England, he would have traveled from Nova Scotia along coastal New Brunswick and soon reach what is now the Canadian–U.S. border at St. Stephen's.

In Louisburg, Nova Scotia, a type of cannon called the "bundled rod" is preserved in the basement of the fort. Two of these were found in the area, the first one in 1849. Since then one of them was lost. They were the same type of cannon that was pioneered by Carlo Zeno. They were lightweight and mounted on a pivot, and, as such, were very effective against the fixed cannons then currently in use. Why is the one remaining cannon not exhibited? Perhaps Nova Scotia has little desire to promote the idea that someone preceded the French and English settlers to their land.

From New Brunswick, a ship following along the seacoast would enter what is now Maine at the Machias Bay area. It is tempting to speculate that mooring holes found on islands from Maine to Cape Cod are evidence of Sinclair's voyage, but they could have just as easily been established and utilized by early Norse explorers.

Recently a discovery of a whaleback ledge "jutting into Machias Bay at Clark's Point, Maine," was made where a "petroglyph of a cross [is] incised beside one of a European ship of the late fourteenth century." Author Andrew Sinclair maintains that this stone is evidence of the voyage of Sinclair and Zeno.[5]

This may be, but Sinclair might not have been the first to land in the Machias Bay area. On my own coastal exploration of Maine, I learned of the belief that Vikings may have also been there. Near the tiny town of Cutler, Maine, is a pond featuring unique stone walls. There is no explanation of them, other than local legend that maintains the Vikings built them.

On the very small island of Manana, offshore of Monhegan Island of Maine, in addition to the standing stones we have discussed earlier, runic inscriptions are found. While the Zeno expedition would most likely have left inscriptions in their own language(s), Monhegan Island presents further evidence of European, pre-Columbian travels. As mentioned in the previous chapter, one such crossing might be no less than the final resting place of King Arthur.[6]

THE SCOTTISH KNIGHT,
CARVED IN ROCK

More intriguing evidence is found farther south. In the small town of Westford, Massachusetts, there is a carved rock memorial to a Scottish knight. The existence of this effigy has been known since colonial times but today is overgrown with surrounding brush. Frank Glynn, an amateur archaeologist from Connecticut, became interested in the tale of the rock carving's existence and set out to uncover the memorial.

After finding the rock ledge on Depot Street in Westford, he cleared the brush. The worn and faded rock was replete with an inscription, and immediately a debate was sparked. Some say the image inscribed appears to be that of an Indian with a tomahawk, and not a knight.

To highlight the inscription, Glynn poured chalk into its punched holes and carved lines. The figure of a knight complete with chain mail and a coat of arms became visible.

Glynn sent a rubbing of the worn stone to T. C. Lethbridge, a British writer, archaeologist, and curator of the Cambridge University Museum of Archaeology and Ethnology in England. Lethbridge researched both the coat of arms and the figure itself in Wales and Scotland. He concluded that it was a depiction of a knight and that this particular knight was important.

The full size of the knight depicted in the memorial carving is six feet. The carving includes a basinet helmet, which came into use in the 1360s and subsequently fell out of use in the fifteenth century. This helped to establish a time frame.

Lethbridge also told Glynn that such effigies in stone were often made during that time period in Ireland and the western isles of Britain. They would be carved at the place where the knight had fallen, usually a place of battle. The detailed carving included the hilt of a sword held over the breast of the knight and a shield with a coat of arms. The coat of arms depicts a "buckle," a crescent, a five-pointed star, and a ship.

Personal correspondence from Lethbridge to Glynn in 1956 described the armor and the crest as being from the outer islands of Scotland circa 1350. A buckle (actually a brooch) on the shield was something shared by only a few families, and after consulting early Orkney medals, Lethbridge was able to narrow down his list of families considerably. He declared that the coat of arms was "clearly the arms of some maternal relation of the Sinclairs."[7] Further research brought new information about the incidences of sable galleys on Scottish coats of arms. Those bearing this heraldic emblem were either Norse kings of the isles or of the lineage of the "Norse jarls" of Orkney, who would have been the Sinclairs.

Henry Sinclair, the discoverer, had been one-quarter Norse.

Finally, the research would pare down the list even further. In medieval Scotland, families in the employ or under the protection of a more important family might take their last name from the clan of their protector. This particular shield and coat of arms belonged to a branch of the Sinclair group, the clan of Gunn, and to a knight who was Henry Sinclair's principal lieutenant, Sir James Gunn.

Sir Ian Moncreiffe, one of heraldry's foremost experts, agreed with Lethbridge's conclusions.[8]

The importance of the Gunn clan connection and the knight in the Westford stone carving is that the Gunn and Sinclair clans were closely linked in Scotland. In the north the Gunns were the "Crowners of Caithness," and tradition held that without their consent, no one could rule over their province in the Scottish northlands. This right was affirmed by the insignia of the brooch on their coat of arms. Sinclair gained the lands through inheritance, but, be that as it may, the Sinclairs ruled only with the consent of the Gunn clan.

Both had strong Norse ties, and this alliance between the two families might have existed from the eleventh century. The history of the

Gunn clan may even predate the recorded history of Sinclair, as we shall later see.

OTHER EVIDENCE IS UNEARTHED

In addition to the carved rock at Westford, a second marker emerged. A Westford farmer had discovered it in his field but did not know what if any significance the inscribed stone had, so he left it in his barn. The stone was of little use in solving the puzzle overall, but it was of the same punched-carving style as the stone featuring Sir James Gunn. The depths of the holes as well as their diameter were identical to that of the first stone. A mysterious "184" and an arrow might have meant something to whoever initially discovered the rock, but it had been moved, thus rendering these markers relatively meaningless. Another ship was depicted on this second carved stone, the design of which fit the style of a Scottish ship of the era (1350–1400).

In any event, the stone was moved to the lobby of the Fletcher library in Westford, not far from the Depot Road granite memorial. A twentieth-century search for a fourteenth-century camp failed to turn up any other nearby evidence of the Sinclair expedition.

There is other evidence farther south, however. The Taunton River in Massachusetts empties into Assonet Bay near Fall River, Massachusetts. On the east side of the bay there is a large rock inscribed with a seven-by-eleven-foot face on which symbols are carved. Described as runic, some say the Dighton Rock is a hoax. Since it was Cotton Mather, the fire-and-brimstone preacher of colonial America who recorded the rock's existence in 1690, it is at least a very old hoax.

In Fall River, in 1831, the skeleton of a man wearing heavy metal-plate armor was dug up at the corner of Fifth Street and Harley. Henry Wadsworth Longfellow wrote a poem about the mysterious "Skeleton in Armor," who he felt built the nearby Norse tower for his fair lady. An 1843 fire in the museum deprived history of any further chance to examine the skeleton of the knight. Anthropologists and experts from Harvard's Peabody Museum would come up with some ridiculous guesses, however. Their best explanation maintained that the armor was that of a Wampanoag Indian.

A CISTERCIAN BAPTISTERY IN NEWPORT, RHODE ISLAND?

The most controversial piece of architecture is a tower that stands guard in Newport, Rhode Island. The Newport Tower, or the Viking Tower as it is often called, is a rounded tower of gray wall set above arches. The centers of these arches are ten feet above ground; earlier a floor had been built above them. The tower itself is eighteen feet in diameter inside, and because the walls are so thick (three feet), it is twenty-four feet in diameter when the measurements are taken on the outside. Its total height is about twenty-eight feet.

The ground floor features eight columns built with rough stones. Twelve feet above the ground there was a floor, as evinced by sockets in the masonry where the floor beams were once attached. A second floor had also existed about seven feet above the first. A roof that is long gone covered the entire structure. The British used the tower as a place to store munitions during the American Revolution. A hasty retreat at the end of the war caused them to simply blow up the munitions, thus destroying the roof. It is estimated that the amount of stone used to complete the structure weighed two hundred tons, four hundred thousand pounds. The man-hours required for such an operation obviously made this a communal effort.

An interesting feature of the Newport Tower is that a stone placed in one of its walls is that of cumberlandite. This type of magnetic rock is found only in Cumberland, Rhode Island, and in the Narrangansett Bay watershed. Scott Wolter has noted that some people call cumberlandite the "stone of the Venus."[9]

The theory that this was a tower built by Vikings is unrealistic.

Vikings were no doubt in the Americas, but they built structures that could be erected quickly and that served a practical purpose. At L'Anse aux Meadows they built sleeping quarters, kitchens, and huts for animals, as well as a boathouse. These structures were most likely built in three months before the onset of winter.

The Newport Tower met some practical needs, but it had other purposes as well. What is not generally known is that it served as an astronomical observatory. Author James Egan demonstrated its use in determining the solstices and even in measuring cycles of the sun and moon.

On its first floor there remains a large recessed fireplace and two flues to vent the smoke to the outside. The fireplace might have served to provide heat and be used for cooking, but it could have also served as a beacon to signal ships. Before houses were built in the area, the tower's position might have provided a lookout for many miles around. While there is evidence that a staircase might have connected the first floor to the second, there is no evidence showing a stairway from the ground level to the first floor. This could indicate that a trapdoor once served to allow or deny entry as necessary.

Because it was built to the exact measurements of a Templar baptistery, the Newport Tower conveyed a message: Sinclair and the Templars had been here. The structure very closely resembled several round and octagonal Templar chapels in the Old World, specifically the Sanctus Clare Chapel in France and the round Orphir Church in the Sinclair-owned Orkney Islands.

Such round and octagonal chapels, churches, and baptisteries are found in Tomar, Portugal, a Templar headquarters; in Mellifont, Ireland, at the site of a Cistercian monastery; on Bornholm Island in the Baltic Sea, which is called the Templar's Secret Island; and in other places where they had been built over pagan sanctuaries.[10]

The knowledge brought home from the Middle East led to a bevy of cathedrals being constructed, with the Templars and their sister order, the Cistercians, in the forefront of that movement. They proved to exhibit extraordinary skills in building strategically located, fortified castles on incredibly difficult terrain. In addition to creating fortresses in relatively inaccessible places, their techniques of fortification were state-of-the-art in their day. Indeed, where they built on rivers and coastal ports they protected their castles with water gates, using hydraulics not generally seen in Europe.

As a result, six hundred years later, Cistercian bridges still exist on the Continent; some even carry automobile traffic. Construction of this nature was not confined to estates and castles, however. The Cistercians and Templars spread circular and octagonal chapels and baptisteries throughout their realm. Jerusalem was the center of the medieval world, and the construction of Templar rotundas symbolized bringing this city of God around the world. The possible connection between the rotundas of larger churches and the round table of grail literature is not mere conjecture or wishful thinking. In a similar fashion, the grail literature was a blend of history and historical novel. The key to appreciating all of it was to be inspired by the symbolism found in both architecture and literature and to understand that beneath the surface of things there was always more to the message.

Templar construction of round and octagonal churches had its basis in the Church of the Holy Sepulchre. Copycat structures are found in Florence and Ravenna and along the coast of the Mediterranean. Other structures are distinctly Templar.

Be this as it may, the argument that the Newport Tower was built in the seventeenth century doesn't hold water either. There is no other colonial structure that resembles the tower, at least none in North America. It would later be called the Old Stone Mill, but it is unlikely anyone would have put a fireplace in a flour mill. Because it was mentioned in the December 24, 1677, will of Governor Benedict Arnold as "my Stone-built Wind-Mill," the claim that Arnold built it began. Those scholars who denied the existence of pre-Columbian contact refer to this as evidence for their belief, although Arnold never claimed to have played a role in the structure's construction.

The most common debunking theory that the Newport Tower is pre-colonial is that a very similar tower, called the Chesterton Windmill, exists in Warwickshire, England. If we are to believe those who say that the Newport Tower is colonial, it must follow that England's most renowned architect, Inigo Jones, somehow interrupted his incredible career to design a windmill.

Inigo Jones is considered England's first great architect. His sponsors, which included the Earl of Rutland and the Earl of Pembroke, paid for his travels in Europe to study firsthand the greatest works. He was then commissioned to build for James I and Charles I as well as for another sponsor, the Earl of Arundel. Jones employed Palladian principles in building the Queen's House, the Royal Banquet Hall in Greenwich, and in designing St. Paul's Church, as well as Covent Garden in London. Would he discontinue the great works for a windmill?

Possibly.

The Chesterton Mill was built for Sir Edward Peyto, at the time a student of Jones, who was designing Peyto's manor house. Sir Edward was an astrologer and a mathematician, and the structure in question was originally built to be used as an observatory.

Newport is where Henry Sinclair built his colony. This was to be the place of refuge for those who wanted freedom from the barbarity of war in the name of religion. The native people of the area would tell the newcomers that this place, Newport, was known to them as Acadia.

THE END OF SINCLAIR

"Prince" Henry most likely made at least one more unrecorded voyage to the place he called Arcadia. He told his daughter Elizabeth of his plans and entrusted her with the knowledge of his colony and directions as to how to get there. She would marry John Drummond, a member of one of the wealthiest families in Scotland, based in the ancestral castle called Hawthornden, one mile east of Roslin.

Drummond and Elizabeth had three sons. The second son decided to leave Scotland and planned to make his fortune on his own. In Madeira he became known as John the Scot. He married Catarina Vaz de Lordelo in April of 1422. Through her family John was now connected to Bartolomeo Perestrelo, whose father had discovered Porto Santo Island. Bartolomeo now had the title of "capitano" of the island. This was the equivalent of governor, and, as a result, the younger Drummond earned a percentage of all production on Porto Santo Island.

Filipa Moniz Perestrelo was the daughter of Bartolomeo; she was originally from the same area as Columbus. She and Columbus would meet in church in the city of Lisbon. She married him and moved to Madeira to be with her family. The family's gift to Columbus was the charts and notebooks of her father, who had discovered Porto Santo while sailing as a Knight of Christ under Prince Henry the Navigator.

In any event, the colony of Henry Sinclair in Newport survived only long enough to leave behind the mysterious tower. What happened to the colony members is unknown. Perhaps they intermarried with Native American women. A darker possibility is that at some point the Indians reacted with violence against the newcomers. There is no public record of just who had come with Henry to Newport, or who went back to Scotland with him. Elizabeth Sinclair Drummond, however, might have brought details of her father's colony to Madeira through her son.

"AND IN ARCADIA, I LIVE"

Possibly one of the greatest authors of the fifteenth century was Jacopo Sannazaro of Italy. He revived the concept of a golden age and a golden place called Arcadia. As we've mentioned previously, Arcadia was originally written about by the poet Virgil. It referred to an ideal place where a virtuous people could live in peace. Virgil described its inhabitants as primitives who "goe altogether naked, except only certain skinnes of beastes."[11]

Sannazaro was a devout Catholic, but he was fierce in his attacks on the church and its princes. At the same time he believed in a goddess, a feminine aspect of the deity, which had consistently been weeded out of Christian theology. His work was at once a lamentation for the innocence lost and the longing to exist in a new world.

Sannazaro's *Arcadia* would receive much attention throughout Europe, and approximately every two years a new edition of it was printed. The book was so popular that its Tuscan dialect would eclipse others to become the official language of a divided Italy.

The pastoral style of an idyllic world would be a theme that was copied by others for years to come. The Arcadia of Sidney, the Diana of Montemayor, and the Bergerie of Belleau would soon follow. There was more to this than a return to Eden. Sannazaro incorporated in *Arcadia* a theme that was woven into the academies of Italy—that of an underground stream of knowledge. It blended Pythagorean, Gnostic, Hermetic, and Kabbalistic teaching and the idea of a higher secret knowledge that was accessible only to the initiate. And although Sannazaro did not invent the pastoral style and theme, the body of writing that followed would be labeled Arcadian.

In France he came across a literary treasure trove, discovering lost and unknown works of Latin poets including *Halieutica,* which was penned by Ovid. Sannazaro devoted himself to these texts. His *Arcadia* was pirated to Venice, where it was published without his knowledge. After the death of his patron, the author returned to Naples and published *Arcadia* again.

THE VERRAZANO VOYAGE TO THE NEW WORLD

Giovanni da Verrazano was born into an Italian family in 1485. Florence at the time was a religious crossroads. Gnostic teachings traveled with silk and wool over its paved highways as Crusaders and notable Templars also passed through Florence. The Templars held Saint John the Baptist in the highest regard, as did Florence. The symbol of both the goddess Venus and the Baptist was the dove. When church backlash struck against the heresies of the city of Florence, Verrazano moved to Lyon. This was another hotbed of heresy; it preserved the cults of Isis and Cybele long after Christianity had begun. The Temple of Cybele was built over with the Notre Dame de Fourvière. "Our Lady" could be regarded openly as the Blessed Virgin Mary but still refer to the goddess.

Lyon was also a city of bankers. The most important of the world's bankers were the Templars, who took their business acumen to other places, notably what would become Switzerland. When the Templar tradition morphed into Freemasonry, it became a somewhat closed society that controlled certain industries. Financing trade fairs along trade routes was a specialty.

Verrazano was no stranger to esoteric societies and had frequent contact with those who were Templars or Freemasons. He believed Arcadia existed outside the pages of Virgil and Sannazaro. He asked for and received the support of France's King Francis. Indeed, his ship was called the *Dauphine* in honor of the French king. It was equipped with fifty men and had provisions to last eight months. The only known crew member was his brother Girolamo, a mapmaker.

Verrazano would sail to Madeira, the home of Christopher Columbus, while his first wife, Filipa, was alive. There he provisioned for the Atlantic crossing. He would leave on January 17, 1524. Forty-nine days out of Madeira, he reached what is now North Carolina. This was around the second week of March, and he headed north to avoid running into the Spanish. At this point he began to give names to some of the places he visited. The first land he saw was called Annunziata, which means "the feast of the Annunciation of the Blessed Virgin." This was on the coast of North Carolina near modern Cape Hatteras. Farther north he called the land between the Outer Banks of North Carolina and New Jersey, Arcadia.

He noted that the strip of land at most points was a mile wide. He had been coasting opposite the Pamlico Sound. The other side of that isthmus can be twenty or thirty miles wide. He declared that it was the only thing separating his ship and the Pacific Ocean. He named the isthmus after himself, Verrazzania, and the area itself Francesca.[12]

If his mission was to find Cathay (China), it is surprising that he did not attempt passage through the numerous breaks in the shoals, or even a portage at some point. Instead he hastened north without recording any such attempt. While such thin strips of coastal land may not have had the access points they do today, one would have to go back in history to find a time when the Chesapeake Bay and the Delaware Bay were "closed," or inaccessible. The narrow point of entrance to the Chesapeake is twenty miles wide. The Delaware is much wider than that. Both would have presented an opportunity as a potential passage into the continent, to what he thought was China, especially if he still believed the Pacific was so close.

Verrazano Reaches New York

Apparently no such investigation took place. Instead Verrazano headed north without stopping until he arrived in New York Bay. He named the bay Santa Margarita after the king's sister, the Duchess d'Alençon. At the place that would be called by others the Verrazano Narrows he sailed north into the upper bay, where he laid eyes on present-day Manhattan. He named it Angoulême, probably in honor of the title that Francis I had held prior to becoming king. Another explanation is that Angoulême is the home of a fourteenth-century Templar fortress near the port city of La Rochelle. The town was in existence from Roman times.

When the Templars became aware of their impending arrests, they may have used the port of La Rochelle to cast off a fleet of ships to find refuge in the New World. Near La Rochelle, the city of Angoulême may have been the site where the treasure from Solomon's stables in Jerusalem, previously stored at the Templar headquarters in Paris, may have been kept before being placed aboard the ships of the fleet. John Calvin, the proponent of Scottish Protestantism, hid in Angoulême. Thus does the small town of Angoulême have other connections with the repressed secrets of underground France.

Its town symbol is a dragon writhing in flames. As Montségur had been the last stand of the Cathars and Paris had been the last stand of the French Templars, both would see their leaders and the faithful go into the inquisitorial flames of church and state.

Verrazano Encounters "the Natives"

From the future New York City, Verrazano coasted the southern shore of Long Island before heading north again. There are a handful of things that stand out among the records, letters, and charts of the Verrazano expedition. At Narragansett Bay he is recorded as receiving help from the natives in guiding him into the inner harbor safely. In both Europe and Asia it was customary to engage a pilot when navigating entrance into a foreign harbor. In this instance, however, the availability of a native having the ability to communicate and having experience in piloting a large ship must be considered to be odd at best.

No less of a source than Samuel Morison, the maritime historian, affirms that Verrazano's ship was "piloted by an Indian." He was guided from Point Judith through the narrow divide between Beaver Tail Point on Conanicut Island and Breton Point on Aquidneck (Rhode Island), past the Small Dumpling Islands, into the inner harbor.[13] This would serve as his anchorage.

With almost all of Verrazano's experience and interactions with America's native populations being awkward in terms of language and intentions, here an "Indian" was found who somehow was trustworthy and knowledgeable enough to pilot his ship! Incidentally, Verrazano did find the two tribes in the area, the Narragansetts and the Wampanoags, to be friendly.

Between Conanicut Island and Newport Harbor he noted the value of certain islands to defend the harbor. He named the islands Petra Viva—after the wife of one of his Italian backers, Antonio Gondi, whose wife's maiden name was Pierre-Vive. Today these islands are known as the Dumplings.

This was the only place where Verrazano records that he spent any time. It was here, near the harbor of what is now Rhode Island, that he interacted with the Wampanoag tribe. He also remarked that some of the native population appeared to be European. He made note of the bay, the mainland, its animals and its trees, as well as the dress and custom of his hosts.

This was the domain of the Wampanoag. They were part of a larger linguistic group known as the Algonquian, and their territory extended into Massachusetts. Verrazano made numerous comments on the charity and chastity of these natives, which may come as a shock given that other European-Amerind contacts were frequently reported to be hostile and licentious.

Could the Wampanoag have come into contact with Europeans before?

It is very likely that a Celtic-speaking people, especially from Ireland, reached New England. Oddly enough the earliest sagas of the Vikings record that they met up with the Irish in the New World. The groups do share numerous words in common. For example, the Celtic/Norse word for boat was *bato;* the Algonquian word was *pados.*

Verrazano's Real Mission

Perhaps Verrazano's real mission all along had been not to find a sea route to China but to locate the alleged Templar colony that had been founded under the leadership of the Sinclair family. In this mission he succeeded. Within the inner harbor of what is now Rhode Island's Newport stood the Newport Tower, which we have identified as a Templar baptistery. Built out of the materials available, it nevertheless resembled European models and shared the same measurements as those built by both Templars and Cistercians.

This Templar baptistery was so out of place in the New World that it would only have caused a shock to a European discoverer. Instead, both Verrazano's letter to the king and the map to his brother do not contain any iota of surprise as to the discovery of this "Norman Villa." Any explorer would have recognized the construction as European, which *should* have been surprising. Verrazano more than most would certainly have recognized the "villa" as something more. The very use of the word *villa* seems like an exercise in disinformation.

Perhaps it is the case that Verrazano's real mission had been disguised, which most likely explains his paucity of comments on the baptistery. Europe had a hunger for records of exploration and the newly drawn maps that would ensue. Before the Verrazano brothers could print their own map wherein the villa would be mentioned for the first time, it was mentioned on the 1526 map of Vesconte Majollo. Mention of it would later be included on the globe of Euphrosynus Ulpius in 1542.[14]

The map of Girolamo yields another clue only slightly secondary to that of the Norman Villa, which Girolamo had indicated on his map as a drawing of a tiny castle. Verrazano and his brother gave a name to the future Newport: Refugio (the Refuge). He does not enlighten us by telling us just who he thought was in need of refuge. One modern guide claims that it was a refuge for a sinking ship. However, Verrazano sailed in a one-ship expedition, and his ship made it home safely. Encountering a European ship would seem worthy of a mention in his records.

Verrazano, searching for the Arcadia that served as a Templar refuge, may have found everything but the people for whom he was searching. Other early maps called the area Norumbega and Anorumbega. Verrazano's Arcadia was supposed to be both an area and a city. The city was said to be located fifteen miles up a river, but just *which* river has never been identified. The Gastaldi map would label everything between Angoulême and Cape Breton as Terra de Norembega. Between the two is the Port du Refuge, a harbor with several islands.

On a large scale Narragansett Bay might be the best candidate for this, as it contains numerous islands and extends to the modern city of Providence, Rhode Island. On a smaller scale the harbor of Newport contains a handful of islands as well.

From the channel between Conanicut Island and the Aquidneck Island Peninsula on which the modern city of Newport is built, it is approximately twenty miles to what is today Fall River, Massachusetts. While the Fall River skeleton in armor and the intriguing Dighton Stone would later be discovered there, Verrazano would not find the city of Norembega.

This journey of Verrazano's would yield only disappointment. The Templar colony had been in the area, as proved by the presence of the villa, but whoever had once settled here was long gone. Likewise, the Arcadia of Sannazaro had been here too, but did not exist anymore.

After failing to locate the colony, Verrazano bid adieu to King Magnus, the Orkney Norse-sounding chief of the Wampanoags who had, surprisingly to the Europeans, been a woman. Verrazano continued along the coast, rounding Cape Cod and heading north to Maine, where he ran into the Abenaki Indians. He noted that their appearance was similar to that of the Wampanoag, but in temperament they were hostile.

Verrazano's expedition begs many questions. First of all, the particulars of his expedition tell a different story than does his letter to the king. He sailed for the North American coast and appeared to target the area that would be the future Newport. There he was guided to a safe harbor and, more dramatically, to a European building.

But why did he spend time only in Newport?

As part of a secret society, Verrazano was privy to secrets that were not to be revealed in letters. He crossed the ocean in search of a colony that had been planted a century before. He knew exactly where to look for the American Arcadia. He found all the evidence he needed to understand that the Templars had unmistakably been there. The baptistery left him no doubt. While it still stood, the Arcadian colony had not survived.

His voyage, while a personal disappointment, did bring him a degree of fame. The crest of the Verrazano family was changed to that of an eight-pointed star. It symbolized, in the gnostic sense, a quest completed and a rebirth, possibly even a new mission.

Indeed, within a few years, his brother tells us they made another voyage to the Americas. This time, most likely on the island of Guadeloupe, Giovanni waded ashore, leaving his men aboard the ship. Experience with both friendly and hostile natives had not prepared him for the Carib people. He was quickly seized, killed, and torn apart. As his men looked on in horror, he was eaten in front of them by cannibals.

Verrazano's explorations were successful only in finding that an English colony had once existed on the continent. If history had been open to the concept of Europeans in America, the answer as to what had happened to the colony might share similarities with the mystery of Raleigh's lost colony. The Refugio of the Templars would not be forgotten. Indeed, many place-names in the area allude to these voyages of long ago.

Verrazano had headed north past Block Island to the future Rhode Island. It would be named after Rhodes, the idyllic landscape in Sannazaro's *Arcadia*. It would later become the name for all of the area in "Rhode Island." As mentioned earlier, in Greek, *rhodes* or *rodos* means "rose." The Greeks also called the island of Rhodes *Helios*, "the island of the sun," as Rhodes was a place of worship for the sun god Helios.

Rhodes is the largest of the Dodecanese islands of Greece. If Dee's colony grew, the newcomers would have been greeted by Lady Occasion, like New York's immigrants are greeted by the Statue of Liberty. It is possible that Verrazano named Block Island "Rhodes" in 1524, Dee named Aquidneck "Rhodes" in 1577, Governor Benedict Arnold (great grandfather to the traitor) followed Dee's naming in 1637 when he bought land there, and colonial leaders continued the tradition of this name in 1644.

The colony was not the only footprint of the Sinclair voyages, however, as we shall soon see.

THE OAK ISLAND TREASURE VAULT

It is believed that when the Sinclair family served as guardians of the Knights Templar and the Freemasons in Scotland, their treasure was hidden in the castles and caves at or near Roslin. With the family needing to preserve the treasure from what would become the Reformation tide and the English who wanted to control Scotland, the treasure was moved. Brought to Nova Scotia (New Scotland), Sinclair picked a spot high on a hill to create what would become known as New Ross. This new Roslin would have a minor fortification to house weapons and those who would work on what would someday become Oak Island's Money Pit. It still exists today. Directly across the road from it is a Freemason lodge.

The history of Nova Scotia and European exploration is much longer than recognized. With physical evidence of a full Norse colony in L'Anse aux Meadows in northern Newfoundland from around 1000 CE, there is no reason to dismiss the evidence of Norse in that future province. The Sinclair expedition most likely followed the early excursions of fishermen from Europe as well. In 1508, Portuguese fishermen laid claim to settlements in Nova Scotia, and specific documents have the Azores family of Pinheiro de Barcelos in Mahone Bay. They were still there in 1568 when documents show them trading cattle with whalers. By 1604 the French may have laid claim to the coast, making it uncomfortable for the Portuguese. However, these French would raise a Portuguese-style "Padrao" cross when wishing to trade with the Portuguese sailors as a symbol of peace.

Catholics attempted to ensure that Nova Scotia would be a Catholic settlement, and in 1632, Isaac Razilly, a member of the Knights of Malta, established a capital at nearby LaHave.

The Nova Scotia repository was the tiny Oak Island, named because it was one of the only islands in Mahone Bay to have been seeded with oak trees. Today the oaks are mostly gone, having been plagued with disease, but the search for the vault continues.

The only thing that is certain is that something was planted deep under the island before 1795. In that year, three boys who rowed out to the island became intrigued by a depression in the ground under a tree where a tackle block hung. They were not aware that in Shakespeare's First Folio there is a line in *Titus Andronicus* that reads as follows: "to bury so much gold under a tree and never after to inherit it." They did have imagination and believed that the depression was a clear giveaway that something was buried below. Mahone Bay had been named for the low-lying pirate ships of the French that were used to steal precious commodities from other ships. Of course, pirates like Captain Kidd might have left a particularly illustrious cache of royal jewels, gold coins, and the booty of Indian maharajahs.

At a depth of three feet the boys uncovered flagstone, which was not otherwise found on the island. This was a further sign that they were on to something. At ten feet a platform of oaken planks convinced them even more.

Removing the barrier they found that the dirt underneath had settled somewhat. This was certainly a shaft that had been dug and then filled in. At twenty feet and again at thirty feet, new oak planks protected the shaft from intruders. By this time the young men had exhausted their own ability to proceed. Attempts at enlisting other men in the area fell on deaf ears; they had *real* work to do.

OTHERS TAKE UP THE CHALLENGE

It was years later when a doctor from nearby Onslow formed a company to continue the dig. The platforms occurred at ten-foot intervals, and they dug until they encountered traps that would not allow them to proceed. After ninety feet the original builders had set up booby traps that allowed the water of the bay to flood the shaft. To do this they had to build coffer dams in the coves on opposite sides of the island, stop the bay's waters, dig tunnels, set drains, and cover up the work before removing their dams.

But what was the treasure really? Was it gold, or was "gold" a metaphor for something priceless that had been handed down through the centuries by the Templars and the Sinclairs?

When physician and Bacon scholar Orville W. Owen of Detroit mounted an expedition to Gloucester, England, some years later in 1911, to investigate what might be an underground repository of Bacon's works, he found only an empty vault under the river Wye. Someone had stopped the river's flow long enough to build the vault, conceivably fill it with the manuscripts, and then allow the river to flow again. Later the manuscripts were moved and the same operation would have then been conducted a second time. The water was diverted, the vault was opened, the manuscripts were removed, and then the water was allowed to flow again.

Employing such hydraulic techniques was nothing new. The body of legendary King Leir had similarly been placed in a vault under the river Soar. The body of Attila had also been buried safely under the Busento River in Italy. In both cases the rivers were temporarily diverted, graves or vaults put in position, and then the river had been allowed to return to its original position.

Although Owen was not successful in uncovering the manuscripts, he was successful in winning over a convert to continue his work. In 1920, Burrell Ruth, who was Owen's student, was on his way to becoming a bona fide Baconian. In time, Ruth came to believe that the manuscripts that had been removed from Gloucester had been brought across the ocean to the Americas.

Specifically, he believed that the original folio of Bacon's Shakespearean works had been moved to a place in Nova Scotia about an hour's drive from Halifax. Here, at Mahone Bay, a search for something had been going on since 1795. The underwater booby traps mentioned earlier had been positioned by builders with an obvious knowledge of hydraulics. Could the same keepers of the manuscripts or their appointed heirs have moved them from one underwater vault to another?

Owen had read the story of the Nova Scotia treasure hunt that was now under the aegis of a New Jersey businessman, Gilbert Hedden. Hedden had gotten wind of the whole affair from a *New York Times* article, and when his family business was sold he had the means to become involved in the search.

Ruth's theory was that before his death Bacon had left detailed instructions as to what should be done with the manuscripts. A ship had left England with the writings of Bacon in it. It sailed to Spain and then to Nova Scotia, where it landed. Why Nova Scotia? In 1610, Bacon and others had been granted land in Nova Scotia by James I.

Two coconspirators in this whole endeavor are believed to be Bacon's chaplain, William Rawley, and Thomas Bushnell, an engineer whose expertise would be invaluable. Rawley was the executor of Bacon's estate. He held all of Bacon's manuscripts and published Bacon's *New Atlantis* shortly after Bacon's death. Bacon's estate was in a shambles, and the creditors seized most but not all of his papers and manuscripts. These Rawley had been asked to publish, which he did, but he also reserved some of the papers for a "private succession of literary sons."

Rawley lived until 1660 so would have had plenty of time to organize a crew to transport and inter Bacon's works. The engineer Thomas Bushnell had worked with Bacon as a young man. His specialty was recovering ore from flooded Cornish mines. After Bacon died Bushnell disappeared for two years.[15] Bushnell lived until 1674. It is possible that as an agent of Bacon's he might have served in a Rawley-sponsored transfer of Bacon's writings. The guesswork and speculation surrounding Oak Island remains.

In my first conversation with David Tobias, the owner of the part of the island where the original shaft is located, he informed me that he believed that the vault had been the work of Sir Francis Drake. I thought back over Drake's life, which I knew well, and couldn't find any time where his presence hadn't been accounted for in the historical record. Drake's life could not only be accounted for, but he also had freely spent his massive wealth, making it probable that he wouldn't have any left over to spend on the building of a secret vault in a land across the sea.

Drake, as a contemporary of Sir Francis Bacon and Dr. John Dee, might have had the ability to carry out such an operation but had died a swashbuckler's death years before the "Shakespearean" plays were even finished.

In recent years the owners of half of Oak Island have broadened their search to other islands in the bay. Tunnels are believed to connect more than one island, and a spiral staircase leading underground has been said to be on an island near Oak Island.

A project as large as the Oak Island treasure vault would have needed to employ hundreds of workers. A modern find was unearthed at the nearby town of New Ross (as in New Roslin?), where stone ruins in disrepair, a well that had been sealed, and the foundations of a structure poked through the earth.[16]

Before leaving Nova Scotia for the next stop on the mystery trail it should be noted that the closest town to Oak Island is Lunenburg. This beautiful little seaport was settled on June 8, 1753, by German, Swiss, and Montbéliardian Protestants under the protection of the English. The principality of Montbéliard, with its fairy-tale name, was actually once a county to the northwest of Switzerland. It was under the influence of Lunen, like other Swiss principalities that were more interested in taxing the land than exercising control. Lunenburg was named for the man who was the Duke of Brunswick and Lunenburg, Augustus, who would later become King George II. He was a Rosicrucian and involved with Bacon. Lunenburg may have also been named for a small town in Germany near Hamburg where in 1586 a meeting of kings and nobles was held. They formed the Confederatio Militiae Evangelicae. Historian Frances Yates says it is possible that John Dee was in attendance and that it connected and united Rosicrucians against the Catholic League.[17]

The history of European settlement in the Americas generally omits the true motives. Some came for land and a New World while many came for philosophical goals. Various Christian sects had everything to fear from the Roman Catholic Church. The Inquisition and the St. Bartholomew Day Massacre are just two examples that show that toleration did not exist. The Americas offered a second chance, and the Rosicrucians were a vanguard toward freedom.

CHAPTER 8

BACON'S NEW ATLANTIS

The early history of Europeans in New England is believed by most to feature predominantly Pilgrims and Puritans looking for a place to practice their own versions of religion. They had no interest in granting freedom of religion to others and exercised stricter practices and punishments than existed back in England.

The history of the European experience in New England actually predates the Pilgrims. It probably initially began with visits by Welsh sailors and Irish monks. It expanded with Viking settlements in Newfoundland and farther south. It continued with fishermen sailing from the Orkney Islands, from Bristol in England, and from the Bay of Biscay in France. The Basques of Spain were also part of the picture. For all of these fishermen, the plan was simply to sail away from home with a boatload of salt and return home with a boatload of salted cod. Religion and utopia had little place in this more mercantile scheme of things.

Between 1490 and 1494 the English city of Bristol claimed to be sending out explorers to find an elusive island known as Hy-Brasil. Or were they? They left England with their holds full of salt, which implies that they were actually looking for cod. The Hanseatic League, made up of merchants from more than a hundred German towns, was trying to claim sole fishing rights to Iceland's waters. Up until this time it mostly controlled trade in the Baltic Sea, but it was constantly expanding its territory. It threatened both the Dutch and the English with its attempts to create a sea-trading monopoly.

VARIOUS EARLY EXPEDITIONS
AND THEIR LEADERS

One British explorer was John Jay. Prior to 1492, Jay wrote a letter to Columbus about explorers from Bristol discovering new lands. Columbus most likely had no inclination to sail the Viking route and had already been to Iceland.

A Thomas Croft was charged with illegal trading, most likely as a pretense that England actually wished to follow agreements with the Hanseatic League, the guild that controlled coastal northern European trade. An English jury found him not guilty and said that his possession of salt could have been for exploratory purposes to sustain a crew seeking to find Brazil. Thomas Croft was a wealthy landowner, a lawyer, and for a time a member of Parliament. Richard Croft, Thomas's older brother, also corresponded with Columbus.

Still another individual by the name of Robert Thorne claimed that his father had sailed to Newfoundland. Since he played an eminent role in exploration and met regularly with other influential scholars, such as the cartographer Mercator, John Dee might have known that Robert Thorne the elder and a Hugh Eliot had made that voyage three years before Cabot.

A series of voyages were made, and it was fairly clear that the voyagers were looking for a utopian colony or a place to create their own utopia: Bacon's New Atlantis. They were also looking for the lost colony of Henry Sinclair and his Refugio. As we know, many of these voyages were the work of a handful of men who were connected to the crown: Francis Bacon, John Dee, and Sir Walter Raleigh. John Dee would be one of several who used the Verrazano map to make his own map. This was in the year 1580. Two years later a relatively obscure explorer by the name of Antonio Brigham would use the Verrazano map to trace

Verrazano's path. There are reasons Brigham does not get the credit other early explorers did. The most important reason was that his voyage was kept secret. John Dee was one of the few in the know. Brigham had two ships and a smaller pinnace and left England in June of 1582. He returned nine months later. It is possible that his was a preliminary voyage, paving the way for Sir Humphrey Gilbert.

Gilbert, who was born in 1539, was a prominent explorer, the half brother of Sir Walter Raleigh, and an active part of Queen Elizabeth's court. He battled in Ireland and was rewarded by being knighted, allegedly in a field of dead Gaels. In Ireland he had worked with one Sir Thomas Smith on an alchemy project. Later he set up another project with Robert Dudley, the Earl of Leicester, who maintained an alchemical laboratory at Limehouse. Much of Gilbert's career was marked by a string of maritime failures. He backed Frobisher's voyage to Greenland, which brought home a yellow mineral that proved worthless. In 1578 he launched an expedition to North America, but his seven ships were hindered by bad weather, which sent them limping home.

One of Gilbert's backers, whose name is not a household name or ever mentioned in the classroom, is Edward Hayes. He may have actually made a pre-1578 voyage to New England with Edward Hoby. Hoby's mother was born Elizabeth Cooke. Her sisters married Nicholas Bacon and Sir William Cecil, respectively. Nicholas Bacon, as mentioned, would serve as the "father" of Sir Francis Bacon.

The role of Bacon and Dee in the earliest English visits to New England becomes clearer. While Dee had a river named for him (more on this below), Bacon's name remains invisible, at least for a time, but references to him can be found as far north as Newfoundland and as far south as Virginia. On June 11, 1578, Gilbert secured a license to explore North America. It had a six-year expiration date, so after the Brigham voyage, in late September of the following year, he set sail.

Gilbert had planned subsequent voyages, but he had problems getting financing. In August of 1580 he gifted John Dee all of Canada and Alaska that was above the 50 degree latitude.[1] As a wealthy man with many connections in the court, including Sir Walter Raleigh, he could simply take possession of Newfoundland for England. He also deeded one and a half million acres to Sir George Peckham, starting at what was called the Dee River and extending westward. The Dee River, a name that didn't last long on maps of New England, was actually Narragansett Bay. This gave Peckham most of Rhode Island and half of Connecticut. Gilbert also granted three million acres to Philip Sidney. Sidney had started his most famous work, *Arcadia,* around this time.

When Gilbert set sail in September of 1579 he did not fare well. One of the ships in his expedition owned by Raleigh and named the *Bark Raleigh* turned back when sickness struck and food ran out. Storms and fog separated the other ships, but they soon made a rendezvous in St. John's Harbor. Gilbert laid claim to Newfoundland in the name of Queen Elizabeth. They were briefly detained by coastal natives because previous explorers had taken slaves. Freed at last, Gilbert, despite his claim, didn't stay long. He then sailed for the graveyard of ships that was called Sable Island. Bad weather and the island's rocky shores brought disaster. A storm near the Azores was the last of Gilbert.

Gilbert would be lost at sea and Raleigh imprisoned, paving the way for Ferdinando Gorges to colonize Maine. He was a commoner with big goals. Knighted for his service in the wars against the Catholics, he aspired to join the landed aristocracy. From his fortress in Plymouth, England, he made plans for building a domain in Maine that he would rule over as lord. His ship *Archangel* was captained by George Weymouth. In 1605, the ship reached the New World, landing first at Martha's Vineyard and then sailing up the coast of Maine. Monhegan Island in Maine was sighted by him. This expedition's patron was Sir Henry Wriothesley, the Earl of Southampton. He had invested in the Cuttyhunk expedition as well, which had not been a success.

Southampton and Gorges both vied for control of the new lands, and it would be up to King James to decide. The year after Gorges's

Archangel had returned to England, the king divided the coast of North America between the two factions. Southampton's group, the London Company, would be given permission to settle south of the Potomac. Gorges's group, the Plymouth Company, was given the land north of Long Island. The Dutch controlled the land in between, and King James didn't want another war on his hands.

It was John Dee who influenced the next voyage of Sir George Peckham. Dee was afraid that the Spaniards would wipe out their intended colony like they had done to a Huguenot colony in Florida. Peckham wrote about Gilbert's ill-fated voyage and, like Dee, reiterated claims that the Welsh prince Madoc had discovered North America. Dee also convinced Peckham that he needed to sail to the place that Verrazano called the Refugio.

THE GOSNOLD VOYAGES

The Refugio of the Templars would not be forgotten, and the push by John Dee had only just begun in 1580 when Dee enticed his queen with tales of Arthur, Madoc, and the friar known as Nicholas of Lynn. Both the search for the Refugio and the search for a home for Bacon's New Atlantis continued. In 1602, a relative of Sir Francis Bacon, Bartholomew Gosnold, would search for it as well. His parents were Dorothy Bacon and Anthony Gosnold, and his backer was the Earl of Southampton. By most standards his was a tiny expedition, for it consisted of only thirty-two men. They set sail in March and set sail back to England mid-June. Gosnold used Verrazano's report as his guide but never made it to Newport. Instead he investigated and named Cape Cod, Martha's Vineyard, and the Elizabeth Islands. He missed the Refugio.

In 1602 a cousin of Sir Francis Bacon's became the choice to found a colony in Massachusetts. Born in 1571 near Ipswitch, in Suffolk, Gosnold and his brothers and sisters lived in a moated castle called Otley Hall, which had been in the family for three hundred years. He was related to royalty[2] and was schooled at Otley Hall, which was frequented by many influential people. His uncle was secretary to the Earl of Essex and sent Gosnold to sea as a privateer attacking Spanish ships in the Azores. Gosnold had returned from his adventure with a plan to reach the Americas using the Azores as a layover.

It was Essex who had intended to fund the New World voyage, but politics got in the way. Gosnold had been trained by Essex. Essex would start a rebellion, and after it ended badly he was prosecuted by Bacon and, having been convicted, was executed, as we know. At this point relations between Gosnold and Bacon became strained given that it was perceived that Bacon had betrayed his friend.

Bacon nevertheless remained the inspiration for the 1602 voyage of Gosnold's, which would end up being sponsored by a group of Bristol merchants together with Henry Wriothesley. Henry had been a longtime friend of both Bacon and Gosnold, and even though he was in the Tower of London at the time, he made a financial contribution to the voyage.

Gosnold's goal was to find a place to plant a colony in New England. The choice was the place that Henry Sinclair had founded his short-lived colony: Newport, Rhode Island. To that end, on March 26, 1602, Gosnold sailed from Plymouth in England to New England. At this time the Plymouth Colony had not yet received its charter. Influenced by Bacon and aware that Verrazano had noted what might be a previous colony, Gosnold knew what he was looking to find. To that end, he was armed with fifteen maps of the New England coast.

Gosnold first reached the coast of Maine, where the Abenaki were not docile like the Wampanoag were known to be. Gosnold then came to Savage Rock, a place that has not ever been located. It is generally agreed upon that it was somewhere on the coast of Maine or as far south as Cape Ann in Massachusetts. Gosnold's reports on the Native Americans were of great interest as the "savages" were actually adept at traveling and trading and were using copper. Gosnold and his crew were approached by eight Mi'kmaq Indians in a Basque shallop. It is unclear whether the Indians had copied the design or stolen the ship. In any case, the natives understood some "Christian" words; apparently they were quick learners.[3]

Gosnold then visited Cape Cod, which he named for the great cod fishing in the area. He visited Provincetown and went ashore there, becoming the first English to set foot in the region. He then sailed around the cape from Provincetown to the Elizabeth Islands, passing Nantucket as he did so. He named Martha's Vineyard after his infant daughter and Elizabeth's Isle after a sister who had married Anne Boleyn's cousin, or possibly after the queen herself.

He (crash) landed at Cuttyhunk in Buzzard's Bay, one of the larger islands, and explored from this base. There are different versions of just where he explored, but apparently he never went far enough west to find the Refugio. He spent twelve weeks on and around Cuttyhunk, ultimately choosing it as his preferred place to settle. Efforts were under way to create the colony when some of the would-be colonists decided they would rather head home. The trip wasn't a total loss, however, as the ship returned to England with a cargo of sassafras, which was used to treat venereal disease.[4]

Along with the precious sassafras, they also brought home an account of the friendly Indians, the Wampanoag, whom they had encountered in Rhode Island. These natives had a quantity of copper, which they used to fashion rudimentary suits of armor. The copper was used for self-defense and decoration; it was incorporated into breastplates and earrings. Asked where they found the copper, the answer was given by pointing a finger in the ground and pointing to the mainland.

The account of natives in armor by John Brereton, who recorded Gosnold's voyage, was followed by a similar report by Martin Pring, who encountered copper-armored natives in the Cape Cod area. Since then such copper has been found in Pemaquid in Maine and Fall River, Massachusetts.

Among the Elizabeth Islands is Naushon, which has been owned by three different families after being discovered. The Winthrops owned it for 47 years, the Bowdoins owned it for 115 years, and the Forbes family owns the preserve today.

Gosnold's voyage might be regarded as a failure. He had spent weeks on Cuttyhunk yet was only twenty easy sailing miles from Newport. Reports of his voyage may have reached the author of *The Tempest* as they would have been sent to the Earl of Southampton, who had sponsored Shakespeare, making Cuttyhunk the possible setting of the play.

Gosnold Sets Sail for Virginia

Gosnold still held on to Bacon's concept of a New Atlantis. He was chosen again soon after returning to England to voyage to Virginia with 107 colonists. Some 40 of these were from Otley, where both voyages had been planned. The expedition included John Smith and Gosnold's cousin Thomas Smith.

Bartholomew Gosnold was possibly the first geomancer in Virginia. Family to Bacon, Gosnold was steeped in the Rosicrucian tradition. He carried a staff with a decorative knob that resembled the staffs of Egyptian and Etruscan augurs. Gosnold's familial relation to Bacon and his affinity implies membership in a secret society or mystery school.

The colony landed at the Jamestown fort, and Gosnold was hit with an unspecified illness. He died on August 22, 1607. Within a month, 67 of the original 107 were dead. While Gosnold gets credit for planning the expedition, the self-promoting John Smith took over after his death and garnered the lion's share of the credit. Gosnold was buried outside the fort's walls. This was not a sign of disrespect; rather, it was tradition that the party leader be buried outside as protection. Inside the rediscovered Jamestown fort, however, Smith's statue stands, not Gosnold's. Although John Smith takes the credit for Jamestown, in reality he was a braggart who exaggerated his own credentials. In truth, he was the son of a farmer and a soldier of fortune. He was set afire in his sleep, burned badly, and put on a ship home.

Of the twenty thousand individuals who would ultimately be sent to Virginia three-quarters of them died—a death rate greater than that of the plague. Those who settled in swampy areas where brackish water led to disease met unpleasant fates. The Indians knew better than to live there, but they did hunt in the swamps.

The colonists had also fought among themselves. With rations tight or nonexistent, the settlers, some of whom were drunken sailors, debtors, convicts, and laborers pressed into work groups off London's streets, fought with each other.

MARTIN PRING

In April of 1603 another of Raleigh's expeditions left for America, captained by a man by the name of Martin Pring, whom we have mentioned briefly before. It reached Maine in late spring and would be responsible for discovering Manana Island, the small island off the coast of Maine that we have also discussed earlier. On it there exists an inscription of a dragon between two rocks called the Serpents. Author Graham Phillips claims that he discovered that the author of the Shakespeare texts may have written a play called *The Birth of Merlin*.[5] At the end of the play two dragons unite into one in the sky: a symbol of Arthur reuniting Britain. Raleigh's secret School of Night was referred to as the Dragon Men.

Pring was in New England in 1603. The Pilgrims would not land until 1620. This means there may have been an English presence there for seventeen years.

In August of 1606, Gorges sent Henry Challons to set up a colony near Pemaquid. He managed to get seriously lost and was captured in the Caribbean by the Spanish. Martin Pring was sent to Maine with supplies, but they never made the rendezvous. Pring went home without starting the colony, and Virginia would claim the right to the first permanent English settlement.

A second attempt had George Popham in charge, with Sir Humphrey Gilbert's son Raleigh as his second. The two quarreled from the first day, and the colony was divided. Popham, who was described as an honest man, wasn't made for the harsh Maine winter and didn't survive. Raleigh Gilbert, described as headstrong and of little judgment, mistreated the local Indians. Little is known of what happened next, but apparently fighting between the Wabanaki tribes and the English led to most of the English leaving as soon as a supply ship arrived.

THE PILGRIMS GAIN A FOOTHOLD

The Pilgrims were a small sect of English Puritans, a splinter group that rebelled against the Anglican Church. Anglicans and Catholics liked dogma and the hierarchy of the church. The Catholic Church based in Rome had their own king, the pope, who claimed to rule the world in many matters. With the Anglicans, the king or queen was head of the church. The Puritans had no set dogma, prayers, and even less ceremony. They may not have played a great role in politics; however, politics played a great role in determining their fate.

Queen Elizabeth had been the target of plots before she took the throne in 1558 and would suffer them after as well. The 1579 plot, called the Ridolfi conspiracy, cost the Duke of Norfolk his head. The Babington plot, seven years later, was headed off by Walsingham, but had he failed, Anthony Babington and John Ballard might have started a Catholic uprising. Mary Queen of Scots tried to put herself on the English throne, but these plots failed as well. The Catholic versus Anglican religious wars were fuel for the Spanish Armada, which was defeated by Dee, Drake, and the weather. The Puritans were then seen as both nonconformists and possibly as fomenting conspiracy. Puritans meeting in private houses were often arrested for doing so.

The small village of Scrooby, England, was the center of a Separatist community. People who played important roles in Massachusetts had their origins in Scrooby. They included William Brewster, who was the postmaster; William Bradford, who was one of the youngest Separatists; and Miles Standish, who was one of the few to have come from a noble family. An ancestor of his was said to have wounded Wat Tyler, the populist revolutionary. Another fought at Agincourt. Brewster and Bradford, as well as John Robinson and John Carver, became the backbone of the Pilgrim Church.

The Separatist community decided that England was becoming too dangerous for them and decided to escape to Holland. Their first attempt cost them much of their money and was a failure as a dishonest sea captain robbed them, stranding them in England. A second expedition was then organized by the postmaster Brewster. Between 1606 and 1609, most of the community was safe in Leyden, Holland. Their self-imposed exile put them in daily contact with others whose religion and language they were not inclined to adopt.

Worse, the king of England was not about to leave them alone. James I attempted to seize a Pilgrim printing press in Holland while Brewster hid out.

The English investors of the London Virginia Company had, by this time (1612), been reorganized as the Company of Adventurers and Planters of London. The Plymouth Company became the Council for New England in 1620. The investors needed a cohesive group like the Pilgrims to brave the rigors of the New World. The Pilgrims needed safe haven. Then Sir Edwin Sandys came into the picture. He was a member of the Council for Virginia, and he accepted Brewster's negotiators and said he'd help promote the Pilgrim cause.

Two ships were employed, and the first group was organized for the expedition. The group included John Alden, who married Priscilla Mullins; William Brewster; William Bradford; and Miles Standish. The passengers numbered 102 in total, 15 of whom were servants. The twenty-four households included families that would go on to consider themselves America's upper crust for centuries: Carver, Brewster, Winslow, Bradford, Allerton, Fuller, Crackstone, Standish, Martin, Mullins, White, Hopkins, Warren, Billington, Tilley, Cooke, Rogers, Tinker, Rigdale, Chilton, Turner, and Eaton. Besides these twenty-four households, a handful of single men were aboard.

The trip took sixty-four days, and on November 9 land was seen; it was Cape Cod. There were suspicions that they had purposefully landed so far north, as Massachusetts was less hospitable than Virginia. Many were concerned about being so isolated.

The *Mayflower* took its time in finding a suitable landing spot. The dangerous shoals and moving breakers that exist around Monomoy pushed them away from some good harbors. Monomoy Point was then called Point Care because of its dangerous breakers. Pollock Rip was then called Tucker's Terror.

They finally agreed on a place where John Smith had landed six years prior. On November 11 of 1620, they rounded the tip of Cape Cod and entered the bay. They fought with each other about settling here as it was cold and bleak. They placed signal fires at Pond Village, Truro, and the village of Great Hollow.

Romantic Notions Crumble as Reality Sets In

The Puritans started with a utopian vision of a new Zion. Instead they battled with each other and were reduced to stealing the native's corn.

In addition to the cache of native corn that they helped themselves to, they took a native canoe as well. They discovered mounds and learned from those in Virginia that these were often the site of elaborate burials. Thus they robbed the native graves for useful items. Ironically, on the opposite side of the bay, at a spot where a native had stolen a harpoon, was Manomet Bluff. This was named Thievish Harbor.

The captain of the *Mayflower* was becoming tired of the bickering between the settlers. Some were ready to settle while others wanted to go to Anguum at Ipswitch, where there were said to be better harbors. Captain Jones warned that he was not planning to winter in the new land. Finally, on December 11, a month after spotting land, they decided to stay. The harbor, which had been given the name Plimouth on a John Smith map, became Plymouth. The natives had called the place Patuxet. The area had been a place of plague in 1617, which had killed almost the entire Pawkannawkut tribe.

The Puritans decided to build a common house first and then arrange small houses along Leyden Street, named for their home in Holland. One by one Pilgrims started dying of illness and disease. In one strange circumstance, Dorothy Bradford fell off the *Mayflower* while attempting to get in a longboat. No one reached her in time to save her.

Colonists Goodman and Browne took dogs to hunt deer and got lost. They almost died before finding their way back to the colony. Fifty-two of the first group of more than one hundred Puritans were dead by the end of 1620.

A second group of Puritans, called Congregationalists, would follow them to Massachusetts. They landed in Portsmouth, then traveled to Salem and Boston, faring much better than the first group had.

The first governor of the Massachusetts Bay Colony was John Winthrop. His son, also named John, came over in 1631. The younger John Winthrop was granted permission to settle and founded a colony in Connecticut, which was named Saybrook. Unlike his father he was an alchemist and became a fellow of the Royal Society during one of his visits to England.[6] As such, he brought quite a different culture to the New World.

Despite all of this progress, elders of the group had no room for democracy, religious tolerance, or a separation of church and state. In this, Massachusetts became an intolerant colony. Roger Williams was cast out in 1636 for differing with the elders. Anne Hutchinson was arrested and brought to trial before being kicked out as well. Both went to Rhode Island, which was quickly gaining a reputation for nonconformity.

In 1647, Rhode Island put together a constitution that didn't require church membership as a prerequisite to voting. Whereas the Plymouth Bay Colony had failed, Rhode Island had succeeded. It was not a utopia, but the colony was stepping in a utopian direction.

Rhode Island, the place where Henry Sinclair had started a colony and what Verrazano had placed on his map as Rhodes, was settled by

Roger Williams, who started a trading post at nearby Wickford and referred to the area as Rode (Rose) Island in 1637.

Official names of this colony were Rhode Island and Providence Plantations. In 1647, early leaders of Providence Plantations decided that it would be represented by the Rosicrucian symbol of an anchor in a blue field. The Arnold family had used the same symbol ten years earlier. The flag has evolved over the years, and the word *hope* now used on the flag refers to the saying, "Hope is the anchor of the soul."

In the next chapter we will take a look at more early expeditions to the New World that were influenced by Sir Francis Bacon. The first focus will be on Raleigh's journeys.

CHAPTER 9

THE COLONY OF THE VIRGIN QUEEN

Sir Francis Bacon (who had created his own order of the Rosi Crosse) and Sir Walter Raleigh (who deemed himself to be the Red Cross knight) belonged to circles that intersected each other but at the same time were opposed to each other. Bacon was the thinker, the philosopher, and the educator. Raleigh was the warrior, the adventurer, and also the author of a history of the world. Both men vied for the attentions of the queen, and they both would organize expeditions to the New World. Both expeditions got off to a bad start.

SIR WALTER RALEIGH'S EXPLORATIONS OF THE NEW WORLD

Virginia had started out as a project of Sir Walter Raleigh's. Raleigh was a Devon man with the sea in his blood. He came to Elizabeth's court when the English were just waking up to the profit potential of the New World. In 1584 he received the queen's permission to sail there and establish a colony somewhere between Newfoundland and Florida.

Within weeks he sent out two ships to the American coast. The expedition scouted the coast of the Carolinas and selected Roanoke Island on which to settle. The island was one of the barrier islands off the coast of what is today North Carolina. Upon their return to England, they would bring back pearls, animal skins, and two native Algonquian. His career was at a high point that he would never see again. In 1585 and again in 1587 he sent out two more expeditions. Famously, the first white child born in the New World was born in the colony. Infamously, the second colony would disappear.

Raleigh's second fleet set sail in May of 1587. After an attempt at finding Spanish ships to attack failed, the fleet dropped off the new colonists at Roanoke. Eighteen men had been left behind from the previous expedition; all were dead. John White learned they had been attacked by Indians. His daughter Eleanor Dare gave birth to a girl. She was the first Christian child born in the colony and was named Virginia Dare. John White would leave for home in August, promising a speedy return with provisions. That return was delayed by Queen Elizabeth who was bracing for invasion, which came in the form of the Spanish Armada that England defeated in 1588. It started badly upon leaving Lisbon and was battered by storms. It ended badly, with a fleet destroyed and eleven thousand lives lost. It would be two years before White would set sail for the New World. By the time he got back to Roanoke it would be too late. The colony had been abandoned.

In 1592, Raleigh was imprisoned in the Tower of London for having secretly married Elizabeth Throckmorton, disobeying the queen. While the imprisonment didn't last, after Elizabeth's death James I put him back in the Tower in 1603. Raleigh didn't want James I to be king and was said to have stated as much, adding that when the queen was dead, England should rule itself. Those words were in part responsible for putting Raleigh back in prison again.

He would not be released until 1616, when his resentment toward Shakespeare led to the Bard's demise. It was most likely Bacon who was behind Raleigh's difficulties, but the illiterate Shakespeare would bear the blame.

On August 10, 1618, Raleigh was put in the Tower for the third and last time. King James was aware that Raleigh was still popular and created a committee of six to investigate him. Bacon was one of the six, as was his longtime opponent Sir Edward Coke. Accused of numerous plots dating as far back as 1603 and for attacking Spanish ships, the six, as expected, found Raleigh guilty. It was Bacon who declared that this was enough to warrant execution. The warrant was then drawn up by Bacon and signed immediately. The still-popular Raleigh had sixty men guard him as he was led to his execution. Although suffering from ill treatment and sickness, he spoke for forty-five minutes in his own defense. He then touched the executioner's ax and said, "This is a sharp medicine, but it is a physician for all diseases."

BACON TAKES CHARGE

Upon his death, Raleigh's enemies replaced him and created the Virginia Company of London. The Earl of Southampton, William Herbert (the third Earl of Pembroke), Thomas Cecil, Henry Neville, Sir Edwin Sandys, and Sir Francis Bacon were among its council.

Bacon was a key member of the Virginia Company of London and the colony's first secretary. William Strachey said he was the "most noble factor in the company"; in fact, he was the lord chancellor.[1] His influence is seen on the Virginia flag, where his Athena is shaking her spear. She also has her foot on the neck of a defeated enemy. The motto on the flag is *Sic semper tyrannis,* literally meaning "Thus always to tyrants" but is generally accepted as meaning "Death to tyrants." There is little doubt that the intention of this colony was that it not be subjected to foreign kings.

Athena is wearing the helmet that, as we know, gave her the power to be invisible. This recalls Bacon's first secret society, which had united with his Rosi Crosse group. They were the Invisibles.

In December of 1606 a little more than one hundred colonists set out on three ships for Virginia. They were gentlemen farmers not ready to get their hands dirty. By the time the year was up only thirty-eight would still be alive.

In June of 1609 the *Sea Venture* was the lead ship of a fleet of nine that set out to reinforce Jamestown, the first city in England's colony of Virginia. The nine ships between them carried a total of six hundred settlers. All was going well until a hurricane caught up with the fleet on July 24, 1609. For days this violent storm pounded the fleet, and when the seas were again quiet the ships of the fleet had separated. Later it was apparent that one of them had been lost in the Bermuda Triangle. Another had broken up on the deadly reef that surrounded the islands of Bermuda.

Four ships found each other and sailed on to Virginia. Then a second group of three reached the port of Jamestown. The lead ship was one of the ships that was presumed to have been lost.

LANDFALL IS MADE IN BERMUDA

The *Sea Venture* wasn't lost, however. Instead it had landed in Bermuda. The archipelago of islands that would later be named Bermuda was named for Juan de Bermudez, who had landed there in 1503. He called it the Isle of Devils. After his visit he advised the king that the island chain might serve as a supply station for Spain, but the pounding surf and the dangerous reef allowed few to land successfully. (As an interesting aside, Bermuda's motto is *Quo fata Ferunt*, "Whither the fates carry us.")

Another visitor to Bermuda was Columbus, who wrote in his log of strange lights and bizarre compass bearings in this part of the world. A Portuguese vessel had wrecked on the dangerous reefs in 1543, and a French vessel was grounded in 1594. Both were able to rebuild and sail on to safety.

The *Sea Venture* survived just long enough for the 150 passengers to launch a small craft and get everyone, as well as a great deal of supplies, to safety. Then it fell apart, having been weakened by the violent storm. Among those aboard were Sir Thomas Gates, who was scheduled to be the governor of Virginia; Sir George Somers, the admiral of the fleet who had served in the military with Sir Francis Drake and Robert Devereux; and William Strachey, a failed civil servant so deeply in debt that the New World was the only refuge he could find from his creditors. (Bacon may have saved him from debtors' prison.)

The survivors quickly found the island to be both a heaven and a hell. Most of them had never performed any real labor before or had any experience living in the wild. The cries of large birds, the crashing of wild boars in the brush, and the noise of the sea crushing their ship into splinters all served to send fear into the hearts of the castaways.

Before the wreck of the *Sea Venture* there were few who had seen the islands of Bermuda. The survivors quickly organized themselves and began building a new ship in which to complete their voyage to Virginia. They built this smaller ship from the wreckage of the *Sea Venture*. Hastily patched together it may not have been ready for the hundreds of miles of ocean between Bermuda and the Virginias, but off it went. Before those remaining on Bermuda could have received any word whether this voyage actually made landfall in Virginia (it wouldn't), they'd built two more ships, the *Deliverance* and the *Patience*. On May 10, 1610, these ships set sail for Virginia and would safely reach their destination with the settlers aboard.

There they found the colony in terrible shape. Their fort was run down, their attempts at agriculture had failed, and, after a series of dishonest encounters, the native population refused to trade with them. While the nearby river was rich with fish, native archers made attempts at fishing deadly. The Bermuda survivors were sorry that they had left the islands of Bermuda behind. Be this as it may, when the news of their salvation reached Europe, the tale of the *Sea Venture* was widely celebrated.

In Virginia, Jamestown, named for King James, was the site of the first permanent settlement and would be its first capital, until 1699. Colonists included John Rolfe, whose wife and child had died in Bermuda. He would go on to marry the famous Pocahontas. Williamsburg became the capital and remained so until 1780, when

Washington and Lafayette would drink together in the Raleigh Tavern in that city. Finally Richmond, named for Raleigh's home in England, would become the capital. Despite Raleigh's falling out with King James, the city's emblem is that of a White Shield and a Red Cross— Raleigh's Red Cross knight.

Virginia played a most important role in forming the democracy that became America, and Bermuda played a parallel role. Friends of Bacon and members of his intellectual circle decided that the Isle of Devils was not so bad after all. While the New World failed to become Bacon's utopia—an island ruled by an intellectual elite—it might serve as the closest example to his concept of a New Atlantis.

Bermuda was given little attention by the crown because it had no gold or resources. It survived on the edges of legitimate trade. In the research for my book *Secret Societies of America's Elite,* I found that illegal smuggling was accountable for one-third of all trade in Bermuda in the eighteenth century. The tiny island chain would become a conduit for goods needed by the colonial revolutionaries against the armies and navies of the English king George III. The colonies needed guns; Bermuda needed food.

Freemasonry was the glue that allowed such trade to be kept secret and when exposed, to go unpunished. The center of trade was the St. George Custom House, where the Lodge of St. George met. This building serves today as a government building whose design might best be described as early Freemasonry. All the trappings of Masonry are in plain sight.

The Source of Shakespeare's *Tempest?*

Many of the survivors of the Bermuda escapade headed back to England, but William Strachey stayed in Virginia. His circle of friends included Henry Wriothesley, Sir Francis Drake, Ben Jonson, Michael Drayton, Sir Philip Sidney, and Sir Francis Bacon. Many of these friends had shared schooling at Gray's Inn and enjoyed London's literary scene. Strachey had dropped out of Gray's Inn to begin what would be a life of failed endeavors.

In the first days ashore in Virginia on or about July 15, 1610, he composed a letter describing the adventure of being shipwrecked in Bermuda. Addressed to a Lady Sara, the wife of Sir Thomas Smith, it was actually more than a letter, for before he had completed it, the text was twenty-five thousand words long. In this missive Strachey describes not only the storm but also the verbal battles of the colonists that brought disharmony to them all. "The tempest of dissension" between the colonists and the tempest of a storm is said by some to have inspired *The Tempest.*

Strachey's letter would not be published until 1635. However, within two years of the shipwreck someone writing under the name of William Shakespeare produced a play called *The Tempest.* According to the First Folio, compiled in 1623, it was the last drama written by the Bard. *The Tempest* was written in 1611 and would be performed onstage later that year.

For those who debate the authorship of Shakespeare's works, *The Tempest*, because of its date and other references, became pivotal to the discussion. *The Tempest* tells the story of a shipwreck in the Mediterranean that strands Prospero, the Duke of Milan, with his daughter, on an island, along with passengers who survive. In it are passages from the Golding translation of Ovid and Florio's *Montaigne*, which are found in several other works attributed to Shakespeare. The most remarkable passage of *The Tempest* is found in act 1 when Ariel visits the "still vexed Bermoothes."

There would be little reason for Shakespeare to have been presented with the letters of those who had reported on the disaster. The survivors reached Virginia in May of 1610. A text called *Discovery of the Bermudas* was written by Sylvester Jourdain, a survivor who returned to England immediately. Next was *A True Declaration of the Estate of the Colonie in Virginia.* It was derived from several sources wishing to show the Virginia Colony in a good light. Third and most important was William Strachey's *True Reportory of the Wrack and the Redemption of Sir Thomas Gates Knight*. This was dated July 15, 1610. Although it was not published until much later, it is likely that Bacon and his inner circle, especially those who had invested in the venture, had the opportunity to view this report. The author of *The Tempest*, if it is based on these reports, either had an inside source or was involved in the Virginia Company itself.

The ship in the play was supposed to be carrying the king of Naples, Alonso. It was reported lost and the king drowned. The fleet of the *Sea Venture* had carried the governor of the new colony of Virginia. The ship sank and the governor apparently drowned.

Strachey's long letter describes the storm as "roaring" and the sky turning "blacke."[2] *The Tempest* says the waters were "roaring" and the sky pouring down "pitch." Both texts describe the men aboard calling out prayers. Both describe the leaky ships. Both ships had their masts cut down. Both describe throwing luggage overboard, both using that term. Both ships are run aground, and both have all passengers surviving.

The island in *The Tempest* and the islands of Bermuda are described in Strachey's letter; in Sylvester Jourdain's text, *Discovery of the Bermudas;* and in "Shakespeare's" play as full of devils. The island being part desert and part temperate is mentioned in both, as is oak and cedar, which was used to rebuild a ship. Strachey and the text attributed to Shakespeare mention owls, beetles, bats, and toads.

Plots against the leadership, dereliction of guard duty, failure to share in the work, and desertion are also described in both texts. Encountering Native Americans and encountering the cannibal Caliban link the stories as well. Strachey, in recalling the very brief history of Bermuda, mentions a Gonzalus Ferdinandus Oviedus, who may have been the first European. "Shakespeare's" characters include Gonzalo and Ferdinand.

Edward de Vere (the Earl of Oxford) often gets the credit for writing the works of Shakespeare. He could not publish under his own name because of the tenuous political climate, but that would not stop him completely. The problem with Oxford having written *The Tempest*, however, is that Oxford was already dead when the wreck occurred. Others claim that Oxford wrote *The Tempest* but hadn't based the tale on that of the *Sea Venture*. Instead, it may have been based either on a ship of Sir Walter Raleigh's that had been sailing in the Bermuda Triangle before Oxford's death or on another wreck involving Bartholomew Gosnold (whom we have discussed before), in 1602. All three voyages shared the same backer: Henry Wriothesley, the Earl of Southampton.

It is more than coincidence that Southampton was Shakespeare's principal patron and provided him with funds to buy his first home in Stratford. Southampton's close circle included Sir Francis Bacon, Edward de Vere, Roger Manners, and others, all of whom are suspected of authoring the plays of William Shakespeare.

If *The Tempest*, with its "Bermoothes" reference, was written after the death of both Oxford and Christopher Marlowe, are there other suspects? Sir Francis Bacon is the best choice. *Players*, by Bertram Fields, contains a list of several lines that are close or exact to those between Bacon's *Promus of Formularies and Elegancies* and Shakespeare's plays. At least one Baconian proverb, "Thought is free," is exactly mirrored in *The Tempest*.

William Stanley, another suspected author of the works attributed to Shakespeare, was the Earl of Derby. *The Tempest* contains a character, Ferdinand, the son of the king of Naples, who may have been named for Stanley's brother.

The greatest candidate, however, for being the author of many of Shakespeare's works always brings us back to Francis Bacon, which brings us back to the stories of Virginia and Bermuda. Like the patron Henry Wriothesley, Bacon was very much involved in the New World. As we know, when Bacon studied at Gray's Inn he founded an invisible knighthood, the Order of the Helmet, with its figurehead Pallas

Athena, depicted with both helmet and spear. The influence of Bacon and others who promoted the Virginia Colony is evident in the way that their goddess remains on the Virginia state flag four hundred years later. It must also be pointed out that the crest of Sir Francis Bacon contains a wild boar, which is identical to the heraldic device of Bermuda.

PLACE-NAMES AND THEIR CONNECTION TO BACON'S COHORTS

In 1612, sixty Englishmen would settle in Bermuda, which is made up of 181 small islands. And like New Orleans, it's divided into parishes. The island was split into sectors known as "tribes," although the connotation must have been different then. Today it is made up of parishes that were named for those involved with the early Virginia Company, who were intimates of Bacon's.

Evidence of Bacon's circle is reflected in nearly every parish. Southampton Parish, for instance, was named after Henry Wriothesley, the Earl of Southampton. He was an initial member of the Virginia Company and joined the Bermuda Company in 1615 before dying in military action in the Netherlands in 1624 at the age of fifty-one.

Devonshire Parish is named for William Cavendish, the first Earl of Devonshire (1552–1626). He was uncle of the Earl of Pembroke and born into great wealth. The community that he was the leader of was initially called the Cavendish Tribe, and members held shares in it. William held the greatest amount. He remained undistinguished as a member of Parliament during Elizabeth's reign but was given a baronetcy by King James I and bought his title as an earl. In 1612 he was a member of the Virginia Company, and when the Bermuda Company was established in 1615, he was a founding member of that as well.

Pembroke Parish was named for the third Earl of Pembroke. This is the man to whom Shakespeare's 1623 folio is dedicated. He was a Knight of the Order of the Garter and actively involved in the Virginia

Company and, like Cavendish, was a founding member of the Bermuda Company in 1615. Through marriage the Pembroke family was related to Philip Sidney, author of *Arcadia*. He may have been the wealthiest peer in England. Pembroke was also a close friend of Bacon. The capricious Queen Elizabeth banned him from the court because of his religious interests, but he did well under King James. He would be the largest shareholder of the Pembroke Parish.

James Hamilton would lend his name to Hamilton Parish. Hamilton Parish had previously been known as the Harrington Tribe, whose Lucy Harrington was influential in the Elizabethan court. James Hamilton, one of the influential Scots who came to London with the Stuart king James, was rewarded by the king with titles and became a Knight of the Order of the Garter as well.

Paget Parish was another early parish in Bermuda. It had been named for one of the early gentlemen adventurers of the Virginia Company. William Paget, the fourth Lord Paget, was born to a Catholic father. He became a Protestant and served with Essex but was still not trusted by the queen. He too would do much better when James came to power.

St. George's Parish is named for George Somers, who was a friend of Raleigh's. He died in Bermuda in 1610. He had captured Spanish treasure ships and warships alike. When he died, his heart was entombed in St. George's Parish; his body was returned home.

Warwick Parish was named for Robert Rich, the second Earl of Warwick. He had his own troupe of actors named the Earl of Warwick's Men, which was managed by Edward de Vere at one point. The company put on plays that were later attributed to Shakespeare. Rich might not have known that Bacon's circle was producing the plays, but he suspected something was amiss. Rich would call Shakespeare "Shakes Scenes" and accused him of both buying plays and stealing scenes. Like Bacon, the Earl of Warwick frequently did not see eye to eye with England's monarchy, which could be very capricious. He was once imprisoned for condemning illegal taxation. Like others favored in the Elizabethan court, including Drake and Raleigh, he would send privateers to the Caribbean to disrupt Spanish shipping.

Sandys Parish was named for Sir Edwin Sandys, a member of Parliament from 1586. He was one of the aristocrats who accompanied James I to London the year the queen died, and he was rewarded by James by being knighted. A very early member of the Virginia Company, he was responsible for enlisting many in the adventure of immigrating to the New World. In 1615 he became a founding member of the Bermuda Company.

Smith's Parish was named for Thomas Smith. A haberdasher's assistant, he rose to become knighted by King James and was made a governor of the East India Company as well as the Somers Isles Company.

BACON'S LAST AND BEST-KEPT SECRET

The city of Williamsburg, Virginia, had been founded according to an architectural plan. According to writer Cort Lindahl, "The layout of Williamsburg and all the associated Rosicrucian and Masonic symbolism indicate that Jefferson may have been carrying out a plan set into motion by Sir Francis Bacon."[3] It is clear that Jefferson had inherited Bacon's plan for a New World, built according to various alignments. He would influence the building of several properties in a fashion that would be echoed later in Washington, D.C., and other prominent cities.

Visitors to Virginia's Colonial Williamsburg Park are able to get a sense of what America was like in the seventeenth century when settlers from England arrived on its shores to create a New World. Tourists walk on quaint streets filled with brick houses and blacksmith shops, hear canned speeches from costumed characters as in a historical Disneyland, and visit souvenir shops for a piece of history to take home. Few know that they are walking over, literally, a secret vault containing the writings of Sir Francis Bacon and others. If they did they might have a truer picture of what Virginia was really all about.

Creating settlements in America was the goal of several secret societies, as we have seen. In Virginia, there was no gold to be stolen from ancient cultures—that took place much farther south. There was no wealth to be derived from the fur trade—that was much farther north. Virginia was an experiment in creating a New World where more than one religion might be tolerated. Bacon's plan for Virginia, as well as the whole continent, was detailed in his *New Atlantis;* it was to be a place where religion would be a matter of choice, where rule would be established by vote, and where science would not be punishable by horrific torture and death. In short, it would be where liberty would be more than a word.

Colonies, however, needed to be funded by businessmen and sanctioned by kings and queens. Royalty might be induced to back their settlement so they could lay claim to glory, or at least to the possible acquisition of large tracts of land that would be given names immortalizing them: Virginia for Elizabeth, or Jamestown for King James, for instance. Investors needed more concrete returns, which tobacco, sugar, rum, and slaves might provide.

Of necessity, the secret societies that were extant at the time had to keep their secrets. Sir Walter Raleigh said of Bacon, "And thy great genius in being concealed, is revealed." Such genius threatened both church and state. But Bacon's pen could not be stopped. Indeed, some believe that in addition to *New Atlantis,* Bacon had sketched out what would become the American Constitution, and his work describes a congress of educated men. William Rawley (Bacon's chaplain) and Thomas Bushnell (a servant of Bacon's who also helped to establish the Royal Mint) were two people who believed this.

Again, Bacon had insisted that these works be kept under wraps until his death. And what better place to hide such secrets than underground repositories? As mentioned earlier, Bacon's chaplain, William Rawley, hinted that Bacon's greatness would be revealed at a later date. The chaplain also served as his secretary and most trusted friend. Some believe that Rawley indeed took charge of his works. Following Bacon's instructions, coded within his writings, Rawley would see that they were protected.

As we have previously discussed but bears repeating here, in 1911, Orville Ward Owen, after deciphering Bacon's codes, led an expedition to try to find a vault under the river Wye near Gloucester, England. They did find the vault, just where Owen said it would be. They also found markings that Bacon had employed. What they did not find was Bacon's manuscripts. Owen believed that the same man who had created the underwater hiding place in the first place had been responsible for moving the documents a second time, to the Americas. As previously established, Rawley, who lived until 1660, may have brought the Bacon documents to America.

Owen would go on to search in the Americas and on Oak Island, Nova Scotia, for the trove of Bacon's writings. Knowing that Bacon had believed that mercury could preserve documents (indeed he had written about this specifically in *Sylva Sylvarum*), Owen checked to see if any evidence of mercury had been found over the years by any of the previous parties searching for the vault. He was informed that a dump on the island had turned up numerous flasks that had residues of mercury in them. In addition, apparently a boatswain's whistle and an old coin dating the workings to the Elizabethan period had also been found.

According to more modern researchers there are numerous vaults in America that might also be likely candidates for being the repository for Bacon's work.

Williamsburg's Bruton Church is one of these. It had been built in Williamsburg to resemble St. Mary's Church in Bruton, Somerset, England, which had been constructed in Saxon times when King Arthur rose to save Briton from the invading hordes. John Dee, the queen's adviser on matters of practicality as well as astrology, had told her that Arthur had come to America, thereby establishing England's claim to the continent.

In the chancel of the English church is the burial crypt of Sir Charles

Berkeley, who had come to Virginia to serve as governor in 1639 and who was responsible for the construction of the Williamsburg church of the same name. It's worth noting that, at this time, Rawley was still alive and was still the guardian of Bacon's writings.

The history of Williamsburg is not accessible on any exact level. Court records were destroyed, and much of its original history has been lost as a result. What is known is that the area called the Middle Plantation was where the Bruton Church was laid out in 1633. Three original wood-built churches and parishes were merged into one, which was then called the Bruton Parish. Bruton Parish would become Williamsburg in 1699.

Somewhere between 1633 and 1699, most likely in 1676, a new church was built of brick. By this time the vault was already in place, twenty feet under the ground.

CLUES ABOUND

In 1938 an excavation took place, revealing the original foundation of the Bruton Church. The church had been moved! And there was more than just a vault twenty feet under the original church. There was also a tunnel system leading to a vaulted brick chamber that was 330 feet long. Tunnels were not uncommon in the colonies—given that they afforded protection from marauding Native Americans—yet few of them were as elaborate as this system of tunnels, which might indicate that something of great importance was being protected. Today, in some locations, parts of the tunnel have been sealed. However, the system still extends to the College of William and Mary at the western end of Duke of Gloucester Street.

To offer some semblance of the significance of this college, four of America's first ten presidents were associated with William and Mary. Indeed, author David Allen Rivera's book *Archaeological Conspiracy at Williamsburg* found evidence that the vault and its tunnels are connected to the home of Martha Dandridge Custis Washington.

Of this network of tunnels and buildings, the Wren building at William and Mary was constructed in 1695. Under the college chapel a crypt houses the remains of many Virginia notables.

In all, the Robert Carter House, the George Wythe House, the King's Arms Tavern, and other notable buildings share underground tunnels with the Wren Building and the Bruton Church.

During her research, Marie Bauer Hall, the wife of Masonic philosopher Manly Palmer Hall, noticed a tomb outside the entrance to the tower in the churchyard. It is the tomb of James Nicholson, who had been a steward at the college of William & Mary.[4] The inscription on the tomb includes a handful of words that are larger than the others. One word, *reader,* was a clue, according to Hall, as to the location of the vault. Another tomb, the Ludwell Tomb, the resting place of Thomas Ludwell, the first person to be buried at Bruton, contained similar references in code through the use of larger letters, offering up the name Francis Bacon.[5] Hall came to no official conclusion, except to be curious about such a coded system of which only few would be aware.

Marie Bauer Hall also mentions that the location of the vault was ten feet west of the grave marker of a woman by the name of Ann Frank. Ann Frank had married a man by the name of Graham Frank, and her tomb marker, which contains the name Ann Graham (anagram), may be a hint that an anagram will provide a clue to the vault.

In Marie Bauer Hall's own book *Foundations Unearthed* she refers to a book written in 1635 by George Wither, the English poet, pamphleteer, and satirist. In the book, published before many of the Williamsburg buildings were erected, are depictions of these future buildings. A Rockefeller restoration official pointed this out to Hall, although the same official was not able to explain how this came to be. More astounding is that that the picture of the book's author, George Wither, was actually a picture of Shakespeare. A device that Bacon created, called the bar sinister, is next to this picture of Wither. The bar sinister device was a known symbol of illegitimacy. To those versed in Bacon's codes, it is a telling sign that this is not an image of George Wither. Rather, it indicates that the illegitimate man is Shakespeare, with Bacon standing behind his mask.

George Wither was known to be one of an inner group of Rosicrucians. Hard to explain is that Wither, writing in England, verified the existence of the Bruton vault. This can only mean that its construction had been planned in England. Henrietta Bernstein in her *Ark of the Covenant, Holy Grail* points out that this indicates that American history was carried out according to a great plan of Bacon and his group.

It has been suggested that, in all, the vault was built to house proof of Bacon's real parents (namely Queen Elizabeth and Robert Dudley, the Earl of Leicester), his writings and those of several others, thirty-three hermetically sealed copper cylinders, a key to the location of other vaults contained throughout America and Europe, and possibly jewels, including a tiara that had belonged to Queen Elizabeth and was later given to Bacon.

Besides Bacon, the other writers who may have been contributors to the literary trove are collectively referred to as the Good Pens. This group includes Francis Drake, Walter Raleigh, Christopher Marlowe, and Ben Jonson.

Some claim that the contents of the vault would be revealed in codes that were embedded in the works of Shakespeare and that might only be deciphered by understanding the cryptography employed therein.

The Bruton vault has also been called the Bacon vault. Bacon's sister and her husband, Bartholomew Gosnold, were at Jamestown and might have been part of the plan to protect whatever Bacon secrets were brought to America. Gosnold's grave was recently discovered just outside of the original boundaries of Jamestown. His remains included a staff resembling the Rod of Ptah from ancient Egypt. Is this still another sign of Rosicrucianism among the early colonists?

Does this reference the long-standing tradition mentioned earlier, that of an architect or leader being buried outside of his work or primary seat of power? Freemasons understand the importance of the architect both as it relates to the "Great Architect above" and the human archi-

tect below. Examples from history abound: Hiram Abiff is the legendary temple builder who was bludgeoned to death by masons' tools by
three men who took turns striking him. Mimar Sinan (1489–1588)
was the chief Ottoman architect and civil engineer for Suleiman the
Magnificent. He built the Suleiman Mosque in Istanbul, which blended
Islamic and Byzantine elements. He is buried in a tomb of his own
design outside the mosque.

Refocusing our attention on the Bruton vault, if such a valuable
treasure exists and is relatively accessible, especially in comparison to
Nova Scotia's Oak Island vault, why is it still underground? The first
possible rationale is that the wealthy and powerful Rockefeller family
owns Williamsburg. They are the inheritors of one of the world's greatest fortunes. They are also considered by some to be the masterminds
behind a plan for a one-world government, given their leadership roles on
the Council on Foreign Relations and the Trilateral Commission. They
might simply desire to avoid unnecessary disruption on their property, or,
as others believe, they may wish to keep any treasure found to themselves.

It's clear that in seeking to find treasure, they spared no expense in
buying and tearing down every structure they could to create the colonial Williamsburg that greets the visiting tourist today. Seven hundred
modern homes were torn down to make room for eighty-one colonial
buildings. Not everyone was willing to sell, however, and the Bruton
Church was one property the Rockefellers had difficulty purchasing.
It came with a cemetery that extended sixty feet around the church.
The land for it had been donated by a man named John Page before his
death in 1692. It is under this land that the vault is located.

Author David Allen Rivera's 2007 book *Archaeological Conspiracy
at Williamsburg* specifically states his suspicion that the Rockefeller
family wishes to locate the contents of the vault. Fletcher Richman, a
leader among proponents of conducting a serious excavation of the site,
shares this opinion in one of his booklets. He believes it may be one of
America's greatest treasures and that the family might simply want to
keep it for themselves.

It may be of no minor coincidence that the Rockefellers played no minor role in the restoration of Stratford-upon-Avon as well. While not as elaborate as Williamsburg, Stratford, complete with numerous restorations, attracts hundreds of thousands of visitors every year.

Marie Bauer Hall's book on the Bruton vault referenced a conversation that claimed everyone knew about the tunnels, "but since the Rockefellers came, it has become a big secret."[6] The tunnel opens on one end at the home of Rockefeller's lawyer, who played a role in getting clear titles to the various deeds of real estate involved in the re-creation of colonial Williamsburg.

Marie Bauer Hall was allowed to excavate to look for the vault in 1938, but despite utilizing ground-penetrating radar, she was unable to locate it. Since that time there have been several other attempts to dig for the vault, almost all unsanctioned. One that was sanctioned in 1991 found no vault or treasure. This does not satisfy the most vocal proponent of a full excavation, Fletcher Richman, who believes the excavators were deliberately misled.

In 2006, just before the four-hundred-year anniversary of Jamestown, Richman was back in Williamsburg. His group, called the Sir Francis Bacon Sages of the Seventh Seal, applied again for permission to investigate and excavate but was told their chances of obtaining said permission were "next to zero."

There was much more intrigue in the settling of Virginia than the history books acknowledge. In Virginia and elsewhere (as we will see in the next chapter), a handful of leaders are known to have avoided accepted religious beliefs and may have been Rosicrucians.

CHAPTER 10

THE ROSY CROSS OVER PENNSYLVANIA

Perhaps no one man did more to ensure that Bacon's vision and the Rosicrucian tradition found a firm foundation in the New World than William Penn. He is the founder of Pennsylvania and the guiding force in bringing the tradition to America.

Born in 1644 in London, by the age of thirty he had conceptualized his own version of a utopia where man was free to worship as he chose. Penn would be given land on both sides of the Delaware River to fulfill his vision. At its center would be Philadelphia, the City of Brotherly Love.

He was the son of Admiral William Penn, and, notably, a Quaker. Today his statue stands tall over the Philadelphia skyline, showing his peaceful and content visage, which was the model, some say, for the image found on the front of a box of Quaker Oats cereal. Despite this pacific image, in his own time Penn was regarded as a rabble-rouser and a rebel, and Quakers were regularly arrested for holding to their beliefs. Penn challenged the English religion, as had Benjamin Franklin. Penn was thrown out of Oxford and then thrown out of his father's home. Like writers of the generation before him he also spent time in the Tower of London for his works. His book *The Sandy Foundation Shaken* dismisses the Catholic concept of the Trinity and the Calvinist theory of justification and therefore challenged official dogma and doctrines.

It did not amuse the king. At one of Penn's trials the jury voted to acquit the young firebrand. The judge, perhaps on orders, then arrested the entire jury.[1]

Four times Penn would be imprisoned, and four times his father successfully interceded on his behalf.

ELEMENTS OF THE ROSICRUCIAN TRADITION EMERGE IN WILLIAM PENN'S SYLVAN WOODS

Penn the younger pushed the envelope quite often and, despite frequent persecutions, wrote a constitution for a colony in the New World. Its coauthor was Algernon Sidney, who was the grandnephew of Sir Philip Sidney and a follower of the Bacon philosophy. This is the same Sir Philip who authored *Arcadia* and who was close friends with Sir Walter Raleigh, Sir Francis Drake, Sir Francis Walsingham, the Earl of Leicester, and Fulke Greville. The School of Night had left its mark, and others would keep its philosophy of independence and the right to civil liberties alive as time continued to pass.

The death of Penn's father revealed that King Charles was deeply in debt to the elder man. King Charles saw a means of killing two birds in one simple act: grant a large landmass in the New World to Penn the younger, providing he left England. What would be called Penn's Woods was the king's idea of honoring the admiral (Penn's father). In such a way was the province of Pennsylvania born. Penn was thirty-six when he received a charter to this land from the king.

And although William Penn didn't get to name the future state, he would get to name his city. However, he didn't specifically name Philadelphia the City of Brotherly Love. Instead he had been influenced by the book of Revelation, chapter 3, which states: "He that hath an ear, let him hear what the Spirit saith unto the churches." Jesus used the same phrase, *He that hath an ear,* numerous times. It allegedly referred to those who had been initiated into the Christian faith—those who could comprehend the lesson of the teaching. The author of the book of Revelation was directing a letter to the "angel of the Church in Philadelphia" (in Asia Minor). The letter states that the Holy One, the True One, will preserve from trial those who keep his word. Philadelphia was the city dedicated to those who kept his word, those "brothers" who formed a community of love. Today, in Philadelphia's city hall, a quote from the book of Revelation is inscribed into the wall.

William Penn crossed the Atlantic in 1682 to create his new world and, specifically, his new city. He hoped it would be a city of brotherly love where all people would get along. This was in contrast to the city of Babel in the Old Testament, where language was confounded by God, thus dividing the populace. He wanted it to be the new Babylon, a city between two rivers. Geographically, Philadelphia met that criterion. Like that city in Mesopotamia (meaning "between two rivers"), Philadelphia was situated between the Delaware and Schuylkill Rivers. The city was laid out in a gridiron pattern with parallel avenues running east and west and crisscrossing avenues running north and south. The great rectangle was not organized perfectly to the east and west but fixed ten degrees south of east. The result is that the sun aligns with the city's streets on two dates equidistant from the two equinoxes.

These two dates, taken together, might symbolize the death and rebirth cycle, which was thinly veiled in Christianity and more openly celebrated in the Celtic tradition.

In 1682, Masonry in England had yet to go public. Instead it was in the process of changing from the tradition of *craft* masonry to *speculative* Masonry. This change from craft to study of high concepts involved the laying out of cities and the building of bridges, churches, and cathedrals. This was Bacon's doing. Masonry would be for those who worked not only with their hands but also those who sought to understand the universe and the sciences.

There is no doubt that William Penn was at least influenced by

Bacon and Rosicrucian tradition. He first broke bread in the oldest tavern in Philadelphia in 1682. Its name was not a coincidence. The name—the Blue Anchor Tavern—invokes a distinctive Rosicrucian symbol. It was by a dock at the corner of Front Street and Dock Street. At the time this was one of the desirable places to live in Penn's city. Much later the water around the dock became polluted, although the tavern itself survived into the nineteenth century.

Northeast from the center of the city is Bensalem. This was named for the Bensalem envisioned in Bacon's *New Atlantis*. In Bacon's Bensalem, all were free to study, experiment, read and write, and worship.

A decade later William Penn would get a full charter for Pennsylvania. It would be known as the Great Experiment. This immediately catalyzed a large number of immigrants to move there. Penn's welcome went out to thousands of Quakers as well as German sects in Europe. George Fox, a friend of Penn's, had initiated the Quaker movement. Fox preached the Inner Light in the late 1640s. Quakers were mystics, unlike the Puritans, who were quite literal. By 1680 there were eighty thousand Quakers throughout the world, and they were often persecuted.

The Quaker doctrine was genuine in religious toleration, and the Quaker Society of Friends was a pacifist organization. Even though Penn himself distinguished between wars of aggression and wars of defense, many in his community were against bearing arms at any cost.

Through his efforts he recruited many Germans from the Continent. By the time of the American Revolution, Pennsylvania was only one-third English. Germantown was settled in response to Penn's invitation to Francis Daniel Pastorius, who would be influential in Pennsylvania's emerging society.

KELPIUS AND THE PIETISTS ARRIVE

The Pietists arrived in 1694. They were led by a young man by the name of Johann Kelpius. Born Johann Kelp in Schassburg, he had attended

Bavaria's University of Altdorf, where he Latinized his name. At the age of sixteen he had obtained his master's in theology and had published several works. Part Pietist and part Rosicrucian, his studies were steeped in what the Catholic Church would say was heresy. He learned from the German theologian Johann Jacob Zimmerman, who wished to create his own Chapter of Perfection in America. Zimmerman was well read in various occult philosophers, from Jakob Boehme to Johannes Valentinus Andreae, and studied the Kabbalah and Rosicrucian texts.

Boehme had written the *Mysterium Magnum,* a commentary on the book of Genesis that opened the eyes and imagination of many. His commentary on the hidden physiology of the human body, the correspondence between parts of the body and the planets, and the relationship between minerals and plants is remarkable. Even more remarkable is that he had been born to illiterate parents and apprenticed to a cobbler.

One day a stranger entered the cobbler's shop and told the young man that he would do great things. The stranger said, "Be courageous and persevere, for God loves thee." Boehme would then go through what can only be described as illuminations, wherein he saw the world and himself from a higher consciousness. His works would influence William Blake, John Milton, Samuel Taylor Coleridge, and various religious groups including the Quakers and Pietists.

Kelpius led the Pietists to the New World in 1694. When Zimmerman died the year before the trip was made, Kelpius had quickly stepped up to lead it, proving himself to be a charismatic mystic who brought medicine, music, and magic to this break-off Protestant sect. He had met Jane Leade in London. She was a prophetess who founded the Philadelphia movement in 1670 and a medium who claimed the ability to channel the Virgin Sophia.

The brotherhood of Kelpius took passage to America in 1694. They landed in Philadelphia at the Blue Anchor Tavern on Saint John's Eve, which was the eve of the feast day of Saint John the Baptist, celebrated on June 24 every year.

They lived as hermits in the wooded area known today as Fairmont Park on the banks of the Wissahickon Creek. Today street names such as Hermit Terrace and Hermit Lane recall the reclusive mystics. They constructed a monastery of wood to await the fulfilling of the prophecy that would be the Apocalypse. A great sign was to appear in the heavens. According to the book of Revelation 12:1 this would be "a woman clothed with the sun, and the moon under her feet, and upon her head a crown of twelve stars."

They called themselves the Society of the Woman of the Wilderness and blended a pagan Druidism with Rosicrucian theology. Many have compared the group to a doomsday cult awaiting the end. The "end" was supposed to happen in 1694, the year they arrived, and the next "end" was predicted to occur in the year 1700. But it was not an end as much as a second beginning that they sought.

Near Hermit Lane is a cave where Kelpius meditated and sometimes gathered together his brotherhood. They measured the skies, practiced astrology, experimented with alchemy, and studied numerology. They would heal the sick without charge, a key Rosicrucian tenet, and they founded the first free public Sunday school. It was nonsectarian, given that they hoped all churches and sects would participate in it.

They also established an observatory, built the first organ in the colonies, and created botanical gardens for research. They built meetinghouses for religious practices. These were not just for themselves; they invited everyone to meet in them and exchange ideas. In short, they created the type of utopia that Bacon had envisioned. On the feast day of Saint John the Baptist they held a celebration that was said to cause visions of angels. June 24 was also acknowledged to be the anniversary of the sect's arrival in Pennsylvania, but to members it was understood as the day the sun enters the astrological sign of Cancer. As had been done from early pagan times on this date, they celebrated by lighting a bonfire.

The brotherhood considered the number 40 to be sacred. Indeed, it was a very important number in both the Christian and Hebrew scriptures. Kelpius's community generally numbered forty members. The wooden monastery they built was forty feet by forty feet, as was their burial ground. Symbols found in Kelpius's cave indicate a Rosicrucian influence, and in 1961 a Rosicrucian monument was placed outside of it.

In 1708, however, the end was near. Kelpius contracted pneumonia, no doubt from the rugged lifestyle he endured. He is said to have placed some important artifacts in a box and instructed a follower by the name of Daniel Geissler to throw the box in the Schuylkill River. Geissler said that he completed the task, but Kelpius knew that he hadn't. He instructed him again, and this time Geissler did the job he was assigned to do. When the box, which was called the Arcanum, hit the water, an explosion took place, complete with thunder and lightning emerging from the water. Legend has it that the box contained the philosopher's stone, a coveted alchemical preparation.

The Wissahickon Creek became the Ganges of the Rosicrucians in America. Ben Franklin and George Washington had connections to the group, with Washington being described as "an acolyte" of the Wissahickon sect.[2] A Pietist he met through the group, Peter Miller, would translate the Declaration of Independence into German for the large local population that did not speak English and for export to Europe. Franklin would keep his connections even after the group had left Philadelphia for Ephrata.

This began to happen as his community drifted apart after Kelpius's death, although not all of them left the city. Six holy men remained, one of whom was Johann Seelig. At his death his staff was thrown into the Schuylkill River, and it too exploded upon hitting the water.[3] As time went on, the Monks of the Ridge, as they were known, were regularly called upon for help in finding a suitable marriage partner or casting an astrological chart.

The formation and settlement of Kelpius and his group in Pennsylvania represented a trend that would continue into the future as similar groups formed and settled there as well. Wave after wave would arrive, the Mennonites, Hutterites, Swiss Brethren, Schwenkfelders, and Amish, fleeing religious persecution or war. Many of the oppressed religions were thinly disguised variations on the Protestant religion. Many of the fleeing individuals were like the Monks of the Ridge, who derided such concepts as predestination and dualism and the limitations they set on the human imagination. They believed that such philosophical points of division allowed religious men to fall into the devil's work. To what point would the True One have his children murdering each other over such concepts? He wouldn't. Love, faith, and good works were stressed.

Again we see echoes of Bacon's philosophy in these peace-loving, tolerant groups.

The last member of the six Monks of the Ridge was an Englishman by the name of Christopher Witt. Witt had studied anatomy and biology in his home country before sailing to America in 1704. He was adept in medicine and was awarded the first medical degree in Pennsylvania. He was also adept in architecture, astrology, botany, and music. His healing powers mixed science and folk medicine and were prized by the community. The Germans regarded him as a *Hexenmeister*—one who can lift curses or, if one willed, place spells. The English equivalent would be a warlock. The Germans who settled farther west, the Amish, are known for their hex signs—said to ward off evil—as well.

In 1718, Witt bought 125 acres in Germantown. He earned his income by farming and practicing astrology and medicine. He lived out his life with Daniel Geissler and kept in touch with the other wizards. When he died in 1765 he was buried alongside Geissler and other monks in the community's graveyard on High Street. Spectral blue flames were said to dance around his grave for weeks. The hermit's grave became known as Spook Hill until an Episcopal church named St. Michael's was built on the site in 1859. A black congregation later took over the church, and it is now known as the High Street Church of God. Daniel Geissler and Witt are said to lie directly under the altar.[4]

By 1720, Rosicrucian chapters were meeting in taverns throughout Philadelphia. According to Robert Hieronimus in *Founding Fathers, Secret Societies,* Franklin had his own lodge.

UNORTHODOXY WAS THE STANDARD FARE

From Francis Bacon to William Penn to Benjamin Franklin a spiritual torch of enlightenment was passed. The dark corners of Europe gave way to the Great Experiment, as Penn called it.

Religious belief was wide open, and new faiths were challenging the old. Not every faith believed in the toleration hoped for by Bacon and Penn, however. Among Protestants, there was hostility against Anabaptists, a branch that had started in Switzerland and southern Germany. Anabaptists were called Swiss Brethren, but even with both Catholic and Protestant Churches against them they were often divided. Amish are their most well-known sect; Hutterites and Mennonites follow. Many members of both of these sects sought refuge in the New World, specifically Pennsylvania.

Radical branches of Moravians settled in Bethlehem, Pennsylvania, while others sought shelter in Philadelphia. Methodists, United Brethren, Church of the Brethren, Brotherhood of Zion, Shakers, Dunkards, Society of Friends, and others changed Pennsylvania dramatically.

With the many sects came a host of charismatic leaders. One from the Palatinate was Conrad Beissel, born in 1691. He was initiated into Rosicrucianism and may have achieved its highest rank. He was knowledgeable as a mystic and familiar with Paracelsus and the Kabbalah. His teachings were described as "Rosicrucian doctrine pure and undefiled."[5]

Beissel had a strong relationship with the Wissahickon hermits, who we have just discussed. They placed a great emphasis on the sciences. Indeed, a clock made by Christopher Witt remains in a structure called the Saron that still stands today in Ephrata. Furthermore, the clock still strikes the hours.

Under Beissel's direction work began on a chapter house that, when completed in 1738, would house the Ephrata community. It would be three stories high, and its ground floor would be used for storage. The second floor was circular and was used for sleeping. The third floor was eighteen feet square and had four windows, each facing a cardinal direction. Secret rites of rejuvenation were practiced in this temple area. Thirteen members would spend forty days and forty nights here, beginning on the night of the first full moon in May. This sojourn involved purging the body through fasting and laxatives, shedding blood, and partaking of the "grain of elixir." Whatever this substance was, it caused convulsions, sweating, and loss of speech.[6]

This Zionitic Brotherhood would be dressed in white. They walked barefoot, like the Essenes had two thousand years before. Such a band of thirteen might draw comparisons to Jesus and twelve apostles or a coven of witches. However, whatever secrets were contained within the chapter house at Ephrata remained in the chapter house.

If Quakers and Pietists were considered unorthodox they were not the only sects to be thought of in this way. Radical groups with alternative views concerning gender, sex, marriage, and community poured into Pennsylvania. They were the first groups from Germany to take any interest in North America. Many of the larger groups were offshoots of the sixteenth-century radical Reformation movement. In addition to the groups already mentioned, they also included the Schwenkfelders, the Waldensians, and the Moravians; these were the sects that established the melting pot that was Pennsylvania at the time.

The Moravians were a radical group from the German-speaking territories (although historians tend to play down their radical beliefs). They were descended from the old Hussite movements of Bohemia and Moravia. Count Nicholas Ludwig von Zinzendorf was their leader.

They lived in close communities in Bethlehem and Nazareth, and their clergy was both male and female. They also counted both male and female members of the nobility among their number. They were divided into groups by sex and age and called these groups choirs. They had rites of communion and baptism and indulged in love feasts, singing, and elaborate rituals that celebrated marriage and sex. Zinzendorf's group was in the Netherlands in the 1730s and sent missions to America.

The Moravians in Bethlehem were a secretive group. Women would generally be housed in buildings on one side of the street and men in buildings on the opposite side. Today, when tour guides give their talks about the early buildings, they can be persuaded to come clean about the tunnels connecting them. Did men sneak through the tunnels under the street to visit the women? Actually their sex lives were a whole lot stranger than that.

The Sun Inn, built on the grounds of the Moravian community in 1758, was said to connect the tunnels, have hidden chambers, and be the hiding place of a treasure belonging to one mysterious cleric by the name of Brother Albrecht. The inn was one more place that Washington slept, as did luminaries such as Lafayette, the Adamses, Pulaski, von Steuben, and the chiefs of several Indian tribes.

For many of the sects this was a time of spiritual exploration. Moravians would take experimentation to new levels, with the towns of Bethlehem and Nazareth becoming central to their economy as well as their spiritual lives. The Moravians would come to believe that they had discovered the feminine Jesus and the androgyny of the Trinity and Jesus. They didn't invent the idea of a female Jesus; this concept can be traced to Gnostics in 80–200 CE. And images of a feminine Jesus abounded in Cistercian communities. At Ephrata, Sophia represented God's femaleness.

Indeed, the Moravians claimed that *all* souls were female. The Holy Spirit had hovered over the waters at the Creation and was Mother. And to them, the Holy Spirit was more the Mother of Jesus than Mary was. She protected him and brought him into the light. Moravians, both male and female, also claimed to hold an erotic love for Jesus. Moravian men may have had homoerotic relations, given that the men were separated from the women.

Gender transformations and single men and women kissing in public had helped get the Moravians kicked out of Europe. Now in Pennsylvania they found that their sexual experimentation was considered obscene to outsiders. Zinzendorf and the Moravians declared that sex between husband and wife was holy, a service to God. Believers received a blessing during intercourse. In Bethlehem, husband and wife slept separately but were allowed to meet for fifteen minutes in a special room for the purpose of having sex. When they were done, the next couple inhabited the room.

Moravians would later burn many of their records.

Their enemies were immigrants from the Lutheran and Reformed movements, which made up a large percent of the Germans arriving between 1730 and 1754. This was a peak period of conflict with the Moravians. Women who were Moravians were allowed to preach in Pennsylvania. The orthodox sects said this was anarchy, and the Reformed and Lutheran sects wanted to stop them.

Today the numerous sects that stretch west from Philadelphia to Ephrata and north to Bethlehem still have a rich, colorful tradition that often remains sub rosa. Visitors to the Moravian Museum of Bethlehem will get a PG version of their history. Yet everywhere hints of the past exist. In tiny Pricetown, Pennsylvania, stands a church that was dedicated on the Friday of the winter solstice.

In the late eighteenth century, Pricetown was home to what was known as the Dunkard or Brethren community. They were pacifists living the utopian dream of Bacon and Penn. As time wore on they did away with distinctive hats and dress, unlike the neighboring

Mennonite and Amish. Their church in Pricetown would, in modern times, be considered a United Church of Christ.

This church contains a marvel of Masonic and Rosicrucian symbols inside, and its altar features two columns more commonly found in a Masonic Temple. The windows, walls, and even the ceiling, are decorated in a Rosicrucian motif. As historian of religion Barbara Brown Zikmund put it, "Yet among the mature we do impart wisdom, although it is not a wisdom of this age, or of the rulers of this age, who are doomed to pass away. But we impart a secret and hidden wisdom of God."[7]

The colonies settled by England were positioned to achieve their religious and philosophical goals. As shown, Massachusetts actually had more restrictive rules and beliefs whereas Virginia had more open attitudes. But Pennsylvania was the colony with true Rosicrucian orientation. It permitted the most variation in religion, and it allowed the ideas of science in the style of Bacon and Dee to flourish.

CHAPTER 11

THE ROSICRUCIANS AND THE AMERICAN REVOLUTION

The American Revolution was the culmination of the hopes of a handful of leaders who sought change. This change included freedom of religion and freedom from the whims of a monarchy that could arrest, charge, and execute with little due process. The revolutionaries included many Freemasons, perhaps a majority of whom wanted nothing more than to be able to enjoy life, liberty, and the pursuit of happiness. They also included those who would benefit financially from restrictions on trade, tariffs, and taxes. According to 33rd-degree Mason and Masonic scholar Manly P. Hall, "not only were many founders of the US Government Masons, but they received aid from a secret and august body existing in Europe which helped them establish this country for a peculiar and particular purpose known only to an initiated few."[1]

FOUR ROSICRUCIAN LEADERS OF THE TIME

Four men stand out as leaders with more than mercantile interests. They are Benjamin Franklin, Thomas Jefferson, George Washington, and Thomas Paine.

Benjamin Franklin

Benjamin Franklin is believed to have been a Rosicrucian. The evidence is circumstantial, but this doesn't mean it can be ruled out. He did travel to Ephrata, and he was connected to Conrad Beissel and Michael Wohlfarth of that community. They had a shared interest in publishing, and both Franklin and the Ephrata community were among the earliest printers in the Commonwealth of Pennsylvania.

Benjamin Franklin was born January 6, 1705. Writer Cort Lindahl pointed out that as the calendar was reformed during his lifetime, that date became January 17. This date may be significant to an initiated few. For instance, the date is at least coincidentally significant as it was celebrated as the feast day of Saint Sulpice, a saint with a high ranking among Merovingians. January 17 is also said to be the day the family of Jesus returned from Egypt after hearing that Herod was dead. It is also the day of Saint Roseline (Rosslyn) of Provence's death in 1329.

It is also the date in 1382 when the revered alchemist Nicolas Flamel performed his first successful alchemical transmutation. Nicolas Flamel had pioneered the art of transmuting metals long before John Dee was born. Flamel's writings had a profound effect on those in Rosicrucian circles who would attempt to accomplish the same thing.

It was a Monday. Flamel was a scrivener, a person who copied books, and he had his own bookstore where he bought and sold books. One day he met a man who sold him *The Sacred Book of Abraham the Jew, Prince, Levite, Astrologer to That Tribe of Jews Who by the Wrath of God were Dispersed among the Gauls*. Flamel and his wife, Perenelle, spent two decades trying to ascertain the secrets this book contained. In 1382, Flamel went to Spain where a Jewish Kabbalist explained the texts to him. He went home, created a lab, and transformed base metals into gold. In addition to the account of his autobiography, the evidence that this is true is the fact that when Nicolas died, he was an extremely wealthy man.

The date of January 17 is also significant because Verrazano left Madeira to sail to America on January 17. In France, the Edict of

Saint-Germain granting toleration to the Huguenots was signed on January 17. In 1893, Bishop Billard purchased Notre Dame de Marceille in Limoux on the date, believing he knew of a great treasure there.

Henry Lincoln wrote the introduction to *Holy Blood, Holy Grail* on that date in 1981 and waited on publication of it for one year, until January 17, 1982. The book revealed the story of the bloodline of the family of Jesus that extended through Mary Magdalene and the Merovingian kings. It was uncovered by a Father Saunière, who would die after suffering a stroke on that date.

An important man in Benjamin Franklin's life was Thomas Denham, a Quaker who took Franklin under his wing. Many of Denham's principles took root in Franklin and inspired some of his writings. The four years that Franklin was employed by Denham led to membership in the Leather Apron Club and a Freemasonry group. After a trip to London both men returned home ill. When Denham died, Franklin lost the person who he said was like a father to him. He was twenty-one.

Robert Hieronimus's *America's Secret Destiny* shows that Franklin frequented a meeting place where those interested in esoteric subjects gathered. He practiced old alchemical formulas, rites, and ceremony. These are hallmarks of the Rosicrucian tradition. He became a Freemason in 1731 and the grand master of his lodge shortly thereafter. Three years later he was the grand master of all of Pennsylvania's Masons.

Franklin was a self-made millionaire. He knew the value of Freemasonry as soon as he moved to Philadelphia. As a printer, lodge brothers referred business to other brothers. Having made his fortune by the age of forty, Franklin went on to establish fire companies, libraries, and a post office. He knew the value of connections, and his post office delivered his newspapers for free. He was also the postmaster. Being a postmaster at this point in time meant being a spymaster, for he controlled the movement of information.

His European counterparts, many in sympathy with the American cause, freely shared information and also spread disinformation when it served to further their cause.

As a Mason and a man of science, Franklin could and did move freely within European society. In England, he was invited to stay at the Medmenham Estate, where the Hellfire Club held weekendlong parties that would shake modern sensibilities. The central figure of the hedonistic group was Sir Francis Dashwood, who had been initiated into Masonry in Italy and whose personal proclivities leaned toward the occult. He was a Rosicrucian as well as being England's postmaster.

He and Franklin shared several common interests. Together they were able to control and disseminate intelligence better than the military could. Dashwood's circle would unite many in England who were prominent and yet who actively promoted the cause of the colonists. One was John Wilkes, who called those who challenged the English king the "Sons of Liberty." The title caught on, and soon resistance groups in several colonial cities were happy to operate as Sons of Liberty as well. England soon became too dangerous for Franklin, with many people calling for his arrest, so he left England for the shores of France.

When it came to becoming a member of a secret society, Franklin never seemed to say no. He was inducted into the Lodge of the Nine Sisters in France and was present when Voltaire was inducted. He was connected to the St. Jean of Jerusalem Lodge and the Lodge of Bon Amis in France as well. In England he traveled in strange circles.

Possibly the most elite lodge, the Lodge of the Nine Sisters, was happy to welcome Franklin as a brother. It included many who would be active in the struggle for liberty. Some were prominent merchants whose ability to supply the colonies with supplies and ammunition was critical. Others were prominent thinkers who could move public opinion. And one was England's top spy in France, Edward Bancroft. Franklin moved in circles that were relatively inaccessible to the average person. Indeed, it would have taken him a lifetime to earn a welcome to them if not for Freemasonry.

The importance of the role played behind the scenes by Franklin and a handful of Americans has been marginalized by history. It was, however, at least as important as the role the military played in the early life of the young country that was America. Not only were connections with the Freemason organization established in France but also those at odds with Freemasonry were enlisted in the cause. The Knights of Malta, ardent Catholics who were loyal to the pope, were not on friendly terms with the Freemasons. Catholics regarded Masonry as an institution that by this time was anti-church. From a practical point of view, however, both viewed England as an enemy in need of comeuppance. Twenty French knights joined the war effort and thousands of foot soldiers came along, including the original French Foreign Legion. The French navy was under the command of Admiral de Grasse, a Knight of Malta who delivered badly needed supplies to Yorktown.

Thomas Jefferson

Thomas Jefferson was at least in spirit connected to Sir Francis Bacon. Jefferson once said, "I'm going to build my secrets into the geometry of these buildings because I know books can be burned but buildings not so easily."[2]

Bacon had said more than one hundred years before, "I have held up a light in the obscurity of philosophy, which will be seen centuries after I am dead. It will be seen amidst the erection of temples, tombs, palaces, theaters, bridges . . . foundations and institutions of orders and fraternities for nobility, enterprise, and obedience; but, above all, the establishing of good laws for the regulation of the kingdom and as an example to the world."[3]

Jefferson envisioned an empire of liberty. He was connected to local Freemasons and regularly attended ceremonies that dedicated new buildings and the laying of their cornerstones. He said it was good to be in the "land of corn, wine and oil."[4] The corn, wine, and oil he referred to were all props in a typical Masonic dedication ceremony.

Jefferson is mentioned in twenty-nine Masonic journals, although nowhere is there a record of his initiation. It is possible it took place in

France. Was he also a Rosicrucian? Like the men in England who eventually came to be known as the Royal Society, Jefferson was a polymath whose interests seemed as widespread as Francis Bacon's.

He studied agriculture and reengineered the plow. He invented the folding chair and the swivel chair although he never patented such inventions. He excavated mysterious mounds that were on his property and wrote about paleontology of the fossils. He was familiar with texts on chemistry, mathematics, and possibly his favorite science, philosophy. He was a true Renaissance man with recorded interests in mechanics, astronomy, meteorology, surgical anatomy, geology, zoology, botany, and even aeronautics. Besides being active in politics, for which he is most remembered, he served as president of the American Philosophical Society.

As far as his religion goes, he was what was called a Deist. He believed in a god but avoided all the trappings that religion had piled onto spirituality. This alone might connect him to the Rosicrucians, but H. Spencer Lewis claimed that Jefferson also embedded Rosicrucian codes in his writings.

While the mystery of Rennes-le-Château would surface after his time, he may have been aware of the importance of the Merovingian kings, and he might have been aware of the claims of a Jewish King Jesus or at least those attesting to his widow having fled the Holy Land for the South of France. Thomas Jefferson toured Languedoc in 1786 and is known to have seen some of the important Cathar and Templar sites including Carcassonne and Béziers. He also visited a lesser-known village called Souterrain St. Ferriol, whose name denotes a subterranean complex of tunnels. It is only three miles from Rennes-le-Château, the site of a treasure that enriched a local priest.

Benjamin Franklin also visited this same region. This prompts the question: Could both men have been introduced to the mysteries of this area when they served as ministers?

Jefferson is said to have edited a book that was written by Joseph of Arimathea in the South of France in 54 CE. This would mean that he was interested in grail literature as well as the area surrounding Rennes-le-Château.

In Nîmes he visited a Roman-built temple that was later renamed Maison Carrée. He wrote to a friend that he spent hours gazing at it "like a lover at his mistress." He would go on to model the Virginia State Capitol after it.[5] Jefferson was self-educated in numerous subjects. One text he discovered was the *Four Books of Architecture,* written by Andrea Palladio of Italy. Jefferson had in fact written to Madison, "We are sadly at a loss here for a Palladio." Palladio (1508–1580) in turn had been influenced by the *Ten Books on Architecture* by architect and engineer Vitruvius.

Jefferson would use the principles of both architects in designing Monticello as well as in the design of buildings for the University of Virginia. He helped his friend Madison in the design for his home in Virginia. Madison would name his home Montpellier after that center of Cathar belief in France.

Thomas Jefferson founded the University of Virginia in Charlottesville in 1817 and designed the property himself. He envisioned an "academical village," the focal point of which would be a temple of knowledge. When the cornerstone was laid, Jefferson, Madison, and Monroe were all present, along with a contingent of Freemasons. By 1822 all the buildings had been completed with the exception of the Rotunda. Jefferson had modeled it after the Pantheon in Rome and designated it as a place of worship and study.

From its very beginning, the university was replete with secret societies, many of which still exist today. They include the Seven Society, the Z Society, the IM Society, Eli Banana, and T.I.L.K.A. Notably, the Seven Society is so secret that members' names are not known outside of the group until their death, at which point a wreath of black magnolias is placed on their grave in the form of a seven. Today the only known way to communicate a message to one of its members is to leave a letter by the Jefferson statue in the Rotunda. Superspy Frank Wisner of the Office of Strategic Services was one member.

While it has been debated whether he was a Freemason, Jefferson's tombstone is an obelisk. Oddly enough, the inscription leaves out his service as president of the United States yet mentions that he was the father of the University of Virginia.

George Washington

George Washington made no secret of his role as a Freemason. At the age of twenty, having just lost his brother to illness, Washington was master of Mount Vernon. Before the year was over he was initiated as a Mason. This might have led to him taking on a military command. Before another year went by he was a master Mason. He might have become the grand master except for his role in the military.

So he carried his lodge with him in his long treks through the country, often from one defeat to another. Half of his officers were "on the level," meaning they were Masons and therefore trusted. According to fellow Mason Lafayette, Washington never advanced a man in rank if he was not a Mason. Twenty-four of his major generals and thirty of his thirty-three brigadier generals were Freemasons.[6] Washington might have been responsible for the mobile lodge that traveled throughout the country to offer fellow Masons a place for their meetings while often on the run and in inhospitable situations. He was a Royal Arch Mason, which is a spiritual degree. Like Thomas Jefferson, he was a Deist. Both men had a pew in Williamsburg at the Bruton Parish Church when Williamsburg was the capital of Virginia.

While it is widely known that Washington was a Freemason, it is not well known that he was also a Rosicrucian. In *America's Secret Destiny*, author Robert Hieronimus quotes sources that describe his reputed involvement with the American Rosicrucian Supreme Council and of Washington's consecration in the Wissahickon Creek.

Washington may have understood that despite founding a nation based on fraternity and equality, there was danger in allowing a secretive force, even Masonry, from becoming too powerful. Truly his own man, Washington declined the rank of grand master, putting an end to discussion that he be made king of America. He condemned the Illuminati and any elite society, especially those that had a political agenda.

The adage later said by Lord Acton in the nineteenth century, "Power corrupts and absolute power corrupts absolutely," seems to apply here. The European concept of kings and inherited nobility was not to be trusted nor allowed in the budding country.

After the Revolution a society of officers who fought together was created. The Society of the Cincinnati consisted of American officers and nearly all of the French Knights of Malta. When Washington found that they planned to limit future membership to descendants he declared that elitism was at work and threatened to quit the group. The order changed the policy. (Washington was also offered a lifelong term as president of the United States, which he refused.)

His cabinet was made up of four men. Jefferson, possibly a Mason, was head of foreign affairs. Edmund Randolph was attorney general and a Mason. Henry Knox was Secretary of War and a Mason. Alexander Hamilton was Secretary of the Treasury and most likely a Mason. Washington had a very active role in mapping out the new capital, and he drew on a tradition of building inspiring landscapes that incorporated astronomy and astrology.

Thomas Paine

A fourth person claimed by modern Rosicrucians as one of their own is Thomas Paine. Paine was from Philadelphia. A Quaker and a Deist, he was a journalist famous for his pamphlets. He had met Franklin while living in England, and Franklin advised him that in America he could forge a career. He wrote letters of introduction for Paine, who arrived in 1774. In January of 1776, Paine's *Common Sense* appeared, which called for a declaration of independence. It sold half-a-million copies, and six months after publication Jefferson penned the Declaration of Independence.

The two most important Rosicrucian groups in America, the

Ancient Mystical Order Rosae Crucis (AMORC) in California and Fraternitas Rosae Crucis (FRC) in Pennsylvania, both claim Paine as their own. The FRC is located in wealthy Bucks County and is famous for a pyramid on its grounds, but it is not well known even by its neighbors. It sits at the intersection of Clymer Road and Richlandtown Road. The FRC says Paine was a member of a supreme council of three that included George Washington, George Clymer, and Thomas Paine. The Philadelphia-born Clymer, while less known, was one of the first Americans to advocate complete independence from England. It was a dangerous stance. He signed both the Declaration of Independence and the Constitution.

Paine could be called a Rosicrucian given that his own personal philosophy echoed Bacon's, and he was not afraid to let people know that he was a Rosicrucian. Paine rejected the monarchy and its divine rights. He called William the Conqueror a "French bastard landing with an armed Banditti and establishing himself king of England," an act that "certainly hath no divinity in it."

The American Revolution would oust the monarchy of England from its position in the New World. Those who signed the Declaration of Independence may have had various motives for so doing, but their overall motive was getting out from under the political and religious yoke of Europe.

Masons made sure that July 4 would be the day to celebrate the creation of their endeavor. Although Hancock signed the Declaration on the first of the month, the fourth was a sacred day to Masons as it marked the rising of Sirius, the Dog Star, which was related in ancient Egypt to Thoth, who brought knowledge to man. Sirius was also connected to the goddess Isis, a most important Egyptian goddess.

The year 1781 was a turning point. The British would be defeated at Cowpens in South Carolina, and the French fleet under Comte de Grasse entered Chesapeake Bay. Cornwallis, expecting help, instead was abandoned at Yorktown and defeated. He surrendered on October 19.

THE SECRET ARCHITECTURE OF AMERICA

The Revolution a success, there was now real work to be done. George Washington was in Georgetown when he issued a proclamation to build a capitol in the city that would bear his name. Pierre Charles L'Enfant, a French engineer who had come over during the war, was hired for the job. He picked out the site of the Congress House, later named the Capitol; the President's House, later called the White House; and the Washington Monument. The gridlike pattern of the city would resemble that of Philadelphia with its echoes of the ancient city of Babylon. Like the plan for Philadelphia, Washington would be built between two rivers, the Potomac and the Anacostia.

The state of Maryland would be the location of the new capital, so named for Henrietta Maria, the wife of King Charles I. Though the many religions brought to America did not conform to the Catholic or Lutheran model, first settlers of this colony were Catholic. The name Maryland raised the feminine principle in Christianity to a much more important role. Many ancient religions had been matriarchal in nature, but Christianity would eclipse that to some degree, with the result being that women, over time, lost their voice. During the Crusades, Saint Bernard implemented great changes and elevated the veneration of Mary, the Mother of God, as well as Mary Magdalene.

The area chosen for the nation's capital bordered "Mary-land" and Virginia. Alan Butler, author of *City of the Goddess,* questions the coincidence. He also points out that the name of the district, Columbia, could refer to the dove—the symbol of Sophia, the divine intelligence, and of Venus and the Holy Spirit.[7] Indeed, the name Columbus was a Latinized version of *Columbia,* meaning "the dove." Columbus had sailed the Atlantic with red Templar crosses splayed across the white sails of his three ships: the *Santa Maria* (St. Mary), the *Niña,* and the *Pinta.* The first two names refer to mother and child, while *Pinta* meant "the painted one," which the sailors referred to as *puta,* "a prostitute." Could this have been a reference to Mary Magdalene, whom the church had branded as a whore? Today she is believed to have been an independent and wealthy woman, but it's more likely that she was a temple priestess.[8]

In the founding of the new nation and its capital in Washington, D.C., two farmers sold their land to the new government so that the district could be created. The ground where the capital stands today was called New Troy. It was granted in 1663 by the second Lord Baltimore to George Thompson. His neighbor was Francis Pope, who apparently had quite the sense of humor, given that he called his land Rome and a small stream that ran through it the Tiber.

L'Enfant was busy drawing up the plans for the capital but in the process was suddenly fired, perhaps due to his temperament and his inflexibility; reportedly he was upset at changes that were being made to his designs for the city.

Washington and Jefferson both contributed their visions and amended the plans of L'Enfant and then replaced him with Andrew Ellicott. Ellicott was an astronomer and a civil engineer who had much to do with laying out the boundaries of the early states. He is often referred to as a Freemason, yet he was a Quaker—and Quakers, at least in general, do not favor Freemasons.

Washington was staying at John Suter's tavern, which was known as the Fountain Inn. It was not Georgetown's only tavern. However, Suter was a master Mason, and his tavern was used as a lodge for Masonic meetings. Washington proclaimed that the ten-square-mile city would begin at Jones Point, bordering Alexandria. The master of the Alexandria Lodge no. 22, Elisha Dick, placed a marker featuring the ceremonial corn, wine, and oil on the spot. Author David Ovason points out that Jupiter was rising over the horizon at 23 degrees of Virgo when this was done.[9]

David Ovason's *Secret Architecture of Our Nation's Capital* points out that the plans for Washington, D.C., entailed so much more than anyone recognized. More than thirty examples of full zodiacs and numerous alignments were utilized in its grand design, representing the maxim "As above so below." A study of the stars and of sacred geometry dictated to the founders of this country why, in what shape, and when monuments were to be built and consecrated, with sacred days frequently marking these occasions. The city was designed to be oriented to the sun. The east-west line is aligned with the spring and winter equinoxes—March 21 and Sept 21, respectively.

While names like Pope and Rome and Tiber may have been whimsy, other names had potent meaning. *The Evening Star,* for instance, was one of the new capital's finest newspapers. The planet Venus functioned as both the Morning Star and the Evening Star, depending on whether Venus (as seen from Earth) is east or west of the sun as it rises and sets. The symbolism of the eagle, which was used in ancient times and by early Masons and Rosicrucians, was meant to represent the nation as well as be an open blind; that is, it was designed to have one meaning to the uninitiated and another to the initiate. The five-pointed star, another popular Rosicrucian symbol, had come to Europe by way of early Christian, alchemical, and Rosicrucian symbolism.

Thus can we see how tenets of the Rosicrucian tradition, as carried on by those of Freemasonry, influenced the building of our nation's capital and came to exemplify the ideals of the young nation.

CHAPTER 12

THE KNIGHTS OF THE GOLDEN CIRCLE AND THEIR PLAN FOR AMERICA

It seems that all of the greatest spiritual leaders from Buddha to Jesus have had their teachings distorted by their followers. In the same vein, Freemasons, Rosicrucians, and other secret societies seem to attract those who would not only distort their message but also turn it on its very head. The Rosicrucian ideals of freethinking, the freedom to invent and to study science, and freedom of religious thought, which had started with a handful of well-meaning individuals, would not last forever. While an elite group—including William Penn, Benjamin Franklin, and George Washington—tried to promote these ideals in America, as time went on and the pressing economic priorities of the new nation came to the fore, other individuals would attempt to subvert them. As the young nation of America continued to grow and develop and it marched forward into the nineteenth century, the principles of the Rosicrucian tradition would be eclipsed by larger concerns having to do with economic livelihood, commerce, and trade—specifically the slave trade.

Paschal Beverly Randolph, a friend of President Lincoln, had been authorized by European Rosicrucians to help bring the Rosy Cross to

America. His father was one of the earliest settlers of Virginia, and his heritage was European, Native American, and Malagasy. As a result, he is described as an octoroon. He had traveled widely and started a career as a writer and a lecturer. His interests were in spiritualism and the occult, and he appeared onstage as a trance medium. One of his books was on pre-Adamic man; it argued that man had existed on Earth at least thirty-five thousand and possibly one hundred thousand years ago. Randolph founded an American branch of the Rosicrucian order in 1852, a year after he became friends with Lincoln. The friendship lasted throughout the Civil War. Upon Lincoln's assassination, Randolph would accompany Lincoln's funeral train to Springfield, Illinois. He was ejected from the train because some of its other passengers objected to a Negro riding with them.

This was a fractious time in America due to escalating tensions pertaining to race relations. The decades leading up to the Civil War saw the movement against slavery growing. The trade had been the province of a handful of merchants united by Masonic lodges stretching from Boston to Newport, Rhode Island, to Charleston, South Carolina. These merchants supported the slave trade because of the profits they derived from it. The slave trade and the agricultural industry it supported did not benefit everyone, but it did benefit the most powerful. As the movement to stop slavery grew, those opposed to abolition became more violent and secretive.

In America's early years it was not unusual for a compromise to be made within a political party. The partnership between President Harrison and Vice President Tyler would be anything but a partnership, however. Harrison was a Virginian in the mold of Washington and Jefferson and against the politics of secession. Tyler was the opposite. He wanted to admit Texas as a slave state. Despite their differences, however, the ticket of "Tippecanoe and Tyler too" won the election. Harrison, however, would only be president for a very short time. After a long inaugural speech given in the rain, he came down with an illness attributed to an intestinal bug. Later it was said that he caught a cold, which became pneumonia. Rumors began to circulate that he had been poisoned. In any case, this remained speculation, given that no autopsy was ever performed. Harrison was the first president to die in office.

In Victorian times it was not uncommon to misdiagnose arsenic poisoning as gastric illness. The symptoms started with abdominal pain, vomiting, and diarrhea. Both of the president's physicians, a Dr. Frederick May and a Dr. William Eustis, were pro-British, and the British endorsed Tyler, believing that, under him, slavery and the vast cotton trade would continue.

Dr. Frederick May had been trained by Dr. John Warren, a Freemason. May's son was an outspoken Tory and a close friend of Benedict Arnold's. Dr. William Eustis was also trained by Warren and had been fired by President Madison because of his actions in the War of 1812. Madison had believed that Dr. Eustis tipped off the British and allowed them to ambush General William Hull on his march to Detroit.

Tyler repudiated the Northern agenda and tried to put Caleb Cushing, a 33rd-degree Mason and slave trader, in office in various roles.

Shortly after the death of Harrison, an organization known as the Knights of the Golden Circle (KGC) was born in Kentucky. George Bickley, who lived in Cincinnati, was its founder, and he traveled widely to recruit new members. Its aim was to build a circle from Canada through Ohio, to Texas and Mexico and the West Indies—in other words, a circle that excluded the free states of the United States.

This was meant to be a secret society that maintained its secrecy through clandestine passwords, temples, and lodges, as well as secret, sworn oaths and supreme councils. The grand seal of the organization was a skull and crossbones, reminiscent of the Knights Templar. Its units or lodges in the Masonic sense of the word were called castles. The KGC attempted to create one large slave state. The result was that Texas became the largest bastion of knights and counted Governor Sam Houston as a member. The organization grew by appealing to Masonic lodge members in the Midwest. Many were farmers who spent much of their time in isolation. As a result, their need to be part of a community was strong.

The Knights of the Golden Circle is described by one author as the most powerful subversive organization in the United States.[1] It would plan the taking of Fort Sumter in Charleston, which basically started the Civil War. Charleston, on the 33rd parallel, is the supreme headquarters of global Freemasonry today. It was, in the 1860s, one of the two most powerful centers of the slave trade in the United States.

SECRET SOCIETIES AND THEIR ATTEMPTS TO ASSASSINATE LINCOLN

Other organizations that fought against the abolition of slavery had been in place from the 1850s. They included the Southern Rights Club, which sent slave ships to Africa, and smaller groups like the Blue Lodges and the Sons of the South. Similarly to Freemasons, theirs were societies of secret handshakes and signs, and they wore hemp in their buttonholes, a sign that they sided with the growers. On December 4, 1855, they attacked a federal arsenal in Missouri and absconded with all the weaponry that it contained.

Although these societies were dangerous, they did not have the scope that the Knights of the Golden Circle had. The KGC could draw upon Masons from all around the country as well as the world. One of its knights was Cipriano Ferrandini, newly arrived from Corsica and connected to Napoleon's family. Ferrandini was part of a plot to assassinate Lincoln in 1861. A man by the name of Lucius Crittenden believed that Lincoln would never make it through Baltimore on his way to Washington, as there was a hotbed of secessionist activity in that city. Ferrandini himself told Allan Pinkerton that Lincoln needed to be assassinated.[2] Other plotters were numerous. The greatest source of their financial backing was England, given that England's mills needed the cotton produced by America's southern states.

Lincoln was aware that funding was coming from England and would arrest and charge no less than thirteen thousand men for disloyalty. The founder of the KGC was charged with spying for England, and General Albert Pike took over. He was a 33rd-degree Mason, handpicked by Mason Jefferson Davis, the president of the Confederacy. After the war, Pike would become the driving force behind the first iteration of the Ku Klux Klan. The Klan would also recruit from Masonic lodges. In some counties, membership in the Klan was limited to Masons.

For many like Pike and his Klu Klux Klan, the Civil War did not end with Appomattox. A handful of conspirators, including John Wilkes Booth—a Mason and a Knight of the Golden Circle—would eliminate Lincoln. Like many assassinations, the investigation would conclude with the death of a patsy or lower level conspirators. Later it became known that Judah Benjamin, Secretary of State of the Confederacy who had ties to Boston's Caleb Cushing, a high-ranking Mason, had raised money not just for the South in general but had also raised one million dollars to fund the assassination of Lincoln.

The plot was put in place in Montreal, where $1 million in gold was made available to John Wilkes Booth.[3] This would be equal to $10 million in today's dollars.

One conspirator by the name of John Surratt had been dispatched two weeks prior to Montreal to get the funds. He had lost his job as postmaster because of his known disloyalty to the president the year before. Booth had listened to a speech by Lincoln in which he had said that not only would he see the slaves freed, but he would also allow them to vote. He swore he would kill the president.

He knew in advance of Lincoln's plan to attend Ford's Theater. President Lincoln invited Ulysses Grant to be his guest that evening but was turned down as Mrs. Lincoln had a reputation of vicious tirades against army generals. At the time, Lincoln's "Secret Service" consisted of one bodyguard, who moved his seat for a better view of the stage.

On Good Friday, 1865, KGC member John Wilkes Booth shot

the president and then, in jumping from the balcony, broke a bone above his ankle. He headed to Maryland, first stopping at Surratt Tavern, then continued on to Beantown and the farm of Samuel Mudd. Despite his descendants' claims that Mudd was innocent, it was Mudd who had introduced Booth to conspirator John Surratt months before. Mudd helped patch up Booth, but he couldn't keep him there. A massive manhunt ensued, and Booth was reportedly seen in a number of places while recuperating from his fracture. When he took flight again, the U.S. Cavalry was on his trail. They pulled people from their houses looking for a number of conspirators. Finally they cornered Booth. He refused to surrender and was shot dead. His body was searched, and officers found money and a picture of his fiancée, Lucy Lambert Hale, daughter of a New Hampshire senator.

While several of the conspirators were executed, Edwin Stanton, who had been implicated in Lincoln's murder by the media, stayed above the fray. He had never been a fan of Lincoln's and had called him an imbecile. While others in Lincoln's government were targeted, Stanton, arguably the next most important man[4] as Secretary of War, was given John Wilkes Booth's diary and before giving it back, removed eighteen pages from it, a fact that Jesse Ventura in his book *American Conspiracies* likens to Nixon's missing eighteen minutes of tape.[5]

Incredibly, John Surratt left the country with the help of a priest, first arriving in Quebec and then fleeing to the Vatican, where he enlisted as a papal Zouave. Later he came back from Italy, married a relative of Francis Scott Key, and became the treasurer of the Old Bay Line (an American steamship line). Dr. Mudd, the man who had helped Booth heal and hide out, was pardoned by President Andrew Johnson, who had succeeded Lincoln as president. Two other conspirators would serve short sentences before being pardoned as well.

The reader is forgiven for thinking that there was at least some help from inside the government to get rid of Lincoln.

OTHER FAMOUS FIGURES OF THE PERIOD
AND THEIR CONNECTION TO FREEMASONRY

Some of the South's craftiest minds ran the KGC. The group was heavy on ritual often borrowed from Freemasonry and Rosicrucian tradition. A thirteen-man inner sanctum ran the group after the war. This group included Colonel Elbert DeWitt Travis, alias William Clark Quantrill. According to a book about Jesse James, the inner sanctum included a few Rosicrucians.[6]

Jesse James and the James Gang

We all know the legend of Jesse James and the infamous James Gang. What is rarely mentioned is that Jesse James was a 33rd-degree Freemason.[7] The gang spread terror throughout the Midwest, successfully robbing one bank after another for years. Sometimes they are seen as Robin Hood types, stealing from the rich and giving to the poor. Other times they are seen simply as robbers, making up for the economic depression that followed the Civil War. The truth is much stranger.

Jesse James began his career during the Civil War. He followed the path of his older brother Frank, who was part of a guerilla operation known as Quantrill's Raiders; they were out to win the Civil War their own way. Even after General Lee surrendered, these guerillas continued their operations. One month after the surrender at Appomattox, Jesse James's gang was composed of one hundred bushwhackers who soon turned to robbing banks. Cole Younger led a group of Quantrill's men in robbing the Clay County Savings Association in Liberty, Missouri, which netted the immense sum, for the time, of seventy thousand dollars.

The James and Younger brothers were not doing this for their own gain or to hand out money to poor Missouri farmers. Their goal was nothing short of being the force that would help the South rise again. They belonged to the Knights of the Golden Circle, which was almost exclusively made up of Freemasons, although many of them were Rosicrucians who were frequently funded by wealthy English merchants. A document called the Holt Report, which was given to Edwin Stanton, claimed that the organization might comprise several hundred thousand members, whose plan was to fund a war for Southern independence.[8] Stanton, however, could effectuate nothing (and, in fact, he may have been involved himself).

The James Gang took the proceeds of their twenty to twenty-five successful robberies and hid them in secret stashes from Arkansas to Arizona. Most remain hidden today, guarded by secret symbols and protected by guardians to ensure they're not pilfered.

Just how independent Jesse James was is still a matter of debate. His older brother Frank had joined William Quantrill in 1863, just before the infamous massacre in Lawrence, Kansas. Quantrill had put together an irregular army of 450 men who attacked that small city. They killed 183 men and boys, anyone old enough to pick up a rifle. It was an act that horrified the Union and made the twenty-five-year-old Quantrill a target. He would live two more years before being mortally wounded in a skirmish against Union forces.

Prior to the end of the Civil War, Frank James surrendered in Kentucky. Jesse attempted to surrender after being caught stealing a saddle and was shot in the lung. His cousin Zerelda nursed him to health, and he married her. Both Frank and Jesse quickly reunited with their former guerillas turned outlaws. After the astounding Clay County robbery they freed former Quantrill members from a jail in Independence, Missouri.

They then went on a series of robberies, shooting lawmen and innocent bystanders alike. As older members of the original raiders were killed, the group became known as the James-Younger Gang.

They continued to rob banks in Missouri, Iowa, and Kentucky, and in one sensational robbery they took on the Second Annual Kansas City Exposition. They held up the ticket booth while thousands of pleasure-seekers were attending the fair. In 1873 they robbed their first train, in Adair, Iowa, killing an engineer in the process.

While they crisscrossed the Midwest they were written up by the *Kansas City Times* editor as heroes. John Newman Edwards wrote "The Chivalry of Crime," which described them as not only defending the South but fighting "with the halo of medieval chivalry" as well. This reference to the Knights Templar was just part of the creation of a myth-history that glamorized the rebels.

The gang managed to operate until August of 1876, when a bank robbery in Northfield, Minnesota, saw some of its members killed, the Younger brothers captured, and the James boys on the run.

They avoided capture for a time. Then, in 1882, Jesse James was shot in the back of the head for reward money—or was he? The alternate theory is that someone who physically resembled him was killed and Jesse became a field commander of the KGC. His mission was to protect the KGC's stash of nearly ten million dollars, an amount equaling one hundred million dollars today.

Albert Pike

Albert Pike, the renowned American attorney, soldier, and writer was a 33rd-degree Mason. While the Freemason organization today says he had nothing to do with the founding of the Klu Klux Klan (KKK), it is claimed that he was nothing less than the grand dragon of the first version of that organization. Certainly he had suspicious connections to the Klan. *K* is the eleventh letter in the alphabet. If $K = 11$, three K's = the number 33. Of course there is more to it than that. Writer Anton Chaitkin maintains that the Scottish Rite Mason organization and the KKK were part of the same agenda.[9]

After the war, Pike was found guilty of treason, but Freemason president Andrew Johnson then met with him and pardoned him. Albert Pike then went on an odyssey around the South to recruit new members. The stashes were protected, but at the same time codes and symbols were created, which would direct other initiates as to just where these caches were and how to get to them. Modern-day treasure hunter

Bob Brewer found KGC maps containing symbols of Masonic geometry and was able to crack codes embedded in the maps. In Arizona he found symbols of hearts, arrows, hooded priests, and Baconian ciphers. They pointed to a grid that had been laid out by engineers, surveyors, mathematicians, and cryptologists over several years or possibly decades. The grid contained several repositories that extended from Arkansas to Arizona. While the treasures of the James-Younger Gang had been stashed away more than a century ago, they were still being guarded in the twenty-first century. Several times Brewer was warned away from the sites, once having been threatened with a beheaded rabbit and twice by helicopters.[10]

CHAPTER 13

ROSICRUCIAN AMERICA TODAY

Today in the United States two major Rosicrucian organizations compete for the title of being the legitimate Rosicrucian order. The largest by far, with 250,000 members, is the Ancient Mystical Order Rosae Crucis (AMORC), which is headquartered in San Jose, California. Here it maintains Rosicrucian Park, which takes up a full city block and features mysterious Moorish and Egyptian architecture. Its website describes the organization as a community of seekers studying the universe. The society welcomes members online and has courses of instruction designed to teach higher levels of learning and self-awareness.

A man by the name of Reuben Swinburne Clymer, a 32nd-degree Mason, came to lead an East Coast equivalent of the Rosicrucian order in the twentieth century. Clymer's order, the Fraternitas Rosae Crucis (FRC), is located in Quakertown, Pennsylvania, just north of Philadelphia in Bucks County. Having approximately one thousand members, it claims to be descended from the original fraternity that was instituted in Germany in 1614. Unlike the AMORC, its headquarters—featuring a pyramid—is closed to the public. The headquarters of the order is said to be a place of learning and worship, but outsiders have no idea what goes on inside. The plaques that adorn the site reveal that it's composed of Supreme Councils of Nine, Seven, and Three. One plaque features Benjamin Franklin as a prominent council member. Another plaque has the Rosicrucian anchor symbol alongside a Templar skull and bones and a winged planet Earth. Underneath is the word *Try*.

THE GUIDESTONE MONUMENT

On a hilltop in northeastern Georgia stands a huge granite monument. It resembles a modern Stonehenge, and it may carry an archaeo-astronomical message. It consists of four guidestones—four solid granite monoliths five meters tall by two meters wide, positioned in a star pattern that emanates from a central monolith. The entire construction, including a slab on top, weighs a quarter of a million pounds and is oriented to the cardinal points. Unlike Stonehenge or Newgrange or any of the similarly mysterious constructions found around the world, this monument was not built by a Neolithic people.

Monuments such as this one *are*, however, found among secret societies, from the Druids to the Freemasons. In *Population Control* author Jim Marrs says, "The monument is therefore proof of an existing link between secret societies, the world elite and the push for a New World Order."[1]

The monument is not ancient at all but was created in Elbert County, Georgia, in 1979, and revealed to the public on March 22, 1980. Elbert County was named for Samuel A. Elbert, a Revolutionary War hero and a Freemason of Solomon's Lodge no. 1 in Savannah. Elbert, along with George Washington, was a member of the Society of the Cincinnati.

The story begins on a Friday in June of 1979 when a man by the name of Robert C. Christian visited the Elberton Granite Finishing Company and inquired about the potential cost of building a monument such as the one described above. R. C. Christian then went to the Granite City Bank and met a man by the name of Wyatt C. Martin, to whom he revealed his true name, after having sworn Martin to secrecy. His name, a vaguely disguised reference to Christian Rosenkreuz, the alleged founder of the Rosicrucian tradition, was no secret to anyone. And Christian Rosy Cross made no attempt to hide his intentions either.

At the base of the monument is a tablet listing some of its details and explaining the astronomic features of the structure. Upon the four outer monuments the ten guides, or rules, are written in eight languages: English, Spanish, Swahili, Hebrew, Arabic, Russian, Chinese, and Hindi. And the four edges of the monument's capstone are inscribed in four *ancient* languages: Babylonian, classic Greek, Sanskrit, and Egyptian. The most striking notice on the tablet is the command to "Maintain humanity under 500,000,000 in perpetual balance with nature." This sounds nice until you realize that the population of the planet is currently above seven billion people. The list goes on.

1. Maintain humanity under 500,000,000 in perpetual balance with nature.
2. Guide reproduction wisely—improving fitness and diversity.
3. Unite humanity with a living new language.
4. Rule passion—faith—tradition—and all things with tempered reason.
5. Protect people and nations with fair laws and just courts.
6. Let all nations rule internally resolving external disputes in a world court.
7. Avoid petty laws and useless officials.
8. Balance personal rights with social duties.
9. Prize truth—beauty—love—seeking harmony with the infinite.
10. Be not a cancer on the earth—Leave room for nature—Leave room for nature.

The message to all is: Let these be guidestones to an age of reason. Francis Bacon couldn't have possibly said it better himself.

And yet, the implication of the message on the stones is far beyond anything Bacon would have advocated. Over time, organizations, like religions, tend to lose the ideals of the founder. Just as they have been since their foundation, secret societies of the elite in our modern age are organized under various umbrellas. Like Bacon and his associates, their members may be known to one another and may work to influence the underpinnings of society. Collectively, these powerful groups influence government, the military, the police, industry, medicine, and media, among other aspects of society. With the message on the Georgia Guidestones, modern Rosicrucians may have shown their hand in announcing to the world the truth.

JOHN DEE'S INFLUENCE ON IAN FLEMING AND HIS JAMES BOND CHARACTER

In this appendix we will examine the influence of John Dee on later culture, particularly the culture of espionage, and more specifically on the renowned English author Ian Fleming. In the tradition of Daniel Defoe and Jules Verne, Ian Fleming created characters in his works who shared some attributes with the Rosicrucians. In Ian Fleming's case, this character took the form of his famous spy, James Bond.

Ian Fleming was born into an immensely wealthy Scottish family. His grandfather Robert Fleming had started managing money as a sideline to his mercantile business; then, in 1873, he'd created a family bank. The bank would survive for a century before eventually being sold to Chase Manhattan Bank (now J. P. Morgan Chase) for $7.7 billion dollars. Grandfather Robert's fortune might have relieved his heirs from needing an occupation, but Ian went to work for Reuters, and his brother Peter became a well-known travel writer. From an early age Ian was inspired by the mystical arts. His father perished in World War I, and he was not close to his mother, Evelyn St. Croix-Rose (Rosy Cross).

Ian Fleming began school at the Durnford School near the estate of the real-life Bond family, whose family motto was "The world is not enough." James Bond movie fans might recognize that as the title of a Bond film starring Pierce Brosnan.

After less than stellar performances at Eton and Sandhurst, Fleming's mother sent him to the Continent when he was about nineteen, the same age as John Dee when he went to Moscow. In Austria, with the Adlerian disciple Forbes Dennis, he studied Jung's works on both alchemy and psychology.

Alfred Adler was an Austrian doctor who had broken with Sigmund Freud and split the science of psychology. Adler was a proponent of feminism, and Freud weeded out any of his disciples who agreed with its tenets. Freud introduced the concept that the dynamics associated with the masculine and the feminine were the key to understanding human psychology. This thinking and Fleming's association with various circles, some bordering on the occult, such as the Cainites, Ophites, and Gnostics, would find its way into his spy novels.

Fleming's circle included members of England's Bloomsbury Set, the seminal group of writers, intellectuals, and artists whose works greatly influenced the twentieth century. Its members included economist Maynard Keynes, author E. M. Forster, feminist writer Virginia Woolf, and scholar Lytton Strachey of Cambridge. Several were also members of the Cambridge Apostles, a group of twelve men that included Keynes, Forster, and Strachey, as well as the spy Anthony Blunt. Their influence on Fleming might have been strong, but it ended as World War I exposed two of them, Anthony Blunt and Lewis Daly, as spies against their own country. Later the *London Morning Post* broke the story of the Bloomsbury Set celebrating the Black Mass. Soon after, their ranks were reduced by two suicides as well as other deaths that were likewise premature.

Fleming's reputation remained unscathed by his connections.

He soon left England and traveled the world for Reuters and the *Times*. It is certain that by 1939, when Fleming was sent to Moscow, he was officially acting as a member of British intelligence. He was soon given the title lieutenant commander in the Royal Navy, as would his avatar, James Bond. Dee of course had been instrumental in setting up the Royal Navy.

One of Fleming's most important roles was in coming up with a defense plan for Gibraltar. His secret code name for the plan was Operation Goldeneye. It had an occult meaning referring to the third eye, or inner eye, necessary to achieve the higher plane of understanding, gnosis. The name of the operation would later serve as the name for his home on the lush island of Jamaica. It would also be the title of another Bond film starring Pierce Brosnan.

Fleming played a role in tricking Rudolf Hess into flying to England. He knew Hess was a student of astrology and could be lured to England by preying upon his interest in the mystical arts. Fleming consulted with the most renowned of Europe's occultists, the Great Beast himself, Aleister Crowley. Crowley was at once a Satanist, a Rosicrucian, and a member of the Order of the Golden Dawn. A plan was devised to lure Hess to England by casting a bogus horoscope for him.

In January of 1941 an astrologer who was secretly a British intelligence agent convinced Hess that he needed to meet the Duke of Hamilton. As a result of trickery and astrology, Hess parachuted into the hands of the Royal Air Force and was captured. This began a purge of occultists in Nazi Germany, which was no small matter as the Nazi Party was full of those who espoused neo-paganism as well as theosophical occultism mixed with a mystical desire for racial purity.

Crowley's role was limited, as he was not trusted in the mission. He would, however, inspire the character of Chiffre (meaning cipher) in Fleming's *Casino Royale*.

Fleming was not the only spy interested in magic and the occult. The logo of the MI5 contained a pyramid and an all-seeing eye.

Possibly Fleming's most important work was in being sent to the United States as part of a joint American-British intelligence network. America was not looking to get into the war against Germany. Parties like America First advocated isolationism, while others even leaned toward supporting the Fascists. British intelligence was on a mission to change all that. It took an active role in courting politicians and the media, and on occasion working against those who worked against Roosevelt's aid policies. The role was more often diplomatic than physical, but there were occasions that sparked Fleming's interest, leading to the creation of his character James Bond.

Rockefeller Center housed the British MI6 (Military Intelligence 6, now called the Secret Intelligence Service, which is the overseas branch of Britain's intelligence) and the early OSS (Office of Strategic Service, then known as the COI, or Coordinator of Information office). The Japanese consul general's office was also housed at Rockefeller Center, which Fleming participated in breaking into late one night. After breaking and entering, he and his cohorts opened the safe contained therein, copied all the Japanese codebooks, and relocked the offices just in time. Fleming would use this adventure in *Casino Royale*.

After the war Fleming went back to writing. There are numerous theories about much of what has gone into or influenced his work. His main character shares the initials J. B. with the two pillars of Freemasonry, Joachim and Boaz. Such pillars have appeared in Masonic temples everywhere for centuries.

When the James Bond spy thrillers were written by Ian Fleming it was no accident that the author had gathered material from the Elizabethan court. Specifically, the occult goings-on in her court interested Fleming. The queen had begun her reign January 15, the same day Fleming started writing his first book, *Casino Royale*. When the queen corresponded with Dee, she signed her letters as *M*. Bond reported to an *M* as well. Was this designation because, as one biographer reported, Christian Rosenkreuz wrote a book titled *Book M*? Dee's code name by Walsingham was Agent 007, preceding James Bond's code name by nearly four centuries.

The Earl of Leicester, a very important member of the court who had been tutored by Dee as a child, would use a similar code. He marked his secret correspondence with two dots, or two zeros, representing eyes. Dee would address his correspondence to the queen with a heading "For your eyes only."

Fleming often wrote from his retreat, Goldeneye. His book *Diamonds Are Forever* features a character by the name of Bill Templar, and he wrote about a flying machine, as did John Dee. Fleming's interest in voodoo was also very apparent, in part no doubt as a result of his living in Jamaica much of the time.

After a heart attack Fleming declared, "I have always smoked and drank and loved too much. . . . Then I shall have died of living too much." A second heart attack saw his prediction come true, claiming his life on August 12, 1964. He was only fifty-six.

While he lived as a man of the world, he is buried in Sevenhampton, a small English village two miles from a bus stop. His grave is marked by an obelisk atop four stones.

From the seventeenth century to the present day, there have been those among us who make great contributions in many fields for the good of us all. Bacon wrote on the advantages of freedom and learning, Dee on the navigation of the world. Several Rosicrucians actually funded and risked their own lives to create colonies in the New Atlantis of Bacon's world. Rosicrucians founded America on principles that had not been previously allowed. With the exception of the Knights of the Golden Circle, Rosicrucians, like Ian Fleming, not only risked their lives but also concealed humanistic messages in their writing.

NOTES

INTRODUCTION.
THE INVISIBLE HISTORY OF THE UNITED STATES

1. *New World Encyclopedia,* s.v. "Albigensian Crusade," page last modified February 18, 2019.
2. James Bailey, *The God Kings and the Titans* (New York: St. Martin's Press, 1973), 29.

CHAPTER 1.
THE SECRETS OF THE ROSICRUCIANS

1. Tim Wallace Murphy, *Hidden Wisdom: The Secret of the Western Esoteric Tradition* (New York: Disinformation, 2010), Kindle.
2. Marie A. Belloc, "Illustrated Interviews: No. XXXIX Jules Verne at Home," *Strand Magazine* (February 1895), 210.
3. Michel Lamy, *The Secret Message of Jules Verne* (Rochester, Vt.: Destiny Books, 1984), 179.
4. Jim Marrs, *Rule by Secrecy* (New York: HarperCollins, 2000).
5. Abraham Cowley, "Ode to the Royal Society." This poem first appeared prefixed to Bishop Sprat's *The History of the Royal Society of London, for the Improving of Natural Knowledge,* 1667.
6. Jim Marrs, *Our Occulted History* (New York: William Morrow, 2012), 217.
7. Johannes Kepler, *Harmonices Mundi* [*The Harmonies of the World*], 1618.

8. De Quincey, "Rosicrucians and Freemasons."

9. Baigent, Leigh, and Lincoln, *Holy Blood, Holy Grail,* 123.

10. Jean Markale, *The Templar Treasure at Gisor* (Rochester, Vt.: Destiny Books, 1984), 66.

11. Frederick J. Pohl, *Prince Henry Sinclair* (Halifax, Nova Scotia: Nimbus Publishing, 1997), 10.

12. Christopher Knight and Robert Lomas, *The Hiram Key* (Beverly, Mass.: Fair Winds Press, 2001), 79.

13. James Egan, *Elizabethan America.*

14. Bill Mann, *Knights Templar in the New World* (Rochester, Vt.: Destiny Books, 2004), 131.

15. Yates, *Rosicrucian Enlightenment,* 2.

CHAPTER 2.
SIR FRANCIS BACON:
THE MAN WHO COULDN'T BE KING

1. Patrick, *View Beyond,* 62.

2. Churton, *Invisible History,* 345.

3. De Quincey, "Rosicrucians and Freemasons."

4. Sobran, *Alias Shakespeare,* 5.

5. O'Connor, *The Secret Treasure of Oak Island,* 109.

6. Ann Somerset, *Elizabeth 1* (New York: Alfred Knopf, 1991), 111.

7. Dodd, *Francis Bacon's Personal Life-Story.*

8. Leary, *Second Cryptographic Shakespeare,* 53.

9. Sarah Gristwood, *Elizabeth and Leicester* (New York: Viking, 2007), 108.

10. Bernstein, *Ark of the Covenant,* 170.

11. Dodd, *Francis Bacon's Personal Life-Story.*

12. Dodd, *Francis Bacon's Personal Life-Story.*

13. Bertram Fields, *Players,* 252.

14. Dodd, *Francis Bacon's Personal Life-Story.*

15. James Baxter Houghton, *The Greatest of Literary Problems* (New York: Houghton Mifflin, 1915), 395.

16. Mark Booth, *Secret History of the World* (New York: Harry N. Abrams, 2010).

17. Ovason, *Shakespeare's Secret Book.*

18. Jean Overton Fuller, Sir Francis Bacon: A Biography (Easton, UK: George Mann, 1994).

19. Pierre Amboise, *Discourse on the Life of Sir Francis Bacon* (Paris, 1631).

20. "Bacon" and "Baconian History," Francis Bacon Research Trust website, accessed June 11, 2019.

21. Mather Walker, "Mather Walker"/"Shakespeare Plays"/"Measure for Measure," Sir Bacon's New Advancement of Learning website, accessed April 23, 2019.

CHAPTER 3.
THE AUTHOR(S) KNOWN AS SHAKESPEARE

1. Donnelly, *Great Cryptogram,* 28.

2. Durant and Durant, *Age of Reason Begins,* 88.

3. Charles Beauclerk, *Shakespeare's Lost Kingdom* (London: Thistle Publishing, 2015), xviii.

4. Fields, *Players,* 40.

5. Peter Farey, "Did Marlowe Die in Padua in 1627?" *The Marlowe Society Research Journal* 9 (2012): 1.

6. Sobran, *Alias Shakespeare,* 178.

7. Gary Goldstein, "Edward de Vere, Earl of Oxford," Luminarium website, accessed August 31, 2006.

8. "Shakespeare Authorship FAQ," The Oxford Authorship site, accessed April 6, 2018.

9. Drabble, *Oxford Companion,* 968.

10. Anonymous (possibly George Puttenham), *The Arte of English Poesie* (black-Friers, neere Ludgate: Richard Field, 1589).

11. Leary, *Second Cryptographic,* 283.

12. *The Shakespeare Conspiracy,* directed by Michael Peer (TMW Media Group, 2011).

13. Donnelly, *Great Cryptogram.*

14. Donnelly, *Great Cryptogram.*

15. Leary, *Second Cryptographic,* 61.

16. Donnelly, *Great Cryptogram.*

17. Leary, *Second Cryptographic.*

18. Fields, *Players,* 5.

19. Leary, *Second Cryptographic,* 28.

20. Shapiro, *Contested Will,* 88.

21. Shapiro, *Contested Will,* 88.

22. Donnelly, *Great Cryptogram,* part 1.

CHAPTER 4.
ALL THE QUEEN'S MEN

1. Catherine Drinker Bowen, *Francis Bacon: The Temper of a Man* (New York: Fordham University Press, 1993).

2. Baigent, Leigh, and Lincoln, *Holy Blood, Holy Grail,* 426.

3. Michael White, *Isaac Newton: The Last Sorcerer* (Reading, Mass.: Addison Wesley, 1997), 138.

4. Yates, *Rosicrucian Enlightenment,* 54.

5. E. G. R. Taylor, "A Letter Dated 1577 from Mercator to John Dee," *Imago Mundi* 13, no. 1 (1956): 56–68.

6. Nicholl, *Creature in the Map,* 307.

7. Drabble, *Oxford Companion,* 663.

8. Stephen Budansky, *Her Majesty's Spymaster* (New York: Viking, 2005), 39.

9. Margaret P. Hannay, *Mary Sydney, Lady Wroth* (Farnham, UK: Ashgate, 2013), 163.

10. Strachey, *Elizabeth and Essex,* 5.

CHAPTER 5.
OCCULT ENGLAND

1. Nicholas Canny, ed., *The Origins of Empire,* vol 1 (Oxford: Oxford University Press, 2001), 112.

2. Yates, *Occult Philosophy,* 36.

3. Joseph R. Strayer, *The Albigensian Crusades* (Ann Arbor: University of Michigan Press, 1992).

4. William Tyndale and Jabor Isidor Mombert, *William Tyndale's Five Books of Moses. Called the Pentateuch* (including prolegomena) (Amazon Digital services, September 1, 2014), xlix.

5. Summers, *History of Witchcraft,* viii.

CHAPTER 6.
KING ARTHUR AND
AVALON IN AMERICA

1. *Annales Cambriae,* entry for the year 516, p. 161.
2. Thompson, *American Discovery,* 203.
3. Morison, *The European Discovery of America.*
4. Gardner, *Mysteries of the Ancient Americas,* 34.
5. Morison, *Great Explorers,* 85.
6. Gardner, *Mysteries of the Ancient Americas,* 34.
7. Holand, *Explorations in America,* 247.
8. Gardner, *Mysteries of the Ancient Americas,* 35.
9. Morison, *The European Discovery of America,* 85.
10. Levenda, *Sinister Forces, Book I,* xix.
11. David Boyle, *Toward the Setting Sun: Columbus, Cabot, Vespucci, and the Race for America* (New York: Walker, 2008).

CHAPTER 7.
ROSLIN, HENRY SINCLAIR, AND
THE DISCOVERY OF AMERICA

1. Frederick J. Pohl, *Prince Henry Sinclair* (New York: Clarkson and Potter, 1974).
2. Johann Reinhold Forster, *History of the Voyages and Discoveries Made in the North* (London, 1786).
3. Pohl, *Prince Henry Sinclair.*
4. William Herbert Hobbs, "The Fourteenth Century Discovery of America by Antonio Zeno," *The Scientific Monthly* (January 1951); Pohl, *Prince Henry Sinclair.*
5. Andrew Sinclair, *The Sword and the Grail* (New York: Crown Publishers, 1992).
6. See *Merlin and the Discovery of Avalon in the New World* by author/explorer Graham Phillips for more on the topic of King Arthur's final resting place.
7. Much of this correspondence between T. C. Lethbridge and Frank Glynn has been preserved and is available at the Westford, Massachusetts library.

8. Pohl, *Prince Henry Sinclair*.

9. *America Unearthed*, Season 1 Episode 12 "America's Oldest Secret," aired March 8, 2013 on the History Channel.

10. Holand, *Explorations in America*, 221.

11. Parkman, *France and England*, 150.

12. Morison, *Great Explorers*, 144.

13. Morison, *Great Explorers*, 155.

14. Holand, *Explorations in America*, 247.

15. Amundsen, *Oak Island and the Treasure Map*, chapter 21.

16. *The Curse of Oak Island* series, The History Channel.

17. Yates, *Rosicrucian Enlightenment*, 47; Yates, *Rosicrucian Enlightenment*, 25–26.

CHAPTER 8.
BACON'S NEW ATLANTIS

1. Morison, *The European Discovery of America*, 480.

2. James W. Mavor Jr., "Bartholomew Gosnold's Voyage to Cape Cod in Verrazano's Wake," *New England Antiquities Research Association* 36:2 (winter 2003): 10.

3. Tony Horwitz, *A Voyage Long and Strange: Rediscovering the New World* (New York: Henry Holt, 2008), 294.

4. Albion, Baker, and LaBaree, *New England and the Sea*, 17.

5. Phillips, *Merlin*, 189.

6. History and Genealogy Unit, Connecticut State Library, "John Winthrop, Jr.," Museum of Connecticut History website, April 1999.

CHAPTER 9.
THE COLONY OF THE VIRGIN QUEEN

1. Bernstein, *Ark of the Covenant, Holy Grail*, 170.

2. Kieran Doherty, *Sea Venture* (New York: St Martins Press, 2007), 33.

3. Bradbury Cort Lindahl, *Axis Mundi* (Self-published, 2015), 247.

4. Bruton Parish Church, "Bruton Parish Churchyard: A Guide with Map" (Williamsburg, Va.: Bruton Parish Church, 1976), 60, cited by David

Allen Rivera, *Mystery at Colonial Williamsburg: The Truth of the Bruton Vault* (N.p.: Rivera Enterprises, 2014).

5. Bernstein, *Ark of the Covenant.*

6. Bernstein, *Ark of the Covenant,* 188.

CHAPTER 10.
THE ROSY CROSS OVER PENNSYLVANIA

1. Brands, *First American,* 36–38.

2. Robert Hieronimus, *Founding Fathers, Secret Societies* (Rochester Vt.: Destiny Books, 1989), 47.

3. Joe Tyson, "The Monks of the Ridge," Southern Cross Review website, 2003.

4. Joe Tyson, "Monks of the Wissahickon: Part IV," *Schuylkill Valley Journal Online,* March 4, 2016.

5. Joseph E. Illick, *Colonial Pennsylvania: A History* (New York: Schribner, 1976).

6. Aaron Spencer Fogelman, *Jesus is Female: Moravians and Radical Religion in Early America* (Philadelphia: University of Pennsylvania Press, 2007).

7. "Archives of Women in Theological Scholarship. Finding Aid for Barbara Brown Zikmund Papers, 1958–2001" (New York: The Burke Library at Union Theological Seminary, Columbia University Libraries).

CHAPTER 11.
THE ROSICRUCIANS AND THE
AMERICAN REVOLUTION

1. Manly P. Hall, *The Secret Destiny of America* (New York: Penguin, 2008).

2. Bradbury Cort Lindahl, *Axis Mundi* (Self-published, 2015), 63.

3. "Mysteries," Francis Bacon Research Trust website, Accessed February 8, 2019.

4. Merrill D. Peterson, *Thomas Jefferson and the New Nation* (Oxford: Oxford University Press, 1975).

5. D'Epiro and Pinkowish, *Sprezzatura,* 36–37.

6. Hagger, *Secret Founding,* 163.

7. Alan Butler, *City of the Goddess: Freemasons, the Sacred Feminine, and the Secret Beneath the Seat of Power in Washington, DC* (London: Watkins, 2011).

8. Lynn Picknett, Mary Magdalene (London: Constable and Robinson, 2003).

9. Ovason, *Secret Architecture,* 49.

CHAPTER 12.
THE KNIGHTS OF THE GOLDEN CIRCLE
AND THEIR PLAN FOR AMERICA

1. Getler and Brewer, *Shadow of the Sentinel,* 15.

2. Keehn, *Knights of the Golden Circle,* 107–11.

3. Keehn, *Knights of the Golden Circle,* 176.

4. Bill O'Reilly, *Killing Lincoln,* 119.

5. Ventura, *American Conspiracies,* 7.

6. Getler and Brewer, *Shadow of the Sentinel.*

7. Getler and Brewer, *Shadow of the Sentinel,* 79.

8. Getler and Brewer, *Shadow of the Sentinel,* 42

9. Anton Chaitkin, *Treason in America: From Aaron Burr to Averell Harriman* (New York: New Benjamin Franklin House, 1984).

10. Getler and Brewer, *Shadow of the Sentinel.*

CHAPTER 13.
ROSICRUCIAN AMERICA TODAY

1. Marrs, *Population Control,* 7–9.

BIBLIOGRAPHY

Albion, Robert, William Baker, and Benjamin Labaree. *New England and the Sea*. Mystic, Conn.: Mystic Seaport Museum, 1972.

Amundsen, Peter. *Oak Island and the Treasure Map in Shakespeare*. Independently published with CreateSpace, 2013.

Anderson, Mark. *Shakespeare by Another Name: The Life of Edward de Vere, Earl of Oxford*. New York: Gotham Books, 2005.

Angell, Marcia. *The Truth about Drug Companies*. New York: Random House, 2004.

Anonymous. *Mysteries of the Rosie Cross*. London: S. J. Brawn, 2011.

Asquith, Clare. *Shadowplay*. New York: Public Affairs, 2005.

Baigent, Michael, and Richard Leigh. *The Elixir and the Stone: Unlocking the Ancient Mysteries of the Occult*. London: Penguin, 1998.

Baigent, Michael, Richard Leigh, and Henry Lincoln. *Holy Blood, Holy Grail*. New York: Dell, 1982.

Barber, Chris, and David Pykett. *Journey to Avalon: The Final Discovery of King Arthur*. York Beach, Maine: Samuel Weiser, 1997.

Bernstein, Henrietta. *Ark of the Covenant, the Holy Grail*. Marina del Rey, Calif.: DeVorss Publications, 1998.

Brands, H. W. *The First American: The Life and Times of Benjamin Franklin*. New York: Doubleday, 2000.

Budiansky, Stephen. *Her Majesty's Spymaster*. New York: Viking, 2005.

Churton, Tobias. *The Invisible History of the Rosicrucians*. Rochester, Vt.: Inner Traditions, 2009.

D'Epiro, Peter, and Mary Pinkowish. *Sprezzatura: 50 Ways the Italians Shaped the World*. New York: Anchor, 2001.

De Quincey, Thomas. "Historico-critical Inquiry into the Origin of the Rosicrucians and the Freemasons." *London Magazine*. January–June, 1824.

Dodd, Alfred. *Francis Bacon's Personal Life-Story*. Exeter, UK: David and Charles, 1987.

Doherty, Kieran. *Sea Venture*. New York: St. Martin's Press, 2007.

Donaldson, Ian. *Ben Jonson: A Life*. Oxford: Oxford University Press, 2011.

Donnelly, Ignatius. *The Great Cryptogram: Bacon's Cipher in the So-Called Shakespeare Plays*. Whitefish, Mont.: Kessinger Publishing reprint, 1887.

Drabble, Margaret, ed. *The Oxford Companion to English Literature, Fifth Edition*. Oxford: Oxford University Press, 1985.

Durant, Will, and Ariel Durant. *The Age of Reason Begins*. New York: Simon & Schuster, 1961.

Egan, James Allen. *Elizabethan America: The John Dee Tower of 1583*. Newport, R.I.: Cosmopolite Press, 2011.

Ellis, Joseph J. *American Sphinx: The Character of Thomas Jefferson*. New York: Alfred A. Knopf, 1997.

Fields, Bertram. *Players: The Mysterious Identity of William Shakespeare*. New York: HarperCollins, 2005.

Fogelman, Aaron Spencer. *Jesus is Female*. Philadelphia: University of Pennsylvania Press, 2007.

Gardner, Joseph, ed. *Mysteries of the Ancient Americas*. Pleasantville, N.Y.: Reader's Digest Books, 1986.

Getler, Warren, and Bob Brewer. *Shadow of the Sentinel*. New York: Simon & Schuster, 2003.

Hagger, Nicholas. *The Secret Founding of America*. London: Watkins Publishing, 2009.

———. *The Secret History of the West*. Winchester, UK: O Books, 2005.

Heironimus, Robert. *America's Secret Destiny*. Rochester, Vt.: Destiny Books, 1989.

Heston, Vernn. *The Mayflower*. New York: Mayflower Books, 1980.

Holand, Hjalmar R. *Explorations in America before Columbus*. New York: Twayne Publishers, 1956.

Honan, Park. *Christopher Marlowe: Poet and Spy*. Oxford: Oxford University Press, 2005.

Howard, Michael. *The Occult Conspiracy*. Rochester, Vt.: Destiny Books, 1989.

Illick, Joseph E. *Colonial Pennsylvania*. New York: Charles Scribner's Sons, 1976.

Incognito, Magus [William Walker Atkinson and Clint Marsh, eds.]. *The Secret Doctrine of the Rosicrucians*. Chicago: Occult Press, 1949.

James, Brenda, and Rubenstein William. *The Truth Will Out*. New York: Harper Perennial, 2005.

Keehn, David. *Knights of the Golden Circle*. Baton Rouge: Louisiana State University Press, 2013.

Kelley, Joseph J. *Life and Times in Colonial Philadelphia*. Harrisburg, Penn.: Stackpole Books, 1973.

Kelso, William. *Jamestown: The Buried Truth*. Charlottesville, Va.: University of Virginia Press, 2006.

Leary, Penn. *The Second Cryptographic Shakespeare*. Omaha, Neb.: Westchester House, 1990.

Levenda, Peter. *Sinister Forces, Book 1*. Walterville, Oreg.: Trine Day, 2005.

Lindahl, Cort. *Axis Mundi*. Self-published, 2015.

Luke, Mary M. *Gloriana: The Years of Elizabeth I*. New York: Coward, McCann and Geoghagen, 1979.

Mann, William. *The Templar Meridians*. Rochester, Vt.: Inner Traditions, 2006.

Marrs, Jim. *Our Occulted History: Do the Global Elite Conceal Ancient Aliens?* New York: William Morrow, 2013.

———. *Population Control: How Corporate Owners Are Killing Us*. New York: William Morrow, 2015.

———. *The Trillion Dollar Conspiracy*. New York: Harper, 2010.

Miller, Lee. *Roanoke*. New York: Arcade Publishing, 2000.

Morison, Samuel. *The Great Explorers*. Oxford: Oxford University Press, 1986.

———. *The European Discovery of America*. Oxford: Oxford University Press, 1971.

Nicholl, Charles. *The Creature in the Map*. New York: William Morrow and Company, 1995.

O'Connor, D'Arcy. *The Secret Treasure of Oak Island*. Lanham, Md.: Lyons Press, 2004.

Ovason, David. *The Secret Architecture of Our Nation's Capital*. New York: HarperCollins, 2000.

———. *Shakespeare's Secret Booke*. East Sussex, UK: Clairview Books, 2010.

Parkman, Francis. *France and England in North America*. New York: Library of America, 1983.

Patrick, Dave. *The View beyond Sir Francis Bacon*. London: Polair Publishing, 2011.

Phillips, Graham. *Merlin and the Discovery of Avalon in the New World*. Rochester, Vt.: Bear & Co., 2005.

Phillips, Graham, and Martin Keatman. *The Shakespeare Conspiracy*. London: Century, 1994.

Pohl, Frederick. *Prince Henry Sinclair*. New York: Clarkson and Potter, 1974.

Quinn, David Beers. *England and the Discovery of America 1481–1620*. New York: Alfred A. Knopf, 1974.

Rivera, David Allen. *Archaeological Conspiracy at Williamsburg: The Mystery of Bruton Vault*. N.p.: Rivera Enterprises, 2007.

Saussey, F. Tupper. *Rulers of Evil*. New York: HarperCollins, 1999.

Shapiro, James. *Contested Will: Who Wrote Shakespeare?* New York: Simon & Schuster, 2010.

Sobran, Joseph. *Alias Shakespeare: Solving the Greatest Literary Mystery of Them All*. New York: Simon & Schuster, 1997.

Steers, Edward Jr. *Blood on the Moon*. Lexington: University Press of Kentucky, 2001.

Stiles, T. J. *Jesse James: The Last Rebel of the Civil War*. New York: Alfred A. Knopf, 2002.

Strachey, Lytton. *Elizabeth and Essex: A Tragic History*. San Diego: Harvest Book/Harcourt Brace, 1928.

Summers, Montague. *The History of Witchcraft*. Secaucus, N.J.: University Books, 1956.

Thompson, Gunnar. *American Discovery*. Seattle, Wash.: Misty Isles Press, 1994.

Ventura, Jesse. *American Conspiracies*. New York: Skyhorse Publishing, 2010.

Wells, Stanley. *Shakespeare and Company*. New York: Pantheon Books, 2006.

Yates, Frances A. *The Occult Philosophy in the Elizabethan Age*. London: Routledge, 1979.

———. *The Rosicrucian Enlightenment*. New York: Routledge, 1972.

INDEX

Academy Royale des Sciences, 20–21

Adam of Bremen, 147

alchemy, 22, 23, 25, 84, 121

Alias Shakespeare, 55

Amboise, Pierre, 40

American Revolution, 4, 228–37

Ancient Mystical Order Rosae Crucis
 (AMORC), 251–54

Andreae, Johann Valentin, 15–18

angels, 88, 120–21

Anglo-Saxons, 130–31

Annales Cambriae, 133–34

Arcadia, 166, 167–68

architecture, secret, 238–40

Aries, 86

Armado, Don Adriano de, 69–70

Arnold, Benedict (governor), 165, 177

Arthur (son of Henry VII), 115, 117

Arthur, King, 130–36

Arthurian myths, 115

Ascham, Roger, 32

Ashmole, Elias, 13

As You Like It, 52

Avalon, 134, 136–39

Bacon, Anne, 34–36

Bacon, Delia, 31, 77–78

Bacon, Francis, 4, 7–8, 9, 10–11,
 13, 14, 16, 100, 111–12, 122,
 198–99

 classic texts of, 26–31

 "deaths" of, 44–45

 early years of, 35–37

 hidden writings of, 208–10

 John Dee and, 89–91

 low profile in English court,
 37–39

 parentage of, 31–35

 place-names and cohorts, 205–7

 royal references to heritage, 39–41

 Shakespeare and, 28–31, 41–43,
 77–79

Bacon, Nicholas, 34–35

Barnes, Richard, 105

Barnham, Alice, 40

bar sinister, 211–12

Beaumont, Francis, 75

Beissel, Conrad, 223–24

Benson, Michael, 12

Berkeley, Charles, 209–10

Bermuda, 41, 199–201
Bernard, Saint, 15, 124, 238
Bernstein, Henrietta, 34, 212
Blount, Charles, 110, 112
Blount, Edward, 104
Blount, Elizabeth, 117–18
Boleyn, Anne, 116, 117, 118, 121
Boone, Daniel, 142–43
Booth, John Wilkes, 245–46
Bouillon, Geoffrey de, 19
Boyle, Robert, 13, 14, 85
Brigham, Antonio, 183–84
Brinknell, Thomas, 108
Brocardo, Giacopo, 83
Brooke, George, 72
Brooke, Henry, 72
Brooks, Robert, 35
Bruno, Giordano, 2, 104, 122, 128
Bruton Church, 209–14
Bulwer-Lytton, Edward, 24–25
Burbage, Richard, 62
Burbage Theater, 50
Burton, Robert, 83
Bushnell, Thomas, 179, 208

Cahokia, 144
Calvin, John, 170–71
Campanella, Tommaso, 122
Carafa, Giovanni, 119
Carey, George, 68–69
Carib people, 175
Carleton, Dudley, 40
carved rock memorial, 160–62
Cassini, Giovanni Domenico, 21
Cathars, 21, 123–24
cathedrals, 23–24
Catherine of Aragon, 114, 117, 118

Catholics and Catholicism, 9,
    10–11, 115–16, 118–21,
    123–24
Catlin, George, 145–46
Cavendish, William, 205
Cecil, Robert, 39, 72, 111
Cecil, William, 30, 33–34, 35, 55,
    97, 102
Champlain, Samuel de, 137–38
Chapman, George, 5, 65, 104
Charlevoiux, Father, 142
chicken pox, 144
Christian of Heidelberg, Prince,
    16–17
Church of England, 116–18
Church of Rome, 117
Chymical Wedding of Christian
    Rosenkreuz, The, 9, 15–18
ciphers, 37–38, 43, 61, 79, 250
Cistercians, 3, 15, 164–65
City of the Sun, 122
Clifford, Margaret, 98
codes, 37–38, 77–78
cod fishing, 154, 182
Coke, Edward, 198
College of William and Mary,
    210–13
Columbus, Christopher, 2, 137, 139,
    146, 148, 149, 152, 167, 183, 199
Cook, Roger, 82
Cooke, Mildred, 35
Corpus Hermeticum, 19, 120
Council of Trent, 127–28
Cowell, James Corton, 47
Cowley, Abraham, 13
Croke, Richard, 116
Crowley, Aleister, 25, 257

Crusades, 2–3, 120–21
Cuffe, Henry, 113
Cuttyhunk, 188–89

Daniel, Samuel, 8
Danvers, Charles, 113
Dare, Virginia, 197
Dark Ages, 131
Dashwood, Francis, 231
Davis, John, 42, 100
de Bry, Johann, 95
Dee, John, 4–5, 10–11, 13, 32, 65,
    80–91, 104, 128, 140–41, 183–85
    associates of, 82–85
    background of, 80–82
    influence on Raleigh, 94
    life at Mortlake, 85–89
    New World and, 130–31
    passes torch to Francis Bacon,
      89–91, 134
Defoe, Daniel, 11–12, 119
demons, 120–21
de Nevers, Louis, 14
Denham, Thomas, 230
De Quincey, Thomas, 18–19
Deryck, Dionysia, 36
de Soto, Hernando, 141, 143
de Vere, Catherine, 56
de Vere, Edward. *See* Oxford, Earl of
Devereux, Robert. *See* Essex, Earl of
Dighton Rock, 162
Disraeli, Benjamin, 31
Donnelly, Ignatius, 78
Dowe, Anne, 35
Drake, Francis, 5, 91–93, 104, 110,
    179–80
Drayton, Michael, 8, 62, 71, 74, 75

Drebble, Cornelius, 82–83
Drummond, John, 166–67
Dudley, Guilford, 32
Dudley, Robert, 31–35, 109
Dugdale, William, 75
Dugua, Pierre, 137, 138

Edict of Saint-Germain, 119–20
Edward III, King, 126, 147–48
Edward VI, King, 35, 84, 116
Egan, James, 21, 164
Elbert, Samuel A., 252
Elizabeth I, Queen, 5, 10, 17, 27, 29,
    31–34, 80, 90–91, 110
    relationship with occult arts, 121–22
    shifting dynamics in England,
      100–101
Emerson, Ralph Waldo, 31
Essex, Earl of (Robert Devereux),
    38–39, 65–66, 100, 102,
    109–13, 121–22
Essex Circle, 65–69
Essex Rebellion, 109

Faroe Islands, 158
Ferrandini, Cipriano, 244
Ficino, Marsilio, 120
Field, Richard, 56, 60–61
Fields, Bertram, 76
Fiorentino, Giovanni, 50
Flamel, Nicolas, 229
Fleming, Ian, 255–59
Florio, John, 29, 59, 104
Fludd, Robert, 13–14, 17, 62, 84–85
Fogg, Phileas, 12
forts, 143–44
Francis I, King, 169, 170

Franklin, Benjamin, 221, 229–32
Fraternitas Rosae Crucis, 25, 251–54
Frederick, King, 17–18
freedom of thought, 13, 22–23
Freemasonry, 5, 15, 217–18, 230–31
Frizer, Ingram, 52
Frobisher, Martin, 57–58, 87, 100
Fromond, Jane, 87

Gardner, Robert, 36
Geoffrey of Monmouth, 133, 135–36
Gilbert, Adrian, 61–62, 93
Gilbert, Humphrey, 93, 100, 104,
  184–85
Gisors, Jean de, 19
Glastonbury, 135
Globe Theater, 62–63
Glynn, Frank, 160–61
gold, 84
Gorges, Ferdinando, 185–86
Gosnold, Bartholomew, 186–90
Great Experiment, 223–27
Great Work, 81
Greene, Robert, 63
Greenland, 147–48
Grenville, Richard, 93
Greville, Fulke, 16, 104
Grey, Jane, 32
Greyfriars, 149
Guidestone Monument, 252–54
Gunn, James, 161–62
Gunn clan, 161–62
Gurdjieff, George, 22

Hades, 8
Hakluyt, Richard, 104, 139, 140
Hall, Manly Palmer, 7, 9, 211

Hall, Marie Bauer, 211–12, 214
Hamilton, Alexander, 236
Hamilton, James, 206
Hapsburgs, 17–18
Hariot, Thomas, 5, 65, 69–70, 84, 101
Hatton, Christopher, 66, 75
Hawkins, John, 91, 141
Hawthorne, Nathaniel, 31
Hayes, Antonio, 184
Hedden, Gilbert, 179
Henry IV, King, 133
Henry VI, 129
Henry VII, King, 114
Henry VIII, King, 114, 115–16, 117,
  127–28
Henry of Lorraine, 14
Herbert, Mary Sidney, 61–62
Herbert, William, 114
heresy, 100, 105, 125
heretics, 123–24
Heydon, John, 27
Hill, Abraham, 13
History of the Kings of Britain, 133, 135
History of the World, 73
History of Witchcraft, The, 128
Hobbs, William Herbert, 156
Hoby, Edward, 184
Hoffman, Calvin, 53
Holy Blood, Holy Grail, 19, 20, 230
homosexuality, 29, 36–37, 105
Howard, Thomas, 57
Hutchinson, Anne, 194
hydraulics, 83, 165, 178–79

Iceland, 136, 147, 155, 182, 183
Igraine, 135–36
Ingram, David, 141

Inquisition, 119, 122
Inuit people, 147
Inventio Fortunata, 147
Invisible College, 1–4, 13–14, 23

James, Jesse, 247–49
James Bond character, 255–59
James I, King, 5, 72, 89, 128, 197
Jamestown colony, 188–89,
    197–99
Jay, John, 183
Jefferson, Thomas, 132–43, 232–35,
    236
John the Baptist, Saint, 22
Jones, Inigo, 166
Jones, Morgan, 142
Jonson, Ben, 62, 63–64, 71–74, 75,
    76, 104, 115

Kabbalah, 9, 23, 128
Kelpius, Johann, 219–23
Kepler, Johannes, 15, 84
Kett, Francis, 105
King James Bible, 14, 61
Knight, Christopher, 20
Knights Hospitallers, 126–27
Knights of the Golden Circle,
    241–44, 247–48
Knights Templar, 3, 14–15, 19,
    23–25, 120–21, 124–27, 164–65
Kyd, Thomas, 62, 97, 103, 104–5

Lancelot, 12
L'Anse aux Meadows, 146, 164, 176
Last Judgment, 119
Lee, Sydney, 59–60
Lethbridge, T. C., 160–61

levitation, 80–81
Life of St. David, 133
Lincoln, Abraham, 244–46
Lindahl, Cort, 207
literature
    authorship of Rosicrucian texts,
        15–18
    popular themes of the day in, 8–9
    seminal figures in, 10–11
    works through time that reflect
        Rosicrucian themes, 11–13
Lodge, Thomas, 8
Lok, Michael, 50–52, 58
Lomas, Robert, 20
Longfellow, Henry Wadsworth, 162
Lost Colony (Virginia), 96
Love's Labour's Lost, 69–70
Luther, Martin, 8, 117, 119

Macbeth, 37, 129
Madoc, Prince, 139–46
magic, 23, 120–21, 128
Maier, Michael, 13, 17
Manannan, 134, 137
Mandan people, 145–46
Mandoag, 141
Manners, Roger. *See* Rutland, Earl of
maps, 88, 148–49, 158, 172–73,
    183–84, 187
Markale, Jean, 19
Marlowe, Christopher, 5, 29, 50–54,
    62, 100, 103–7
Marrs, Jim, 13, 15, 252
Mathers, Samuel, 25
Matthew, Tobie, 43
McKay, James, 142
Medici, Catherine de, 95, 119

Medici family, 3, 19, 120

Mercator, Gerardus, 81, 84, 87, 148–49

Merchant of Venice, The, 50–52, 53, 57–58, 61

Merlin, 136, 138

Merrick, Gilly, 112, 113

Michelangelo, 119

Middle Ages, 21

Monas Hieroglyphica, 86

Monas Hieroglyphica symbol, 10, 86

Moncreiffe, Ian, 161

Monhegan Island, 159–60

Moravians, 224–26

More, Thomas, 118

Morison, Samuel, 171

Morse, Samuel, 77–78

Murphy, Tim Wallace, 7

musical codes, 62

Narragansett Bay, 173–74

Nashe, Thomas, 29, 63, 65, 68–69, 101, 104

Native Americans, 141–46, 157, 171–72, 174–75, 187–88, 193

Nazis, 13

Neile, Paul, 13

Nennius, 133

New Atlantis, 5–6, 17, 27, 81, 137–39, 182–91

New Atlantis, 9, 27, 40, 83, 122, 179, 208

Newfoundland, 128–39, 147–48, 155, 185

Newport Tower, 163–66, 172–73

Newton, Isaac, 13, 81, 85

New World, 5, 11, 88, 137–39, 168–76, 196–98. *See also* New Atlantis.

Nicholas of Lynn, 87, 147–49

Northumberland Folder, 78

Nova Scotia, 159, 176–77

Oak Island treasure vault, 176–81

occult, 114–15, 120–21, 127–29

Oconostota, 145

Oracle of Delphi, 22

Order of the Helmet, 8, 28–29

Othello, 58–59

Ovid, 56

Owen, Orville Ward, 79, 178, 209

Oxford, Earl of (Edward de Vere), 30, 54–59, 100, 107–9, 203–4

Paine, Thomas, 236–37

Pallas Athena, 8, 28

Paris Observatory, 21

Paris Temple, 125

Paul IV, Pope, 119

Peasants' Revolt of 1381, 126–27

Peckham, George, 141, 185, 186

Penn, William, 5, 215–18

Pennsylvania, 215–23

Perceval, 12

Percy, Henry, 5, 65

Peyto, Edward, 166

Philip, King, 32

Philip II of Spain, 119

Phillips, Graham, 138, 190

Pico della Mirandola, Giovanni, 120, 121

Pietists, 219–23, 224

Pike, Albert, 249–50

pilgrimages, 135
Pilgrims, 191–95
Pillars of Hercules, 28
piracy, 92–93
plague, 144
Plymouth Company, 186, 192
Pohl, Frederick, 20, 157
Poley, Robert, 106
Ponce de Leon, 148
Powel, David, 141
Prague (city), 17, 88
Pring, Martin, 138, 188, 190–91
Priory of Sion, 14, 19
Protestant sects, 118
Pucci, Francesco, 83
Puritans, 191–95, 218

Quakers, 215, 218, 219, 224, 239

Raleigh, Walter, 5, 13, 64–65, 69–71,
    72–73, 93–99, 101, 103–4, 106,
    185, 196–98
Randolph, Paschal Beverly, 241–42
Rape of Lucrece, The, 29, 56, 69
Rawley, William, 8, 40–41, 179, 208–9
Red Cross, 9, 10, 19, 94, 201
Red Cross knight, 65, 94, 95, 196, 201
Reformation, 116, 117, 118, 123
Reform Club, 12
Refugio, 173, 183, 186
Rhode Island, 194–95
Rich, Robert, 206–7
Richard II, 39, 55, 68, 109, 112, 121
Richard II, King, 131, 133
Richard III, King, 114–15
Ridolfi plot, 57, 106, 191
Rivera, David Allen, 213

Robsart, Amy, 32, 33–34
Rockefeller family, 213–14
Romano, Julio, 57
Rooke, Laurence, 13
Rose Cross, 8
Rosenkreuz, Christian, 7, 19–20,
    253, 258
Rosicrucianism and Rosicrucians
    in America today, 251–54
    anchor symbol, 5
    connection to Knights Templar,
        23–25
    explanation of, 18–20
    far-reaching nature of, 14
    popular themes reflected in
        literature, 8–9
    source of name, 20–21
    tradition of, 7–8, 21–23
Roslin/Rosslyn Chapel, 7, 20, 24,
    150–52
Rosy Cross, 16
Rowe, Nicholas, 75
Royal Society, 13–14, 23, 101
Roydon, Matthew, 104
Rudolf II, King, 86, 88
Ruth, Burrell, 79, 178–79
Rutland, Earl of (Roger Manners),
    65, 67, 108–9, 166, 204

Sanders, Patrick, 83
Sandys, Edwin, 207
Sannazaro, Jacopo, 167–68
sassafras, 188
Saxons, 132
School of Atheism, 70
School of Night, 5, 65, 66, 70, 97,
    103–4

Scott, Reginald, 128

Sea Venture, 199–201

Shakespeare, William, 28–31
  aftermath of death, 74–76
  ascendency of, 62–64
  backstory in Elizabethan England, 64–65
  Circle of Essex and, 65–69
  de Vere and, 54–59
  identity of, 46–47, 59–61
  Marlowe and, 50–54
  pen as a sword, 69–71
  scant knowledge of, 47–50
  skeptics of, 76–79

Sidney, Philip, 14, 62, 95–96, 100–101, 185, 216

Sinclair, Henry, 20, 152–56, 166–67

Sinclair, William, 7

Sinclair-Zeno expedition, 152–56
  documents corroborating, 155–58
  evidence of Sinclair's presence, 158–60

slave trade, 241–44

smallpox, 144, 145–46

Smith, John, 188–89

Smith, Thomas, 207

Smith, William H., 78

solstices, 20, 164, 226

Somers, George, 206

Somers, John, 41

Southhampton, Earl of (Henry Wriothesley), 29, 31, 59, 67, 68, 100, 101–3, 113

Spanish Armada, 110

Spenser, Edmund, 8, 13, 42, 62, 75, 82, 94, 104

Standish, Miles, 191–92

Stanley, Ferdinando, 98

Star Chamber, 112

St. Clair/Sinclair family, 20, 24, 150–52, 161

Stewart, Isaac, 142

Stoker, Bram, 25

Strachey, William, 201–4

St. Sulpice, Church of, 20–21

sub rosa, 10–11

Summers, Montague, 128

Tapper, Ruwart, 128

Tempest, The, 41, 59, 129, 202–4

Templar colony, 172–76

Temple of Solomon, 124

Thirty Years' War, 17

Thorne, Robert, 183

Throckmorton, Elizabeth, 70, 96–97, 197

Titus and Andronicus, 59–60, 177

Tobias, David, 179–80

tolerance, 13

Tower of London, 99, 101, 109, 121, 127

treason, 105

Trismegistus, Hermes, 120

Tudor, Francis, 34

Tudor, Mary, 32

Tudor, Owen, 114

Tudors, 114–15

Twelfth Night, 52, 56

Tyndale, William, 128

United States
  and invisible history, 1–6
  and modern Rosicrucianism, 251–54
  and secret architecture, 238–40

Varennes, Pierre Gaultier de, 142
Vaughan, Thomas, 13, 84
Vaughn, William, 52
Vautrollier, Thomas, 61
Venus and Adonis, 29, 56, 60–61
Verendrye, Gaultier de la, 142
Verne, Jules, 12, 24
Verrazano, Giovanni da, 168–76
Vikings, 146, 147, 163–64
Villeneuve, Saint Roseline de, 21
Virginia Company, 28, 41, 192, 198, 205
Vortigern, King, 132
Voyage of Mael Duin's Boat, The, 134

Wales, 132–33
Walsingham, Francis, 53, 96, 101, 103, 105–7, 258
Warner, William, 104
Washington, George, 221, 225, 235–36, 237, 239, 252
Wat (Raleigh's son), 71, 73

Watson, William, 72
Wat Tyler's Rebellion, 126–27
Westford rock, 160–62
Westminster Abbey, 53, 58, 75
Weymouth, George, 185
Whateley, Anne, 49
White, John, 197
White, Michael, 85
Whitman, Walt, 31
Whittier, John Greenleaf, 64
Wilkes, John, 231
Williams, John, 142
Williams, Roger, 110, 194–95
Williamsburg, Virginia, 207–14
Wilmot, James, 31, 46–47, 76–77
Wither, George, 29, 211–12
Witt, Christopher, 222–23
Wren, Christopher, 13
Wriothesley, Henry. *See* Southhampton, Earl of
Wyatt Rebellion, 32
Wycliffe, John, 126
Wynne, Peter, 141